Media and Youth

For my father, Dr. Marvin Kirsh, whose unconditional love and support, not to mention his daily questioning about how many new pages I had written, helped bring this book to fruition. And for my wife, Sudha, and children, Michelle and Daniel, whose insatiable appetite for media has allowed me to purchase three high-definition TVs, every video game system under the sun, and a Blu-Ray DVD player.

Media and Youth

A Developmental Perspective

Steven J. Kirsh

WILEY-BLACKWELL

A John Wiley & Sons, Ltd., Publication

This edition first published 2010
© 2010 Steven J. Kirsh

Blackwell Publishing was acquired by John Wiley & Sons in February 2007. Blackwell's publishing program has been merged with Wiley's global Scientific, Technical, and Medical business to form Wiley-Blackwell.

Registered Office
John Wiley & Sons Ltd, The Atrium, Southern Gate, Chichester, West Sussex, PO19 8SQ, United Kingdom

Editorial Offices
350 Main Street, Malden, MA 02148-5020, USA
9600 Garsington Road, Oxford, OX4 2DQ, UK
The Atrium, Southern Gate, Chichester, West Sussex, PO19 8SQ, UK

For details of our global editorial offices, for customer services, and for information about how to apply for permission to reuse the copyright material in this book please see our website at www.wiley.com/wiley-blackwell.

The right of Steven J. Kirsh to be identified as the author of this work has been asserted in accordance with the Copyright, Designs and Patents Act 1988.

Library of Congress Cataloging-in-Publication Data

Kirsh, Steven J.
    Media and youth : a developmental perspective / Steven J. Kirsh.
        p. cm.
    Includes bibliographical references and index.
    ISBN 978-1-4051-7948-5 (hardcover : alk. paper) – ISBN 978-1-4051-7947-8 (pbk. : alk. paper) 1.   Mass media and children. 2.   Mass media and teenagers. 3.   Technology and children. I.   Title.
    HQ784.M3K5678 2010
    302.23083–dc22

                                                                    2009025993

A catalogue record for this book is available from the British Library.

Set in 10/13pt Palatino
by SPi Publisher Services, Pondicherry, India
Printed and bound in Malaysia by Vivar Printing Sdn Bhd

1   2010

Contents

Preface

Media and Youth: A Developmental Perspective provides a comprehensive review and critique of media effects research conducted on infants, children, and adolescents. Across development, youth vary cognitively, emotional, physically, and socially. As such, throughout the text, theories and research are evaluated from a developmental perspective. In doing so, the effects of media on youth, as functions of age and developmental status, become clearer. A developmental analysis also allows for age-related gaps in the literature to be identified. In order to highlight the importance of development in media effects research, each chapter ends with a section entitled "Developmental Points of Interest," which places the empirical findings, underlying theory, and suggestions for future research in the context of developmental change. Finally, the text addresses five important questions in the study of media effects across development: How much media do youth consume, and why do they consume it? What are the theoretical rationales given to explain the impact of media consumption on infants, children, and adolescents? What are the specific positive and negative effects associated with consuming different types of media across development? How strong an influence are media in the lives of youth? And which techniques can be used to reduce the harmful consequences associated with media consumption?

Acknowledgments

I would like to thank Carolyn Emmert, Alexis Everson, and Thomas Marchhart for their feedback on earlier drafts of the manuscript. I am especially grateful to Janice and David Zalk for producing my three wonderful nephews, Joshua, Jacob, and Jesse.

1

Media in the Lives of Youth

As I walked toward the study, I heard the unmistakable clicking of a keyboard in use. My daughter, Michelle, who was 13 at the time, was rapidly typing away at the computer. Given that it was 3:30 in the afternoon, I was impressed, not only by the speed and accuracy of her typing, but also by the fact that she had actually started her homework without my prodding. But what was even more remarkable was that she was able to successfully complete her homework while simultaneously listening to *Grease* on her iPod, instant messaging her friends, checking her e-mail, and managing a stable of virtual horses. Like many teens, Michelle was deeply immersed in media. Immersion in media, however, is not limited to adolescence, as it occurs throughout children's formative years. Consider the following as just a thin slice of the vast media pie that youth consume: Babies are exposed to Mozart in an effort to increase their intellect; toddlers watch videos of a friendly purple dinosaur with the hopes of learning to identify colors and picking up a few social skills; preschoolers get a jump-start on their ABCs by playing computer games; grade-schoolers give virtual nurturance to an electronic pet and blow away villains in virtual battles; and teens constantly instant message each other, blog their lives, and update their Facebook pages. Such copious amounts of media consumption have proven to be a great source of concern for parents, researchers, and policy makers. But such concerns are not new, as they have accompanied media since its inception.

A Brief History of the Perceived Power of the Media

For millennia, media has been thought to influence those who consume it, and more often than not, the effects were thought to be negative.

In ancient Greece, youthful morals and values were thought to fall prey to the spoken word, as Socrates' trial and execution were meant to illustrate. In the 1700s, the written word was labeled by the Church as a bastion of evil, a belief that would persist for centuries. In the late 1800s, scholars believed that reading novels led to bloated imaginations, overexcited nervous systems, and distorted views of reality. Similarly, newspapers were thought to cause unnatural, rapid shifts in attention, which ultimately undermined the mental health of the reader. When combined with images, as was the case with newspaper comics of the early 1900s, the written word was perceived to be especially threatening to the morals, manners, and health of youth. Similar to newspaper comics in design and content, the comic books of the 1940s–1950s were believed to glorify violence, encourage homosexuality, stimulate unhealthy ideas about sex, laud delinquency, and teach lawlessness. Simply put, throughout history, the spoken and written word were vilified as "evil influences" on youth (Starker, 1989). Inflicting ills upon the world, however, was not limited to speech, newspapers, novels, and comic books.

By the early 1900s, the much maligned newspapers ran editorials denouncing the then newest medium, film. Movies were thought to teach depravity and immorality, and the cinema was marked as a training ground for criminals. Concern over the potential negative influence of movies grew over the next 20 years. In fact, the first large-scale empirical study of media on youth, conducted circa 1930, investigated the impact of viewing movies on children and adolescents' health, affect, behavior, and cognitions. The findings were primarily negative, with movie viewing linked with the creation of negative stereotypes, poor sleeping habits, low levels of cooperation, and increased anxiety (Jowett, Jarvie, & Fuller, 1996). However, the introduction of a new form of a medium does not guarantee the moniker *evil influence*, as such terms were primarily directed toward the most popular and widely owned media of the day (Starker, 1989). For instance, radio was not perceived as a threat to youth until receivers were found in nearly 90% of American homes, some 40 years after its introduction to the public. It was only then that numerous critics decried the most popular radio fare of the day, such as *The Shadow* and *Sam Spade*, as glorifying crime and giving youth dangerous ideas.

Starker's (1989) contention that as a medium's popularity rises, so too does its perceived power and negative influence on youth, has been repeated numerous times in the last 75 years. From 1950 to 1980, the primary negative influence of youth was perceived to be television, and in particular violent television (U.S. Surgeon General's Scientific Advisory Committee, 1972). In the 1990s and early 2000s, video games replaced TV as the primary threat to the good behavior and mental health of youth. For instance, in 2000, research on the aggression-promoting effects of violent video games was discussed in U.S. Senate subcommittee hearings (Anderson, 2000). Today, one of the greatest threats to youth appears to be from the Internet, with sexual predators lurking in chat rooms meant for youth and pornography merely a click away. Of course, "media" itself is neither bad nor good. Rather, it is the content of media that affects those who consume it. In addition to producing negative effects, media also has the potential to positively influence youth. For instance, comic book stories have been used to teach youth about AIDS, and video game play during medical procedures can reduce the perception of pain.

Historically, the perceived threat of media on children and adolescents was primarily based on conjecture and anecdotal evidence. That is, the reported harm that youth incurred from reading newspapers, watching films, and so on was based on testimonials or unsubstantiated accounts of youthful misdeeds and misgivings. Although lacking in number, testimonials can be very persuasive, as my closet full of Chia Pets, graveyard of seamonkeys, and unused Bedazzler illustrate. The use of anecdotes in advertisements makes sense, as retailers are trying to sell products: caveat emptor, after all. But, if anecdotal evidence is so flawed, why was it repeatedly used to vilify various forms of media for hundreds of years? Because of their generality and vividness, anecdotes have emotional power and, therefore, can appear to strengthen an argument, even though the "evidence" lacks scientific validity. More often than not, anecdotes provide a clear "take home" message. For hundreds of years, the messages were simple: Media is powerful, and media is bad for youth. Historically, it was the message that was important and not the research on which the message was based.

In contrast, in today's society the message does need to be justified by the means. It is only when the likelihood that biases and inaccuracies in observations are significantly reduced that a phenomenon can be said to be validly demonstrated. Currently, empirical evidence of media's effect on youth abounds. Some of the newer effects identified are indeed negative, whereas others are benign. But, based upon these studies, whether good or bad, one simple conclusion can be drawn: Media exposure *does* influence infants, children, and adolescents! There *is* power in the media, both perceived and real.

Investigating Media Effects Across Development

Before delving into the research, it is important to understand the general age-related periods of development that scientists use. *Infancy* refers to the period of childhood immediately following birth through 12 months of age. *Toddlerhood*, which is often signified by walking without support, takes place between 12 months and 3 years of age. *Early childhood*, also known as the preschool years, occurs between the ages of 3 and 5. Elementary school–aged children between 6 and 10 years of age are classified as being in *middle childhood*. *Early adolescence* refers to youth ranging from 11 to 13 years of age. *Middle adolescence* is composed of 14- to 16-year olds, and *late adolescence* refers to individuals aged 17 to 19. Of note, in their studies, researchers also make use of the age-related terms *childhood* (toddlerhood through middle childhood), *tweens* (8 to 14 years of age), and *adolescence* (early adolescence through late adolescence).

When studying children, extrapolating the findings from adults to youth, or from older children to younger children for that matter, can lead to incorrect and misleading conclusions. For instance, according to functional magnetic resonance brain imaging (fMRI), the neuroanatomy involved in the processing of a single word and basic judgments involving numbers differs between adults and children (Ansari & Dhital, 2006; Schlaggar et al., 2002). Moreover, young adults have been shown to process information nearly two times faster than youth in early adolescence or younger (Hale, 1990). The results of these and other studies lead to the following conclusion: The greater the difference in age between adults and children or between older youth and younger youth, the greater the likelihood that they will differ physically, cognitively, socially, and emotionally. As such, it is always important to keep developmental status in mind when considering the effects of media on infants, children, and adolescents.

What are the positive and negative outcomes associated with media consumption across development? Are youth more vulnerable to the effects of media at certain ages more so than at others? How big an influence does media exert on the behaviors, thoughts, and emotions of youth? These are but a few of the many questions to be addressed in the coming pages. So, where do we start our investigation of media effects on youth? We begin by exploring just how much media infants, children, and adolescents actually consume.

Media Ownership Across Development

Media in the Home

Televisions, VCR–DVD players, radios, and CD players are found in nearly every home in the United States. In fact, for families with adolescents, trying to find a home without these types of media is extremely difficult, as 99% of homes have each of the aforementioned items. For families with children between 0 and 10 years of age, the number of TVs, radios, and CD players is virtually identical to that reported for homes with adolescents. But, for some unknown reason, in homes with youth under 10 years of age, 5% fewer DVD–VCR players (93%) are found.

Computers with Internet access are becoming increasingly common, with around two thirds of children under the age of 10 and 75% of youth 11 years of age and older finding themselves able to access the World Wide Web from home. Similar percentages can be found for ownership of video game consoles during adolescence, as around 80% of youth between 8 and 18 years of age own at least one. However, only 50% of families with younger children have video game consoles in their homes. As costs for computers, Internet access, and gaming systems decline, it is expected that these transmitters of media will be found increasingly in the homes of American families, even those with the youngest of children. For instance, the percentage of children under age 7 who have computers with Internet access in their homes increased 6%, during a recent 2-year period. Moreover, the percentage of homes with high-speed Internet access has more than doubled, from 20% to 42%, during that same period (Rideout & Hamel, 2006; Roberts, Foehr, & Rideout, 2005).

Media in the Bedroom

It is a given that most children and adolescents want TVs, computers, and video game consoles in their bedrooms. In fact, prior to writing this chapter, my 10-year-old son asked me to put a video game console in his

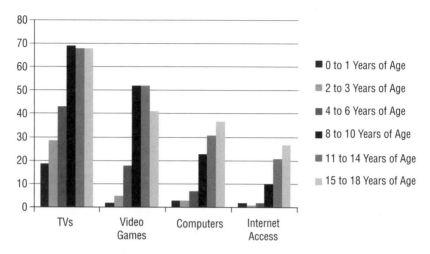

Figure 1.1   Media in the bedroom by age.
Source: Rideout and Hamel (2006), and Roberts et al. (2005).
Note: There are no data available for 7-year-olds due to data collection issues.

bedroom. I said, "No." My daughter, who is 3 years older, tried a more sophisticated approach. First, she asked me for a horse, and when I said, "No," to that, she then asked for a TV. Again, I said, "No." However, the fact that my children do not have TVs and video game consoles in their bedrooms places them in the minority amongst their peers.

During infancy, toddlerhood, and early childhood, a very small percentage of children younger than 4 years of age (5%) have video game consoles in their bedrooms. However, between 4 and 6 years of age, that percentage more than triples (18%), and by the time youth reach age 8, and consistently thereafter, approximately 50% of children will be able to play video games in their bedrooms. (See Figure 1.1.) This is especially true for boys, as two out of three boys have video game consoles in their bedrooms. At a significantly higher percentage, the likelihood of finding a TV in a child's bedroom from 8 to 18 years of age stabilizes at around 70%. In contrast, only 33% of children younger than age 6 have TVs in their bedrooms. Surprisingly, during infancy TVs can be found in one out of every five bedrooms. Computers with Internet access are the least likely type of media to be found in the bedrooms of children and adolescents. In fact, less than 30% of adolescents between 15 and 18 years old can access the Internet privately from their bedrooms. Not surprisingly, as the age of children decreases, so too does the likelihood that they will be able to access the World Wide Web from their beds. For instance, Internet access is virtually nonexistent (2%) in the bedrooms of children under the age of 6. Across development, gender differences are prevalent, with boys having more personal media (e.g., TVs, DVD players, and computers with Internet access) in their bedrooms than girls (Rideout & Hamel, 2006; Roberts et al., 2005).

Media in the bedroom aids sleep: A myth in need of busting
Relative to other youth, children and adolescents with TVs in their bedrooms stay up later at night, get less sleep, have more sleep disturbances (e.g., waking up in the middle of the night), and feel more tired the next day. Similar sleep-related problems have been reported for youth playing computer games, accessing the Internet, and listening to music at bedtime. The lone bedtime media-related activity that does not appear to adversely affect sleep is reading (Eggermont & Van den Bulck, 2006; Paavonen, Pennonen, Roine, Valkonen, & Lahikainen, 2006). Moreover, for youth between the ages of 8 and 18, having media in the bedroom increases overall media exposure by 2 hours per day (Roberts et al., 2005).

Why do parents allow media in the bedroom?
Do you think that any parents would allow a neighbor who they have never met to talk to their 13-year-old daughter about sex or provide her with sexually graphic content? Do you think any parents would want that same neighbor to show their impressionable 4-year-old son imagery that glamorizes violence and displays graphic and disturbing images of death? The answer to both of these questions is "Of course not!" Why, then, do parents allow media that do most, if not all, of the aforementioned activities into their children's bedroom?

A recent study by Rideout and Hamel (2006) asked parents of young children (6 years old or younger) that very question. The most common answer given (55%) was that placing a TV in their child's bedroom frees up TVs in the main part of the house. By doing so, other family members can watch what they want, thereby reducing family conflicts involving program choices and use of the remote control. If fact, 23% of parents report that having a TV in the child's bedroom reduces fights between siblings. Less conflict and fewer fights between family members mean that parents will have fewer hassles to deal with.

The second most common answer given (39%) was that placing a TV in their child's bedroom keeps the child occupied, thereby allowing parents to do chores around the house or get some "downtime." Simply put, the TV becomes a readily available babysitter. Finally, nearly 20% of parents justify placing a TV in their child's bedroom because they believe that television acts as a nonmedicinal sleep aid. Thus, after saying goodnight to their child, parents will not have to return to help a fidgety, sleep-fighting child get to sleep. As the most common parental answers illustrate, parents place TVs in their children's bedroom because it makes the parents' life easier and more hassle free.

Despite the fact that many parents allow unsupervised use of media in their children's bedroom, two out of three parents express "significant concerns" that youth are frequently exposed to inappropriate content when consuming media. As an example, more than half of parents believe that, for adolescents, sexual media contributes "a lot" to sexual behavior; and 43% believe that media violence contributes "a lot" to aggressive behavior. Although parents express concerns about the influence of media on youth in general, they tend to be less concerned about the influence of media on their own children. In fact, only 20% of parents are worried that *their* children are exposed to "a lot" of media content unsuitable for youth (Rideout & Hamel, 2006).

By monitoring the content of TV shows, video games, music choices, instant messages, e-mail, "buddy lists" and the like, parents believe that they can effectively protect their children from inappropriate media content. It is the perceived control of content that gives parents confidence that their children are safe from harmful media. However, as children age and parents' ability to monitor, and thus control, their children's media exposure decreases, the percentage of parents believing that their progeny have been exposed to inappropriate content in the media more than doubles (14% for parents of children, and 30% for parents of teens; Rideout & Hamel, 2006). Despite these concerns, TVs, video game consoles, and the like continue to remain in their children's bedroom, and sleep continues to be disturbed.

Media Consumption Across Development

Measuring Media Use

Prior to relaying media consumption patterns evident across development, it is crucial to understand how such data are collected. For a critical consumer of research, it is important to be aware of the advantages and disadvantages of the assessment procedures involved in any study.

Global time estimates

When using a global time estimate (GTE), respondents (e.g., a child or parent) answer a series of questions regarding the amount of time spent engaging in a particular media-related activity during the previous day or week. For instance, a typical GTE question would be "How many hours did you spend watching TV this past week?" This type of measure is easy to administrate, requiring relatively little work for the respondent. The trade-off for ease of use, however, is imprecise data. In less than 30 seconds, the respondent is required to recall all relevant media-related experiences, estimate the amount of time spent engaged in each activity, and create a summary tally to report (Board on Children, Youth & Families, 2006).

Moreover, such assessments are prone to *social desirability*, which refers to the situation in which socially acceptable answers are provided, rather than what the participant truly thinks, believes, or knows. Most parents want to appear caring and thoughtful regarding the welfare of their children. Given the negative publicity surrounding the effects of media use on aggression, obesity, and so on, it is reasonable to assume that many parents would respond to media-related questions in a socially desirable manner. As a result, parents may underreport the amount of time youth are actually exposed to media. For adolescents, the opposite may occur. Rather than responding in a socially desirable way, some adolescents may respond in an antisocial manner. Examples of antisocial responding include making patterns in the data, randomly responding, and answering the opposite of how one really feels. Currently, there is no research on antisocial responding in the developmental literature.

Time use diaries

In contrast to the simple and easy-to-use GTE, time use diaries (TUDs) offer a more accurate and complete picture of an individual's daily media consumption in the context of the day's activities. Over a 24-hour period, respondents record all of their activities, including those activities not involving media use (e.g., playing baseball). The beauty of the TUD is that it relays the individual's day as it unfolds. In this very labor-intensive method, respondents are required to note the primary activity they are engaged in (e.g., TV shows watched), the duration of that activity (e.g., 5:00–5:30), people present during the activity (e.g., Mom), and other events going on while engaging in the primary activity (e.g., talking). Although TUDs are useful at capturing routines and daily events, respondents frequently refuse to include activities that they would consider private (e.g., surfing the Internet for porn). Additionally, TUDs assess only primary and secondary activities; tertiary activities and beyond are not recorded. Finally, noncompliance with the requirements of the task (i.e., failure to record an activity in the log) becomes compromised for events of brief duration, especially those that are recurring. For instance, respondents may decide that recording every time they check their e-mail is cumbersome, and refuse to record the activity. Moreover, similar to GTEs, TUDs do not provide information regarding the content of the media consumed. Given the difficulties in getting data, TUDs are rarely used in media consumption research with youth. Instead, researchers make use of a modified TUD: the media diary.

Media diaries

In essence, media diaries are TUDs that spotlight media use. Because media use is targeted, participants easily record their media consumption by circling an answer on a user-friendly grid. For instance, listed across the top of the survey used by the Kaiser Family Foundation to assess media habits in youth (Roberts et al., 2005) are half-hour increment time slots, such as 6:30–7:00 and 7:00–7:30. Down the left side of the grid are a series of questions (e.g., "What was your main media activity?" and "What else were you doing?"). At the cross section of the question and the time slot is a rectangle within which are a series of potential answers. For example, response rectangles for the question regarding the main media activity consumed list responses such as *listening to music* and *watching TV*. All that the respondent is required to do, therefore, is circle the appropriate answer during the appropriate time slot.

Reading ability is an important factor to consider when having children and adolescents fill out a media diary. Youth cannot provide accurate responses if they do not understand the questions. Not only is reading comprehension important, but reading speed is as well. Children need to be able to complete a media diary questionnaire before losing focus. For this very reason, during the Kaiser Family Foundation study (Roberts et al., 2005) mentioned above, third grade children filled out a media diary with fewer questions than the one completed by adolescents. When media diaries are used with children 8 years of age and under, it is the parent who typically fills in the grid. Thus, as with GTE, social desirability can play a role in parents' willingness to illustrate the totality of their child's media use. An additional limitation of the media diary method is that the amount of media usage needed to trigger a response is specified by the researcher. The Kaiser Media grid, for example, asks youth to circle a response on the grid when they have consumed at least 15 minutes of the 30-minute time block. Thus, media use of 10 minutes would not be recorded. The possibility exists, therefore, that 20 minutes of media consumption per hour (10 per 30-minute slot) go unrecorded. Finally, similar to previous media consumption measures, media diaries fail to log the type of content consumed.

Electronic monitoring

Rather than relying on parents or youth to fill in grids or log media consumption activities, electronic monitoring systems (EMSs) collect such data automatically. In EMS, data are collected through the use of a stationary meter connected to a television set or a smaller, portable meter carried around by the individual. Both types of meters function like a media diary, recording the time of day and amount of media consumed. However, EMSs go beyond GTEs, TUDs, and media diaries because they also record the type of content (e.g., the genre) consumed. This is a clear advantage over the other methods, as the content consumed is just as important to understanding media consumption patterns across development as is the total amount of media consumed. Nevertheless, EMS is not without flaw. In order to identify the primary consumer of the media and the amount of time attending to the media, participants need to punch in activation and termination codes on the meter. This is the Achilles heel of EMS, as failure to log in or log out can produce erroneous data. Additionally, EMS is limited in the types of media tracked. Computers, video games consoles, handheld devices, and CD players cannot be assessed with EMS. Currently, EMS is primarily used for commercial assessments of radio and television use across development; rarely is EMS used for academic research purposes. However, the future of media consumption research will most assuredly use these devices, as they are easy to use, provide accurate data when used properly, and have the potential to reduce social desirability (Vandewater & Lee, 2006).

Evaluating media use assessments

Little is known about the accuracy of EMS in relation to actual media use. However, when comparing media diaries and GTEs, media diaries clearly win out. In comparison to GTEs, estimates of media use based on diary entries correlate the highest with objective recordings of television use in the home. Despite this fact, estimates of media use (at least for television) generated by ESMs, GTEs, and media diaries are remarkably consistent. Vandewater and Lee (2006) reported that estimates of average TV consumption by adolescents vary by no more than a half hour amongst the various measurements. Although the measurement technique used to assess *general* media use does not appear to matter that much, when making *predictions* from media use to an outcome variable (e.g., sexual behavior), measuring techniques matter. As such, Vandewater and Lee suggested that researchers attempting to relate media consumption to individual behaviors or attitudes should eschew GTEs in favor of EMSs or media diaries.

Media Use During Infancy, Toddlerhood, and Early Childhood

A recent study by the Kaiser Family Foundation (Roberts et al., 2005) found that even very young children consume significant amounts of media on a daily basis. On an average day, approximately 88% of infants (over 6 months of age) listen to music, 56% watch TV, 24% are entertained by DVDs, 2% use a computer, and 1% play video games. One to 2 years later, daily consumption of music remains consistent, as 84% of toddlers are exposed to it. However, during the toddler period, media consumption increases: 81% watch TV, 41% watch DVDs, 12% use a computer, and 8% play video games. Preschoolers listen to music and watch TV daily at levels consistent with those of toddlers (78% and 79%, respectively). However, there is an increase in the percentage of preschoolers using computers (26%) and video games (18%). As a result of these increases, the percentage of youth watching DVD entertainment drops nearly 10% (to 32%).

It is worth noting that 39% of children under the age of 2, 12% of toddlers, and 10% of preschoolers do not consume any screen media (TVs, DVDs, computers, and video games). For those youth who do consume media, the following data apply. Infants consume about 1 hour per day of screen media. That number doubles to slightly over 2 hours per day of screen media for children between 2 and 6 years of age. Moreover, throughout infancy and early childhood, children listen to music for about 1 hour per day, while being read to for about 45–50 minutes. In case you were wondering, children younger than 6 years of age spend about 1 hour per day playing outside, if in fact they do go outside, as nearly 20% do not (Rideout & Hamel, 2006).

Media Consumption During Middle Childhood and Adolescence

In general, media consumption increases from early to middle childhood, stabilizing thereafter. Research indicates that youth between the ages of 8 and 18 spend nearly 8½ hours per day consuming media, more than twice the amount of time that younger children spend engaging in the same media-related activities. For youth over the age of 8, approximately 4½ hours per day are devoted to screen media (i.e., TV, DVDs, and movies), with an additional hour for audio media, print media, video games, and computer use. Interestingly, the percentage of youth consuming screen media on a daily basis is consistent with that of earlier years (85% listen to music, 81% watch TV, and 42% consume DVD entertainment). Virtually all youth (97%) play electronic games on computers or video game devices (Lenhart et al., 2008; Roberts et al., 2005).

There are two developmental findings worth noting. First, from middle childhood to late adolescence, video game play decreases. Second, computer use and listening to music rise in popularity. By the end of high school, adolescents spend just as much time, if not more, listening to music as they do watching television. In fact, music is the medium of choice for youth engaging in non-media-related activities, such as doing chores, walking to school, or riding on the bus (Foehr, 2006). Many researchers feel that music may be the medium with the greatest perceived importance to adolescents. In support of this contention, consider the following: when asked what medium they would want with them if stuck on a desert island, the number one choice of adolescents was music (Roberts, Christenson, & Gentile, 2003).

However, computers are encroaching into the hallowed ground of music. With increasing age, adolescents spend more time on their computer and online, a finding that can explain the reported decrease in console and handheld video game play. Whether it is writing e-mail, instant messaging a friend, or blogging, computer activity becomes increasingly important to youth with development. The fact that computer use more than doubles from middle childhood to late adolescence illustrates the increasing importance of computers in the lives of teenagers. However, in addition to simultaneously surfing the Internet, engaging in discourse, and sending messages to others, adolescents can also use the computer to engage in their other favorite activity, listening to music. How can they accomplish all these tasks at once? Media multitasking is the answer.

Media multitasking

Youth are media multitasking (i.e., using more than one media-related activity at the same time) in increasing numbers. In fact, between 1999 and 2005, the percentage of time media multitasking increased by 10%, to an overall level of 26%. According to Foehr (2006), media-related activities least likely to be multitasked by youth were TV watching and videogame play, with computer use being multitasked the most. However, 20% of youth between 8 and 18 do not report any media multitasking behaviors. In general, children and adolescents who media multitask have at least one of the following characteristics: (a) They consume high levels of media, (b) the TV can be viewed while sitting at the computer, (c) the TV is "on" in the house the majority of the time, (d) they possess a personality characterized by sensation seeking, and (e) they are female. The first three characteristics seem sensible, as each affords youth the opportunity to multitask. It also makes perfect sense that sensation-seeking youth media multitask more than others, as the process of multitasking involves heightened sensations. But why are girls more likely to multitask than boys? Foehr posited two primary explanations for this finding. First, due to evolutionary pressures associated with being the "gatherer" in a hunter–gatherer society, girls are genetically predisposed to multitask. The second possibility is much more parsimonious, requiring no assumptions about the application of evolutionary processes to modern-day life. Specifically, girls may multitask more than boys simply because they consume more media that allows media multitasking to take place. For example, boys watch more TV and play more video games than girls (Roberts, Henriksen, & Christenson, 1999), and each of these media is associated with little multitasking behavior.

Why Youth Consume Media

Children and adolescents spend the majority of their out-of-school activities with media. But why is media consumption so psychologically appealing to youth? To answer this question, two primary theories have been forwarded: (a) the uses and gratifications perspective, and (b) self-determination theory.

Uses and Gratifications Approach to Media Consumption

According to the uses and gratifications perspective, enjoyment is the key to understanding media consumption. Although the needs of youth are many and varied, multiple "uses" and associated "gratifications" of media consumption have been identified. The most frequently cited uses and gratifications include arousal, companionship, escape, habit, learning, passing time, and relaxation (Sparks, 2001).

Companionship
For youth, media consumption has the ability to promote friendships and maintain relationships. For instance, youth can watch television, play video games, and listen to music with their friends. Additionally, the Internet allows relationships to be maintained across distances, as youth can IM one another, chat online with people they know, and play online games against family and friends. Imaginary relationships with characters in the media (both real and fictional) can also give youth the *feeling* of companionship, a phenomenon referred to as a *parasocial relationship* (Rubin & McHugh, 1987).

Parasocial relationships are one-way interactions in which the individual feels an emotional, even intimate, connection toward a media-based character. Moreover, people involved in parasocial relationships maintain a vast knowledge base regarding their parasocial friend, even going so far as to believe that they know how that character will think, feel, and behave. Over time and media exposure, parasocial relationships strengthen in intensity. Such relationships seem so real to individuals that they experience anxiety and depression when forced to "break up" with their parasocial friend (e.g., due to a show's cancellation or a character dying; Eyal & Cohen, 2006). Unfortunately, little is known about the nature of parasocial relationships during childhood and adolescence. However, a recent study with adolescent participants found that teens engaging in *moderately* intense parasocial relationships perceive themselves to have poor relationships with their parents but good relationships with their friends. Thus, parasocial relationships might provide teens with "friends" that can be gossiped about without any real-world repercussions. However, youth espousing *strong* and *intense* parasocial relationships tended to feel alone and were deficient in real-life friendships. For these teens, parasocial relationships appear to take the place of the real-life relationships that they are lacking (Giles & Maltby, 2004). However, it should be pointed out that parasocial relationships do not provide the same benefits to health and well-being that real relationships provide.

Escape

Doing chores, completing homework, and dealing with annoying siblings are daily occurrences for youth. In order to experience a respite from this burdensome reality, youth consume media. Children and adolescents can escape to virtual worlds in cyberspace, immerse themselves in the lyrics of their favorite musical group, and otherwise get lost in the content of the media that they use. Does media use truly allow youth to escape reality? Although there is not enough research to validate this contention, what has been done points in this direction. For instance, Johnston (1995) found that many adolescents report watching horror movies to circumvent dealing with real-world problems. These same adolescents, however, also used drugs to avoid dealing with troubling interpersonal issues. Thus, although media can be used to escape reality, it remains to be seen if doing so provides a health benefit to the youthful media consumer. In fact, if using media to escape reality becomes commonplace, it becomes a habit.

Habit

Sometimes youth watch TV, play video games, and check their e-mail because of unconscious desires to do so, and because of feelings of relief or comfort when engaging in the activity. Such behavior indicates that a media habit has been formed, and when media habits strengthen over time, youth may display symptoms characteristic of an addiction (McIlwraith, Jacobvitz, Kubey, & Alexander, 1991). Media addiction is a controversial topic, for unlike alcohol and drug addictions, foreign chemicals are not introduced into the body when using "plug-in" drugs, like television and video games. Media addiction, therefore, is similar in nature to the recognized psychological disorder known as gambling addiction.

Those purported to be addicted to media have the following characteristics: (a) They use media excessively, (b) they use media more than intended, (c) attempts to reduce media use are unsuccessful, (d) media consumption prevents the individual from engaging in other activities (e.g., schoolwork), and (e) they feel psychological withdrawal symptoms (e.g., irritability, unhappiness) once media use stops. However, the American Psychiatric Association (S. Bakshi, July 2008, personal communication) currently does not recognize media addiction as a true psychopathology. Instead, it believes that more research is necessary to determine if "media addiction" is a diagnosable mental disorder (ScienceDaily.com, 2007). Regardless, for some youth, media use can disrupt and interfere with their ability to function in the real world.

Learning

At times, children and adolescents intentionally seek out media to obtain information. For instance, with just a click of a mouse, the Internet provides youth with a plethora of informational websites. One such website, Wikipedia, has even replaced the need for printed encyclopedias in many homes. However, not all media-based learning is good for youth. As an example, research has shown that viewers of violent television "learn" that the world is a mean place, with potential harm around every corner (i.e., the mean world effect; Gerbner, Gross, Morgan, & Signorielli, 1994). However, youth do not seek out violent TV with the intent of learning this "fact." Rather, the mean world effect was an *unintended* artifact of media consumption. Thus, learning can take place during media consumption, even if the intent to learn is absent.

Passing time

In the poem "Time Is" by Henry Van Dyke, the perception of time varies as a function of the emotional state of the individual, as "time is too short for those who rejoice" and "too long for those who grieve." Recent research supports Van Dyke's poetic contention that emotion influences time perception. Specifically, Campbell and Bryant (2007) demonstrated that time is perceived to go by slowly for novice skydivers fearing their first jump but quickly for those looking forward to it. Like those individuals positively anticipating their first jump, media use can make time fly by (with the added benefit of not having to worry about your parachute opening; Rau, Peng, & Yang, 2006). In fact, one recent study found that nearly all (99%) adolescents and adults playing video games reported losing track of time (Wood, Griffiths, & Parke, 2007). It should come as no surprise, then, that media is a frequent companion for youth who are waiting in line, being transported between activities, or otherwise bored. It addition to passing time, media use can help reduce boredom-related frustration, anger, and hostility (Zillmann, 1998).

Relaxation
When my kids are wound up (i.e., they are annoying me), I send them to their bedrooms to "chill out." And in order to chill, my daughter listens to music or reads, whereas my son plays with his Legos and listens to books on tape. Using media to relax is a commonplace occurrence across development, although little research on children and adolescents exists. Of note, the key to media-based relaxation is choosing media with relaxing content, like classical music. Highly arousing video games and exciting television shows will not engender a relaxed physiological state in the user. Remember, though, even relaxing media can keep children up at night, as they may refuse to put the media down (or turn it off) until the content is finished.

Sensation seeking
In the summer of 2007, public outrage followed the airing of the final episode of the HBO series *The Sopranos*. Were viewers upset at the gratuitous violence displayed during the point-blank shooting and subsequent head squishing by an SUV of New York mob boss Phil Leotardo? No. Did people cancel their HBO subscriptions because AJ Soprano seemed to get over his depression by dating an underaged girl and becoming an assistant movie producer? AJ certainly is whiny and annoying, but no. Rather, the public was outraged because after a period of foreshadowing and suspense associated with the potential killing of Tony Soprano, the screen went blank, thus ending the series. It was the *lack* of stimulation that caused the furor, not the presence of it. Users of media want to feel their hearts race, their blood flow, and their palms sweat. Media use can be exciting and stimulating. For this very reason, children and adolescents seek it out (Zukerman, 1994).

Self-Determination Theory

Self-determination theory (SDT; Deci & Ryan, 1985) focuses on the factors that influence human motivation. Recently Ryan and colleagues (Ryan, Rigby, & Przybylski, 2006) have applied SDT tenets to media consumption in order to explain media's motivational pull, that is, clarify the reasons as to why so many individuals are drawn to media. Of particular interest is the SDT contention that media consumption can help fulfill three basic psychological needs, and in doing so enhance feelings of well-being (e.g., self-esteem, positive emotions, and vitality) in the user. The three psychological needs of note are autonomy, competence, and relatedness.

Autonomy refers to the sense of control that individuals feel when doing something on their own. Thus, feelings of autonomy are primarily invoked during activities that youth *choose* to engage in, rather than those that they were *forced* to do. Media-related activities engendering autonomy include using the TV remote control, choosing the songs to be played on an iPod, regulating the impact of content when reading comic books, and navigating an avatar through a virtual world. Although there are no empirical studies demonstrating that feelings of autonomy result from media use, there is research illustrating the importance of an autonomous worldview (i.e., locus of control) to the health and well-being of children and adolescents. For instance, feelings of autonomy have been linked with higher academic achievement and better problem-solving abilities in youth (Halloran, Doumas, John, & Margolin, 1999).

The second psychological need, *competence*, refers to the successful completion of tasks, especially those that are challenging. Relevant media-based examples include completing all levels of a video game, finishing an online Sudoku puzzle, knowing the details of every *Star Trek* episode ever made, and creating your own Youtube.com video. As these examples illustrate, certain types of media-based experiences (e.g., completing a video game) create an immediate feeling of task-oriented competence. Other media-based experiences, in contrast, may lead to feelings of competence only long after the media was consumed. For instance, knowing the minute details of *Star Trek* Episode 2 ("Charlie X") might lead to feelings of competence only during a *Star Trek* convention years later.

Competence is remarkably similar to the developmental notion of *self-efficacy*, which refers to the feeling that one can independently complete a variety of tasks. Research on children and adolescents has demonstrated that mastery experiences (i.e., excelling at some ability) lead youth to believe that through hard work and practice, they will also be able to successfully complete future tasks. Additional benefits associated with having high levels of self-efficacy include better peer relationships, lower drug use, and higher academic achievement (Ausbrooks, Thomas, & Williams, 1995). Thus, competence does appear to be an important contributor to the well-being of youth. The question that remains, however, is whether media consumption can also positively influence competence in youth. Currently, the data suggest that the feelings of competence engendered by media consumption may be limited to the media consumed, and not enhance general feelings of competence.

Over a decade ago, Funk and Buchman (1996) found that girls reporting the greatest amount of video game play rated themselves as the least competent in academic, athletic, and social settings. Why would this be? Should not the competence associated with high levels of video game play lead to general feelings of competence? Not necessarily. Harter (1987) contended that in response to doing poorly in areas traditionally valued by society (e.g., academics and athletics), youth attempt to cognitively reduce (i.e., discount) the importance of these competencies. At the same time, these discounting youth attempt to cognitively increase the importance of nontraditional competencies in which they excel. For instance, a poor athlete may devalue the importance of athleticism to his future because he is a music-mixing master. Adolescents are thought to engage in discounting to help maintain a positive view of the self. However, if traditional competencies are deemed to be socially unacceptable, then valuing nontraditional competencies, such as video game play, does not aid the sense of self. In fact, as the Funk and Buchman (1996) data indicate, it may actually hurt it.

According to SDT, relatedness is the final psychological need deemed important for well-being. *Relatedness* refers to a sense of connection with others. Media-based activities that lead to feelings of relatedness include online video game play (with text or aural messages), e-mail, instant messaging, blogging, as well as written and video-based discussions. Research during middle childhood and adolescence indicates that youth frequently engage in relatedness activities through media, and that such use enhances current real-life bidirectional relationships (e.g., friends; Valkenburg & Peter, 2007a). However, as the previous discussion on parasocial relationships illustrated, relatedness may also occur in a unidirectional manner, from the media consumer to the entertainment character.

Additional Reasons for Media Consumption

Beyond SDT and the uses and gratifications perspective, there are three additional reasons posited to explain the psychological appeal of media: identity formation, social status, and mood management. Each is presented in turn.

Identity formation
Children and adolescents may use media to help establish or maintain their individual and social identities. *Individual identity* refers to the traits and attributes used to describe the self, such as beautiful, smart, and outgoing. *Social identity*, on the other hand, refers to the self-assigned social group membership to which one belongs, and the emotional significance attached to that membership. Thus, whereas individual identity allows youth to answer the question "Who am I?" social identity helps youth answer the question "Where do I fit in?" For instance, listening to death metal music may help youth maintain the view of themselves as a nonconformist (individual identity) and a member of the Goth community (social identity). Multiple studies have shown that media use can influence identity formation in youth, especially during early adolescence (e.g., Huntemann & Morgan, 2001).

Social status
During middle childhood, children begin to evaluate and compare themselves to their friends in a variety of areas, such as academic prowess, athletic ability, and physical appearance—a phenomenon known as *social comparison*. The social comparison process is used to help youth establish their identity and figure out their place in the larger group (e.g., the best baseball player). When my son was 9 years old, he repeatedly asked me to buy him violent video games rated as inappropriate for youth younger than 17 years of age (i.e., M-rated). In order to support his case, he reported to me that many of his friends already played M-rated video games (e.g., *Doom 3* and *Halo*). It is clear that through the process of social comparison, my son's friends were bragging about their video game experiences in an attempt to elevate their social status

in the peer group. This anecdotal story matches Zillmann's (1998) contention that boys, more so than girls, use media for such purposes. However, there is little research in this area, and none from a developmental perspective.

Mood management

When I was in college, I had a friend who was rejected by a girl that he had a crush on. Shortly thereafter, I found him repeatedly listening to Led Zeppelin's classic ballad, "Stairway to Heaven." This example illustrates the use of media as a means for controlling one's emotional state (in this case, maintaining sadness), a phenomenon commonly referred to as *mood management*. However, the above example is not typical of mood-matching behavior in adolescent males, as males tend to use music to match angry moods. Girls, in contrast, tend to use music to maintain solemn moods (Roberts & Christenson, 2001). Although the vast majority of research in this area has involved the influence of music on mood, all forms of media can be used to create or modify one's emotional state (Zillmann, 1998). Other than during adolescence, however, little is known about the use of media for mood management.

Catharsis: A mood management perspective   One area of mood management that is of particular interest to media researchers is anger reduction. According to Freud, anger and aggressive urges build up over time and, if not properly released, result in violent outbursts. *Catharsis* refers to the situation in which volatile pent-up anger and aggressive feelings are freed, thereby preventing future violence. It is commonly believed that playing violent video games and watching violent programs on television provide a cathartic release for youth, resulting in a reduction of angry feelings and aggressive behavior. Fortunately, beliefs can be tested, and over a period of 60 years, there has been little empirical evidence forwarded in support of this contention (Bushman, 2002).

Developmental Points of Interest

Youth consume copious amounts of media across development. Regardless of the type of media involved, each has the potential to provide infants, children, and adolescents with rewarding experiences (Palmgreen, Wenner, & Rayburn, 1980). Of course, those rewards are tied to the specific needs of youth. For instance, some youth may play video games because they want to alleviate boredom, whereas others play because of a desire for the company of friends. In general, the uses and gratifications perspective focuses on the gratifying experiences and positive emotions associated with media consumption. However, each use and associated gratification are idiosyncratic, without any over-arching theory to explain the connection. In fact, research has yet to investigate how the uses and gratifications of media change across development. Moreover, many researchers feel that there is more to media consumption then immediate gratification, as not all media-based experiences are positive. For instance, being unable to finish a level in a video game can cause frustration and anger in the gamer, hor-ror movies can scare the viewer well into the night, and documentaries such as Spike Lee's *When the Levees Broke* can cause great despair in the viewer. Thus, when looking beyond joy, it becomes clear that media consumption occurs as a result of strong motivational forces, such as those identified by SDT. Specifically, individuals are drawn to media that can engender autonomy, competence, and relatedness.

Although SDT adds insight into why youth consume so much media, there are several issues that remain unresolved. First, how do feelings of autonomy, competence, and relatedness change as youth age? Second, across development, which medium (e.g., video games and TV) has the greatest influence on basic psychological needs? Third, which of the three processes (i.e., autonomy, competence, and related-ness) is most likely to be influenced by media? Fourth, are the benefits of media consumption on well-being limited to the context surround-ing the media experience (e.g., video game self-esteem), or can media use effect a greater, more general change in well-being (e.g., global self-esteem)? Fifth, just how many experiences are needed to move short-term benefits to long-term changes in well-being? Finally, SDT focuses on media use in general, devoid of content. Do the supposed health benefits to youth apply to media content involving drug use, porno-graphy, and violence?

There are many different reasons to explain why youth consume media. It would come as no surprise if each of the aforementioned explanations accounted for child and adolescent media consumption at some point during development. In addition, understanding differences in the psychological appeal of media, from infancy through adolescence, may provide insight into the changing nature of media consumption across development. For instance, although "learning" may be the primary explanation for media consumption during the preschool years, identity formation may explain media's appeal during adolescence. Also, different media may serve youth in different ways. As an example, youth may watch educational TV to enhance learning, listen to rebellious music to form an identity, and play violent video games to feel competent. As these examples illustrate, the *content* of the media consumed (e.g., sex, drugs, and rock-n-roll) is just as important to the understanding of the psychological appeal of media as is the media itself.

Finally, the potential influence of media consumption on youth may vary as a function of the reasons given to justify its use. In support of this contention, Johnston (1995) found that after watching horror movies, sensation-seeking adolescents reported more positive emotions than youth who watched these types of films in an attempt to alter their mood. Thus, the gratifications sought *prior* to media use may explain not only the psychological appeal of that particular media but also the potential *impact* of that media on the individual. However, little developmental research has been conducted on this issue.

2

Media Effect Theories

"Where's the rent?!" So yells the foul-mouthed, beer-toting, slightly buzzed property owner, Pearl, in the Funnyordie.com video offering *The Landlord*. Pearl, played by the director's 2-year-old daughter, has many lines that are less than appropriate for a toddler to say, including, "I'm gonna smack you," "I need to get my drink on," "You're an asshole," and "I want my money, bitch." Besides being absolutely hilarious, this 2 minute and 25 second video sparked outrage across the country. Numerous TV talk show hosts even wondered if the pint-sized toddler had been "damaged" by the experience (Zumbrun, 2007). Did the video go "too far," as the talk show pundits proclaimed? Just what would the damage to Pearl be? Is she destined to a life of cussing and debauchery? Fortunately, the developmental concept known as socialization helps answer these types of questions.

Socialization and Theory

Socialization is the process through which youth acquire the rules, standards, and values of a culture. Unless experiences are particularly traumatic, socialization takes time, with repeated exposure required before rules, standards, and values can become engrained (DeHart, Sroufe, & Cooper, 2004). With this in mind, there really was no need to worry about Pearl in the first place. Having her repeat sentences that she does not understand is by no means traumatic. Even though she might have picked up a few swear words along the way, it is doubtful that Pearl will be asking her preschool teachers to pass the "damn" juice. In fact, her father reports that in real life, Pearl does not use any of the foul language from the video (Jones et al., 2007). Despite the limited impact associated with the infrequent use of swear words at age 2, the controversy

Table 2.1   Media Effect Theories

• Hypodermic needle or magic bullet theory	• Social learning theory
• Excitation transfer theory	• Social cognitive theory
• Cultivation perspective	• Script theory
• Priming	• Universal media model

surrounding *The Landlord* raises three broader psychological questions. First, just what are the environmental factors that act as socializing agents of infants, children, and adolescents? Second, what are the specific effects associated with media-related socializing experiences? Finally, what are the mechanisms that allow media to socialize youth?

The answer to the first question is simple. Just about anyone (or anything) can be an agent of socialization. Whether it is in school, on the playground, or at a restaurant, youth are exposed to rules, expectations, and values that shape their thoughts, attitudes, and behaviors. Although there are many potential socializing agents, the most common socializing forces of youth are parents, siblings, peers, and, of course, the media. The answer to the second question, which focuses on the socializing effects of media consumption on the behaviors, emotions, and thoughts of youth, will be dealt with in subsequent chapters. Of note, the first and second questions are empirical in nature, with answers being illustrated through data. In contrast, the third question, and the focus of this chapter, is to explain *why* media exposure has the ability to influence children and adolescents. The answer to this question goes beyond raw facts and into the world of constructs, principles, and conjecture. In other words, explaining why media socializes youth requires the use of theory.

Media theories are composed of interrelated ideas that, when put together, can accomplish the following: (a) Explain *why* specific outcomes occur as a result of media exposure; (b) make *predictions* regarding the effects of media use on thoughts, feelings, and behavior; and (c) detail the means through which the typical outcomes of media use can be *controlled* (i.e., increased or decreased). Over the last 100 years, researchers have put forth many theories to explain the socializing effects of media on youth. Some of these theories focus on the impact of media on thoughts, whereas others spotlight feelings and/or behavioral outcomes. Below, the most relevant of these theories will be illustrated and discussed from a developmental perspective (and see Table 2.1 for a list of media effect theories).

Hypodermic Needle or Magic Bullet Theory

During the first half of the 20th century, there were few formalized media effect theories. Instead, the impact of media on consumers was explained by a very simple and general theoretical overview: Media consumption affects everyone, and everyone is affected by media in pretty much the same way (Sparks, 2001). Today, this orientation is commonly referred to as either the *magic bullet* or *hypodermic needle theory*. According to this theory, media is like a hypodermic needle injecting its messages into consumers or a magic bullet that upon hitting its target creates uniformity in thought and action. The magic bullet theory is exemplified in the horror movie *The Ring*, in which all viewers of a cursed videotape will die exactly 7 days after watching the tape (unless, of course, the tape is copied and viewed by someone else). Today, the magic bullet theory is thought to drastically oversimplify the manner in which media influences infants, children, and adolescents (Sparks). Moreover, numerous studies have shown that media does not influence everyone in exactly the same way (Kirsh, 2006). As such, this theory is no longer considered a valid media effect theory.

Excitation Transfer

At first, I could not identify the smell. All I knew was that it was not pleasant; it was rancid, really. I noticed "the odor" about halfway through the sci-fi action movie *Transformers*. Then, as I sat there in the theater with my family, I looked to my right, and saw my son's sockless feet atop the empty row of seats in front of us. The odor and its source were now clear to me, and I was not happy. In fact, I was really angry— angrier, though, than I should have been. But why did I have such a pronounced negative reaction to a smell (albeit bad) that I was quite familiar with? Excitation transfer is the answer.

Excitation transfer theory contends that because physiological arousal dissipates relatively slowly, the arousal generated from one event can be added to the arousal associated with a subsequent event (as long as the two events are temporally close). The end result of excitation transfer, then, is an intensified level of arousal for the latter event (Zillmann, 1983). In relation to the negative moviegoing experience mentioned above, the arousal from enjoying an action-oriented movie was added to the arousal associated with smelling rancid feet, resulting in an intensification of the negative emotional state associated with encountering foot odor. The beauty of excitation transfer theory is that it works for all types of emotional experiences and all sources of physiological arousal. Regardless of whether the emotional experiences are positive or negative, excitation transfer can occur between the two. Even arousal associated with exercise, frustration, sex, and so on is equally transferable from one event to another. Thus, excitation transfer theory provides a biological mechanism to explain why media consumption can influence the emotional experiences and behaviors of youth that occur shortly after the media has been turned off.

Cultivation Perspective

Without the vision of the artist, a block of clay remains just that: a block. But with precise finger movements and through the pruning away of excess clay, a new, more complicated form can be realized. Like an artist molding clay, so too can media transform the reality of those who consume it. At least, that is what the cultivation perspective proposes (Gerbner, Gross, Morgan, & Signorielli, 1994). According to this viewpoint, television is an omnipresent force that, like a magic bullet, acculturates *all* viewers into beliefs and attitudes that are consistent with those displayed on TV. However, in contrast to the immediate and strong effects proposed by the magic bullet theory, the cultivation perspective posits that the engendering of viewpoints takes time, with the strongest impact of TV occurring for those who watch it the most. Thus, in comparison to light viewers of TV, heavy viewers are thought to espouse beliefs and attitudes that are more consistent with the world of television. In fact, multiple studies have provided support for this contention. For instance, adolescents watching the greatest amount of sexual content on TV are the most likely to (a) approve of casual sex (Bryant & Rockwell, 1994), (b) consider unusual sexual behavior as normal (e.g., oral sex parties; Greenberg & Smith, 2002), and (c) feel the most dissatisfaction with being a virgin (Courtright & Baran, 1980).

Since its original inception, the concepts of mainstreaming and resonance have been added to the cultivation perspective. Both of these concepts reflect the fact that television and real-life experiences interact when influencing beliefs and attitudes. *Mainstreaming* refers to the situation in which heavy TV viewers develop a convergent outlook that is impacted to a lesser extent by most real-life experiences. For instance, regardless of income level, heavy viewers of television espouse similar beliefs regarding crime rates in their neighborhood (Gerbner et al., 1994). In contrast, real-life experiences are thought to have the greatest impact on the personal beliefs and attitudes of light viewers of television.

There is an exception to mainstreaming, for real-life experiences can at times amplify cultivation effects, a phenomenon known as *resonance*. However, for resonance to occur, there needs to be a high degree of similarity between an individual's real-life experiences and those displayed on TV. Consider, for example, the effects of watching sexually explicit television on adolescents' attitudes toward sex. The concept of resonance predicts that cultivation effects (e.g., concordance between televised beliefs and personal beliefs) will be the strongest for individuals who (a) are the most sexually active and (b) watch the most sexually provocative TV.

In the preceding paragraphs, Gerbner's cultivation perspective was discussed in terms of television viewing, rather than general media consumption. Why? Because the cultivation perspective requires that a large number of people view similar content, which television, more so than any other media, affords. Remember, Gerbner developed his theory in the 1970s, when most homes were without cable or satellite television. At that time in history, there was no public access to the Internet, nor was there a video game industry that generated billions of dollars in revenue. Because large audiences can now be reached through media other than TV, the cultivation perspective has been generalized to a variety of media, such as video games, music, and the Internet. For instance, Van Mierlo and Van den Bulck (2004) found evidence of cultivation effects associated with violent video game play in middle school children. Specifically, positive associations were found between violent video game play and the perceived prevalence of violent crime. Interestingly, in that same study, the strongest cultivation effects were found for violent television viewing. So, maybe Gerbner was right; TV might just be the primary source of cultivation effects for youth. However, more research is needed to assess the magnitude of cultivation effects as a function of the type of media consumed.

The cultivation perspective has been one of the most popular media effect theories in the last 30 years (Bryant & Miron, 2004). It is only recently, however, that the underlying mechanisms behind the effect have been elucidated. Research validating the cultivation perspective has relied heavily on participants estimating the probability of events, such as the likelihood of being victimized or the prevalence of drug use in a neighborhood. As such, factors that influence estimation also influence the cultivation effect. Shrum and Bischak (2001) suggested that three information-processing heuristics underlie Gerbner's cultivation effect: the availability heuristic, the simulation heuristic, and the representativeness heuristic.

The availability heuristic contends that estimation is based on the ease with which information can be retrieved from memory, with easily remembered events being perceived as more common than events that were difficult to remember. For instance, research has shown that people tend to overestimate the occurrence of homicides and robberies, in part, because they are effortlessly able to retrieve out of memory well-publicized crimes. Moreover, routinely encountered events on TV become salient (i.e., important) in the minds of the viewers, thereby increasing the ease with which such events can be remembered. In contrast, the representative heuristic suggests that the similarity of features between an event and the memory of a prototype (i.e., the best example of a category) influences estimation. The closer the resemblance between the event and the prototype, the more probable the event is perceived to be. Finally, according to the simulation heuristic, events that can be easily *imagined* are perceived to have the greatest chance of occurring (Tversky & Kahneman, 2005). The cultivation effect works because media-based content creates memories, reinforces engrained memories, and makes existing memories more readily available for use. In turn, through the heuristics mentioned above, estimates of occurrence and probability of the real world tend to match those portrayed in the "reel world."

Priming

Beyond triggering heuristics, media can prime related networks of emotions, thoughts, and concepts. Think of priming as a "readying process" in which inaccessible information becomes immediately available for use. Thus, when one emotion, thought, or concept is primed, similar emotions, thoughts, and concepts are also triggered. Moreover, an activated network can aid in the processing and interpretation of information. For instance, imagine each of the following words: *cowboy, horse, barrel,* and *saddle*. Now, fill in the missing letter in "r _ p e." I bet most of you filled in an *o* to make the word *rope*. Why would this occur? Because your thoughts were primed by the rodeo-related words mentioned above, the word *rope* readily comes to mind. Now do this exercise again with a friend, but rather than using rodeo-related stimuli, have that person imagine the following words: *peach, pear, banana,* and *cantaloupe.* Given that fruits were the source of priming, your friend will probably enter an *i* into the missing slot to make the word *ripe*.

Similar to having fruit-related words prime the word *ripe* and rodeo-related words prime the word *rope*, so too can different types of media prime, and thus activate, different types of networks. Sexual media can prime sexual thoughts and feelings; drug-related media can prime drug-related thoughts, emotions, and concepts; and media violence can activate aggressive networks. However, priming is not limited to a single network, as the same content can activate multiple networks. For instance, watching police officers chase down and tackle a shirtless, mullet-wearing drug peddler on *Cops* can prime both drug-related and aggressive networks, as well as networks devoted to bad hair. Priming, however, does not just result from consuming media content, for the media itself can act as a prime. Seeing a television set, for instance, can prime thoughts related to your favorite TV show, which in turn can activate a broader network of thoughts and concepts (e.g., aggressive or prosocial).

Linked networks can be activated through an internal cognitive process (e.g., thinking about something) or primed externally through environmental experiences, including media exposure. Furthermore, the more often a network is used, the greater the likelihood that it will be activated in the future. In fact, with overuse, networks can be chronically activated, thereby biasing an individual's available thoughts, emotions, and concepts. For instance, the chronically activated networks of highly aggressive youth tend to involve emotions, thoughts, and concepts related to aggression. As such, during ambiguous situations in which the intent of another person is in question, aggressive youth tend to perceive hostile intent, when they just as easily could have perceived intent that was benign (Dodge, 1986).

Social Learning and Social Cognitive Theory

Social learning theory and social cognitive theory were both developed by Albert Bandura (1965, 1986). The former has been one of the most highly cited media effect theories in the modern era, as its "learning" orientation can effectively explain the influence of media on the acquisition of most behaviors (Bryant & Miron, 2004). Simply put, social learning theory posits that behavior is a learned response resulting from observations made in the world. In contrast, social cognitive theory represents a theoretical expansion of Bandura's earlier work to reflect the fact that behavior is more of a "choice" than a "response" to the environment, and that there are also cognitive, emotional, and motivational influences on behavior.

Social Learning Theory

If you ever have the misfortune of meeting a zombie, avoid running into a farmhouse. Although you will be safe there for a few hours, by the next day you will be surrounded by the walking dead. Also, when inside, never stand next to a boarded-up window. Zombies can sense that you are there and will quickly break down the barrier, pull you through, and eviscerate you. Be careful not to let strangers into the house, as one of them is hiding the fact that he has been bitten by a zombie, and after his death and demonic resurrection, he will attempt to eat your brain. Finally, do not trust anyone in a military uniform, as they have great difficulty telling the difference between zombies and humans and will most likely shoot you in the head. Just to be clear, I have never actually had an encounter with a real-life zombie. So, how do I know so much about zombie–human interactions? I learned them from watching countless horror movies; and learning without personally experiencing a consequence falls under the purview of social learning theory.

Bandura's (1973) social learning theory posits that children and adolescents learn by observing the behaviors of others, a process referred to as *observational learning*. For instance, research has shown that after watching an action adventure television show replete with martial arts violence (e.g., the Power Rangers), children in grade school imitated the flying kicks, punches, and blocks that they had just seen (Boyatzis, Matillo, & Nesbitt, 1995). Whereas for some children, the imitated karate moves represented the acquisition of new behaviors, for others, the playground activities involved the use of previously learned ones. According to social learning theory, the consequences experienced by the model influence whether or not an observed behavior is imitated.

Specifically, when models are reinforced for their actions, similar behaviors in real life are more likely to follow than when such behaviors are punished. It is worth noting that when *no consequences* are levied against a modeled action, the observer perceives the behavior to have been tacitly approved of. For instance, Bandura (1965) found that after watching a short movie of an adult hitting, kicking, and yelling at an inflatable "Bobo" doll, preschoolers imitated these behaviors under two conditions: (a) The models were reinforced for their combative actions; or (b) no consequences were levied against the models. In contrast, when models were punished, preschoolers imitated the observed behaviors to a much lesser extent.

Video games, television, comic books, the Internet, and so on all provide youth with ample opportunities for observational learning. Regardless of the type of media consumed, children and adolescents are constantly witnessing media-based characters being reinforced, being punished, or not experiencing any consequences for their actions. For instance, on television, nearly 70% of the violent actions *illegally* committed by "heroes" go unpunished, with 32% of such actions being rewarded (Wilson et al., 2002). Of course, characteristics of the model, and of the modeled behavior, also influence the likelihood of observed behaviors being imitated. For instance, children and adolescents are more likely to ape media-based behaviors that have been glamorized (i.e., made to look "cool" or glorified). Moreover, observational learning is especially strong when the modeled behaviors are performed by individuals who youth are attracted to (e.g., models of similar and/or slightly older ages; Bandura, 1986; Hoffner & Cantor, 1991).

In addition to explaining how behaviors are acquired, social learning theory clarifies how learned behaviors are maintained over time. First, behaviors are maintained when they successfully satisfy personal needs, thus becoming self-reinforcing. For instance, if feeling "unique" is an important aspect of the self, then youth might engage in behaviors (e.g., such as listening to 1980s punk music) that reinforce one's uniqueness. Second, behaviors are maintained when they are socially sanctioned by peers or otherwise extrinsically rewarded by them. Similarly, when consuming media, youth observe the consequences of behaving in a particular manner, and as such, their own behaviors are modified accordingly. Finally, media can provide *direct* experience with both reinforcements and punishments, thereby maintaining learned behaviors. For instance, during video game play "good behaviors" are reinforced with bonus points and "bad behaviors" are punished, via the loss of points or lives.

Social Cognitive Theory

Traditionally, social learning theory is presented alongside the behavior-based "learning" theories, operant and classical conditioning. However, Bandura considered social learning theory to be more of a cognitive theory than a behavioral one. To reflect this cognitive orientation, Bandura revised his original theory and renamed it *social cognitive theory* (Bandura, 1986). Under the revised version, behavior is explained using three key influences: behavioral, personal, and environmental factors.

Behavioral factors refer to previously acquired actions available to the individual, such as a child's current repertoire of prosocial behaviors (e.g., helping and sharing). *Personal factors* consist of an individual's expectations, beliefs, goals, self-perceptions, desires, and intentions—in other words, internal motivation. *Environmental factors* are nonendogenous influences (e.g., media, friends, and family members) that affect the individual through direct experience or observational learning. Under the tenets of social cognitive theory, behavioral, personal, and environmental factors interact with one another to influence human actions, thoughts, and feelings, a phenomenon referred to as *reciprocal determinism*. Thus, unlike social learning theory, which forwards unidirectional effects (e.g., from environment to behavior), social cognitive theory posits bidirectional interactions between behaviors, internal motivations, and the environment.

In general, social cognitive theory posits that human adaptation and change are results of self-organizing, proactive, self-reflecting, and self-regulating behavior, rather than simply being reactions to environmental experiences or internal drives. Under this revised theory, human agency (defined as the exertion of control over thoughts, motivations, emotions, and goal achievement) drives the acquisition and maintenance of behavior. Moreover, the influence of the environment on the individual is thought to be at its apex when there is an alignment between the agentic self and the messages relayed in the environment. Thus, media should influence the behavior of youth to a greater extent when there is a high degree of similarity between the internal motivations of the individual and the content of the on-screen modeled behaviors, relative to when these factors are not in agreement.

Script Theory

Movies, television shows, comic books, and video games are based on screenplays, scripts, or storyboards, each of which orchestrates a story from beginning to end. In real life, children and adolescents use scripts as well. Here, though, the script is a cognitive account of what typically happens during the beginning, middle, and end of interpersonal interactions (e.g., going on a date), events (e.g., attending a football game), and situations (e.g., ordering a pizza). Cognitive scripts provide detailed information regarding both the sequencing of events (e.g., paying for a delivered pizza before eating it) and the appropriateness of an action during any given situation (e.g., tipping the driver is optional if the pizza is late; Huesmann, 1986).

Youth have many scripts to choose from, though not all are appropriate for the situation. For instance, scripts for playing catch with a baseball are suitable for a playground, but not for inside a house. Thus, when choosing a script to enact, children and adolescents engage in a two-step process: First, youth must assess the similarities and differences between the current situation and the content of all accessible scripts. Second, youth need to consider the potential consequences of using the script and whether or not the script is consistent with socially acceptable behavior (i.e., a social norm). In general, most children and adolescents choose scripts with perceived positive consequences, as well as those that are consistent with social expectations. However, youth do make poor choices. Children and adolescents act aggressively, engage in drug use, and commit crimes. According to script theory, deviant and nondeviant youth differ in four script-related areas: (a) script content, (b) decisions regarding script appropriateness, (c) anticipated consequences of actions, and (d) desire to follow social norms (Huesmann, 1986).

Cognitive scripts develop as a result of observational learning and direct experience. Thus, media can alter or even create the scripts that children and adolescents use to interact with the world. For instance, in *Scarface*, the antihero Tony Montana provides a script for finding a female companion: "In this country, you gotta make the money first. Then when you get the money, you get the power. Then when you get the power, then you get the women." OK, maybe it is not the best dating advice for everyone, but it seemed to work well for Bill Gates. Once scripts are developed and in use, they tend to be resistant to change.

In other words, once youth start using scripts, they continue to use them. Moreover, new experiences cause little change to the content of well-established scripts. Script inflexibility is not necessarily a problem for prosocial youth, but resistance to script change is one factor contributing to juvenile delinquency.

Because scripts are cognitive entities, like concepts, they cluster in associated networks. Script networks are based on social behaviors that emphasize similar actions. For instance, classroom and lunchroom settings are comprised of different scripts (e.g., rule based for the classroom, and chaos based for the lunchroom). However, because each of these scripts involves a school setting, they both belong to the same cognitive network. As such, the activation of one script (e.g., talking about traumatic lunchroom experiences) should also prime other school-based scripts (e.g., traumatic classroom experiences).

Script theory details the behavioral decisions made by youth and emphasizes the importance of social norms when making decisions about script choice and enactment. Thus, factors that influence social norms will indirectly influence the behaviors of youth. This is where the power of the media comes into play. With repeated exposure to media, scripts will be formed and/or maintained. Moreover, script entrenchment will result in children and adolescents seeking out environments that are consistent with their script-linked beliefs. Thus, youth will seek out opportunities to not only use acquired scripts but validate them as well. Media provides ample opportunities to validate scripts. For instance, sexual teens will seek out sexually charged television content, and aggressive children will seek out media laden with violence (Bryant & Rockwell, 1994; Kirsh, 2006). Although traditional media (e.g., television, music, and movies) does not afford opportunities to enact scripts, this does occur during video game play and many online activities.

Universal Media Model

With the exception of social cognitive theory, all of the aforementioned theories are limited in scope: Excitation transfer theory focuses on arousal-related emotions; priming, script theory, and the cultivation perspective all focus on cognitions; and social learning theory primarily addresses the role of observation on learned behaviors. Although social cognitive theory contends that behavior is influenced by a multitude of factors, it fails to

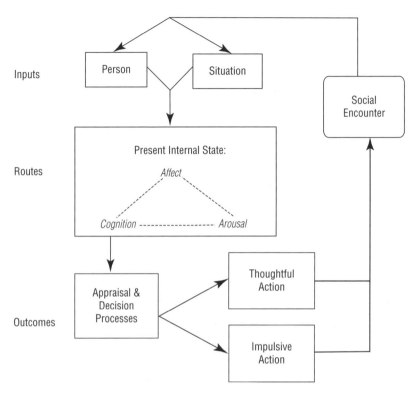

Figure 2.1   The general aggression model.
Source: From Anderson and Bushman (2002). Reprinted with permission.

provide a detailed explanation of how cognitions, emotions, behaviors, and motivations influence decision-making processes, and ultimately behavior. This is where the universal media model (UMM) comes in.

In order to explain the influence of media consumption on thoughts, feelings, arousal, and behavior, UMM combines elements from the preceding theories (with the exception of the magic bullet theory) into a single model. But first, I need to give credit where credit is due: UMM is an applied version of Anderson and Bushman's (2002) general aggression model (GAM). According to GAM, input variables, routes, and outcomes cyclically interact to influence aggression. Now, replace the word *aggression* with *behavior*, and you have explained UMM. In fact, without any changes whatsoever, the details of UMM can be seen in the original figure used to clarify GAM processes (see Figure 2.1). With that in mind, let us look at UMM in greater detail.

Input variables are made up of person and situational variables. Person variables are composed of those person-based characteristics that affect an individual's preparedness to act in a specified manner (e.g., prosocially, sexually, or aggressively). Included in this variable are stable and/or preexisting biological factors (such as genetic predispositions and hormone levels), attitudes, beliefs, personality characteristics, and scripts. Situational variables are context dependent, in that they refer to the environment-based interactions currently being experienced, as well as general elements within that environment (e.g., a hot room). As children and adolescents change settings, the person variables remain the same, but the situational variables change along with the setting.

According to UMM (and GAM), person and situational variables indirectly influence behavior by modifying the individual's present internal state, which consists of three routes: affective, arousal, and cognitive. The affective route details the moods and emotions evoked as a result of the input variables. The arousal route refers to current levels of physiological arousal, as well as any excitation transfer–related arousal resulting from personal and situational variables. The cognitive route involves the priming and creation of thoughts, scripts, and networks associated with the input variables. Similar to the concept of reciprocal determinism, UMM theory contends that affective, arousal, and cognitive routes are bidirectionally interconnected. That is, each route directly influences, and is influenced by, the other routes. For example, sexual feelings can increase sexual thoughts, which in turn can increase levels of sexual arousal, which then influence sexual feelings.

After information is processed through internal state routes, the current situation is evaluated. Given that priming, network activation, excitation transfer, and the like have already taken place, the appraisal process may be biased along the lines of internal state predilections. As such, the decisions regarding behavioral choice and enactment that follow may also reflect this bias. However, the decision to enact a behavior (biased or not) occurs only after information is evaluated through one of two appraisal processes: immediate and thoughtful. Immediate appraisal processes assess the perceived emotions, intent, and goals of the parties involved in the current situation. Moreover, the immediate appraisal process is automatic and unconscious, and if the outcome of the appraisal goes unchecked (for instance, due to lack of resources), impulsive action will follow. However, if sufficient resources are present and (a) if decisions based upon the initial appraisal appear to produce an unsatisfying outcome, or (b) if the situation involves important decisions, a reappraisal will take place. During the now conscious reappraisal process, new information is sought out, potential courses of actions are reevaluated, and past decisions are brought to mind. Behavior resulting from the reappraisal process is referred to as *thoughtful action*. Finally, UMM has cyclical features that utilize a feedback loop. Specifically, after impulsive or thoughtful action takes place, the current social encounter becomes, in effect, an input variable for the ongoing interaction. The behavioral cycle is now complete, as current interactions influence both person and situational variables, starting the cycle anew.

Let us now look at how UMM handles the following situation. Suzy, an unusually helpful child, watches an episode of *Sesame Street* in which Big Bird helps Cookie Monster find his lost cookies. Suzy, who is relaxing at the time, then notices that Bobby is looking for his lost shoe. According to UMM, Suzy's input variables will contain a personal variable replete with prosocial scripts and a positive attitude about helping others. The TV show acts as a situational variable, and, in this case, one that emphasizes helping behavior. The consistency between both personal and situational variables should activate cognitive, affective, and arousal routes related to prosocial actions. In all likelihood, Suzy will help Bobby look for his shoe, as both the immediate appraisal and reappraisal processes result in helping behavior. In turn, Suzy's helpful behavior will act upon her person variables by reinforcing her already well-established helping scripts.

Developmental Points of Interest

By definition, developmental theories explain not only the course of development but also why developmental changes occur. Do any of the traditional media effect theories reviewed meet the criteria for a developmental theory? No! Absent from every single one of the aforementioned theories are tenets that discuss media effect in the context of the physical, cognitive, social, and emotional changes occurring throughout development. Although the above theories are not developmental, current developmental findings can be integrated into their tenets in order to make media effect–based predictions for youth of different ages.

To clarify this issue, let us consider a time of development when youth appear particularly vulnerable to the effects of media, namely, early adolescence. Early adolescence is a time of pronounced change. Youth must adjust to the physical changes in their bodies, increased sexual feelings, academic and socioemotional challenges at school, and changes in their relationships with parents and peers. Although most adolescents cope well with these challenges, early adolescence is also a time of increased negative emotions and depression (Steinberg, 2001). Additional research suggests that early adolescents experience levels of physiological arousal greater than those of younger children or older adolescents (Spear, 2000). Moreover, during adolescence youth lose one half of their prepubertal neocortical synapses, ultimately resulting in a more efficient brain during adulthood. However, the brain of the early adolescent has experienced limited synaptic pruning, thus reducing their ability to make sound judgments (Brownlee, 1999). According to Yurgelun-Todd's (1998) research on brain imaging, early adolescents respond to emotionally laden situations with less cognitive activity than older individuals, potentially leading to "gut" and impulsive reactions.

Now, with this information in hand, let us examine the potential impact of media exposure on UMM processes during early adolescence. The heightened physiological arousal experienced by early adolescents should interact with internal state arousal caused by media to create a cumulative level of internal state arousal that is higher than at other points in development. Although media will enact scripts, engage cognitive networks, and prime thoughts, the cognitive deficiencies experienced by early adolescents should limit the impact of cognitive internal state routes on subsequent UMM processes. In contrast, the emotional routes of UMM should be very strong during the early teen years, and as such, media should create the strongest emotional response during this developmental period. As a result of limited cognitive resources and heightened physiological and emotional responding, reappraisal is less likely to occur during early adolescence than at other ages. Ultimately, relative to other developmental periods, these changes should result in young teens engaging in more impulsive action than thoughtful action.

Remember, media theories allow for the explanation, prediction, and control of behavior. As the example above illustrates, a theory's ability to accomplish these goals is enhanced when developmental issues are taken into consideration. Moreover, the incorporation of developmental concepts into theory helps social scientists identify research avenues that have yet to be fully explored.

3

Media and Academic Effects

A commonly held belief during childhood is that elementary school teachers not only teach in their classrooms but live there as well. After all, teachers are at school before children arrive, and they remain in their classrooms long after children go home for the day. For youth, the realizations that teachers have real lives and that they do not actually live at school can be shocking. As Amelia wrote on a website specializing in childhood beliefs (www.iusedtobelieve.com, 2007), "I used to believe, probably like many other kids that teachers lived at school. I thought during the summer, they just camped out at their desks. I was proved wrong when I saw my fifth grade teacher at the mall in *Victoria's Secret* ... buying a thong. I was never the same." Just as children eventually learn that there really is no Santa Claus and that the Easter Bunny is just a myth, so too do they come to realize that teachers have families and homes to go to when the school day is done. However, there exists another type of educator that lives either at school or in the homes of youth, and rarely travels between the two. In addition, you never have to worry about these teachers purchasing embarrassing undergarments. As you probably have already guessed, these lingerie-free educators are not made of flesh and bone. Instead, they are made of plastic, glass, wire, and an assortment of electronic chips. Collectively, they are referred to as *educational media*.

With promises of future success for their bright and ready-to-learn children, parents often sit their progeny in front of the TV and turn the channel to *PBS*, *Nickelodeon*, or whatever station is airing "educational" content. Parents are also purchasing educational media in droves. In fact, the educational media business is booming, with cumulative sales in the billions of dollars range. For instance, *Dora the Explorer* DVDs and interactive games, alone, have grossed nearly $4 billion since their introduction into the marketplace in 2000 (www.commercial freechildhood.org, 2007). But do children and adolescents actually learn from electronic teachers? That question will be explored further. But first, because not all media has educational benefits, it is also important to understand the potential academic *hazards* of general media consumption.

Is Media Consumption Detrimental to Academic Achievement?

Over a 30-year period, numerous studies have assessed the relationship between general media use and academic achievement (e.g., school performance and scores on standardized achievement tests). Typically, these studies forward a reduction hypothesis, which contends that excessive media consumption leads to poor academic performance (Valkenburg & van der Vort, 1994). Recently, Shin (2004) identified three potential mechanisms through which the reduction hypothesis operates: *time displacement*, *mental effort and passivity*, and *impulsivity*. These mechanisms are hypothesized to either inhibit intellectual processing in youth or lead to behaviors that impede academic success. It is worth noting that these mechanisms were developed to explain the impact of television exposure on academic achievement. Below, I extend the reduction hypothesis to all types of media consumption.

Mechanisms Behind the Reduction Hypothesis

The time-displacement hypothesis posits that media use takes time away from activities that are intellectually challenging and/or related to school performance, such as homework and studying for tests. Watching TV, listening to music, and playing video games are perceived by youth to be a lot more entertaining and enjoyable than school-related cognitive tasks, which at times can be tedious, difficult, and boring. Consequently, because media use displaces learning-related activities, cognitive growth is stunted, and as a result, current and future academic achievement suffers. As the old adage goes, "Use it or lose it." Sounds great in theory, but there is a dearth of empirical evidence to support the contention that media use *displaces* activities that promote academic achievement. Instead, media use (e.g., playing video games) tends to displace media use (e.g., watching TV) or other forms of leisure activities, such as going for a walk and hanging out with friends at the mall (Schmidt & Anderson, 2006). Despite the lack of evidence, the belief that media displaces intellectually stimulating activities persists. Even children and adolescents believe this media myth (Ballard, 2003).

The mental effort/passivity hypothesis contends that media use leads to mental laziness. The hypothesis proposes that media consumption "spoon feeds" information to the brain, requiring little mental effort on the part of the user. Slack-jawed, glassy-eyed stares at the television are thought to be indicative of cognitive passivity. Over time, passive thinking becomes the norm, and the desire to exert cognitive effort wanes. Thus, when faced with challenging cognitive activities (e.g., reading or solving math problems), youth exert little effort and/ or avoid doing them altogether. In turn, this type of prolonged cognitive passivity leads to a reduction in cognitive growth.

As with the previous hypothesis, there are no empirical data to indicate that media use actually impacts subsequent cognitive effort when solving problems in school or at home. Moreover, there is little evidence to support the contention that media use induces cognitive passivity. In fact, recent research has shown that when consuming screen media, children are cognitively active. For instance, when confused by a teen-related topic being discussed in the movie *Transformers*, my prepubertal son loudly blurted out to the entire theater, "What's masturbation?" Beyond this anecdote, empirical research has demonstrated that children frequently ask questions and discuss on-screen content when consuming media (Alexander, 1990). Of note, the questioning and discussion of content demonstrate an active mind, not a passive one. Thus, the mental effort–passivity hypothesis is also relegated to the realm of media myth.

According to the impulsivity hypothesis, the arousing nature of media and its rapid-fire presentation of information shortens attention spans, discourages sustained activities, and impedes task-oriented behaviors. At the same time, such stimuli are thought to induce hyperactivity and encourage impulsive behaviors. Thus, the impulsivity hypothesis posits that media use reduces academic achievement because (a) it makes it more difficult for children to sustain their attention in relatively less arousing environments, such as the classroom; and (b) it leads to impulsive behavior, which also can impede learning.

Even educational television shows, such as *Sesame Street*, were once heavily criticized as having a negative impact on the attention spans of preschool viewers (Hartmann, 1996). However, the impulsivity hypothesis appears to be nothing more than a media myth. Across development, there are no data to support the contention that activity levels and attention spans are adversely affected by media consumption (Schmidt & Anderson, 2006).

Does media use cause ADHD?

Attention deficit/hyperactivity disorder (ADHD) is characterized by a long-standing pattern of inattention, impulsivity, and hyperactivity. Recent correlational research indicates that a history of frequent television consumption significantly contributes to ADHD behaviors during early childhood, middle childhood, and adolescence (Chan & Rabinowitz, 2006; Christakis, Zimmerman, DiGiuseppe, & McCarty, 2004; Miller et al., 2007). However, as Stevens and Mulsow (2006) pointed out, when important environmental factors (e.g., socioeconomic status [SES] and parental involvement) were statistically accounted for, television consumption failed to predict ADHD behaviors. Moreover, the lone study that found a significant effect of video game play on ADHD behaviors during adolescence (Chan & Rabinowitz) failed to assess potential confounds in the environment. As such, the validity of these latter results is called into question.

Correctly diagnosing ADHD is a complex process that involves a clinical evaluation that includes input from parents, teachers, and the child or adolescent of concern (McGough & McCracken, 2000). Due to time constraints and the financial costs involved, research in this area has focused on the impact of media on the presence of ADHD *symptoms*, rather than an actual ADHD *diagnosis*. However, the presence of ADHD symptoms in a child does not guarantee a diagnosis of ADHD. Moreover, most media effect studies have failed to report if the amount of ADHD symptoms observed fell within the "clinical" or diagnostic range (i.e., the level of symptoms typically shown by those with an ADHD diagnosis). Rather, such studies tend to only point out if media use was associated with higher levels of ADHD symptoms. It is quite possible for children to show increases in ADHD symptoms but still have their behavior fall within the "normal range" of development. Thus, it is inadvisable to equate an increase in ADHD symptoms with the presence of an ADHD diagnosis.

Research Linking Media Use and Academic Achievement

Although the mechanisms underlying the reduction hypothesis have yet to receive a great deal of empirical support, the contention that media use reduces academic achievement (with mechanisms unknown) is still frequently forwarded. Thus, with the reduction hypothesis in hand, let us venture into the world of empiricism. It is safe to say that the research on media use and academic achievement is muddled. Although some studies report strong negative correlations between television viewing and academic achievement, other studies find no significant links between the two. Still, the majority of the studies conducted tend to support the reduction hypothesis (Thompson & Austin, 2003). For instance, Ennemoser and Schnieder (2007) found, that over a 4-year period, heavy viewers of entertainment TV demonstrated the least progress in reading achievement. One study even found that television consumption during childhood and adolescence was negatively associated with academic achievement in early adulthood, some 20 years later (Hancox, Milne, & Poulton, 2005). Taken together, these studies suggest that, in addition to negatively influencing academic achievement in the near future, the effects of media consumption during childhood and adolescence can last for decades, a contention that is particularly worrisome.

Williams and colleagues (Williams, Haertel, Haertel, & Walberg, 1982) suggested that the inconsistent findings surrounding the reduction hypothesis occur because there is a curvilinear relationship between television consumption and academic achievement. Specifically, as long as television viewing remains less than 10 hours per week, academic achievement tends to increase as the amount television consumed goes up. However, once the 10 hours per week barrier is breached, academic achievement decreases as television consumption increases. Interestingly, developmental status does not appear to impact this curvilinear relationship, as it is found for both children and adolescents alike. Of note, the first half of the curvilinear relationship suggests that academic achievement is actually enhanced through media use. These data support the stimulation hypothesis, which contends that media use fuels the brain, resulting in greater academic achievement. Research on Internet use also supports the stimulation hypothesis. One recent study found that the number of hours spent using the Internet was positively associated with greater levels of academic achievement (Jackson et al., 2006).

So, which is it? Does media consumption impact academic achievement negatively through the reduction hypothesis or positively via the stimulation hypothesis?

Evaluating Research on the Reduction and Stimulation Hypotheses

In the studies reported above, the medium was the message, meaning that the observed effect was driven by the *amount* of media encountered rather than the *nature* of the media consumed (i.e., the content). Under this type of effects model, as long as media programs are consumed for the same amount of time, watching shows with disparate content, such as *MTV Cribs* and *60 Minutes*, should have an equal impact on academic achievement. Similarly, hours spent playing violent video games, like *Doom 3*, should have the same effect on academic achievement as watching an equivalent number of hours of educational television, such as *3-2-1 Contact*. Do you think content matters for academic achievement? I do, and so do most contemporary media effect researchers (Schmidt & Anderson, 2006).

In fact, there is evidence to suggest that media lacking in educational value really can be detrimental to academic achievement, especially for preschoolers (Wright et al., 2001). Even still, the possibility exists that the consumption of copious amounts of noneducational media (i.e., entertainment media) during childhood and adolescence reflects a lack of investment on the part of parents in their children's education. Thus, more so than the content of the media consumed, parents' general failure to value, encourage, and support the cognitive growth of their children leads to poor academic achievement (Zhan, 2006). In support of this contention, when parental expectations regarding academic success are taken into consideration, many studies find that media use no longer predicts academic achievement (Schmidt & Anderson, 2006). Nevertheless, more research is needed that specifically focuses on the academic effects associated with consuming entertainment media, in the context of achievement-related family factors and developmental status.

The Benefits of Educational Media

It is one thing to suggest that entertainment media does not negatively impact academic achievement. It is quite another to contend that educational media can produce measurable academic benefits across development. Television shows, such as *Sesame Street* and *Blue's Clues*, provide toddlers and preschoolers with learning opportunities. Are these shows really advantageous for young children? Do older children gain knowledge and skills from watching programs that spout scientific fact and theory, like *Zoom* and *Bill Nye the Science Guy*? Can adolescents benefit from educational programs aired on the Discovery Channel and the Learning Channel? The answer to each of these questions is found in the next part of this chapter, which focuses on the cognitive and educational enrichment resulting from educational media consumption.

Televised Educational Media

During the 1980s, the perceived negative influence of entertainment media at the expense of educational alternatives resulted in the creation of national policy that would ensure that children and adolescents had access to educational content on television (i.e., the Children's Television Act [CTA], 1990). The CTA required networks to air educational and informational (E/I) programs designed for youth. Unfortunately, the CTA did not establish guidelines for what constituted E/I programming or when such programming should air. Not surprisingly, networks classified shows with dubious educational content, such as *Biker Mice From Mars*, *The Power Rangers*, and even reruns of *Leave It to Beaver*, as E/I programs. In contrast, many programs with real educational value were being aired when most children were asleep. As such, the Federal Communications Commission (FCC; 1996) established the "Three Hour Rule," which mandated networks to air a minimum of 3 hours of E/I programming per week. Importantly, these programs were to be shown at times when most children could actually view them (i.e., between 7:00 a.m. and 10:00 p.m.). Furthermore, the new FCC policy established criteria for classifying shows as E/I, as well as specified that E/I programs must be at least 30 minutes in length. Two major categories of E/I programming were identified: academic and prosocial. Programs labeled as academic E/I focus on science, nature, history, English, and social studies, that is, general academic content. In contrast, prosocial E/I content (addressed in the next chapter) depicts prosocial behaviors, such as sharing, helping, and the acceptance of diversity. See Table 3.1 for examples of E/I programming.

Table 3.1   Examples of E/I Programming by Target Audience (in Years)

Age Group	Program Name
Toddlers	*Teletubbies*
Early Childhood	*Boohbah*
	Sesame Street
	New Adventures of Winnie the Pooh
	Dora The Explorer
Middle Childhood	*Bill Nye the Science Guy*
	Doug
	Time Warp Trio
	Tutenstein
Adolescence	*Saved by the Bell: The New Class*
	Young America Outdoors
	Jack Hanna's Animal Adventures
	NBA Inside Stuff

When thinking about E/I programs, shows directed at preschoolers, such as *Sesame Street* and *Mr. Rogers' Neighborhood*, easily come to mind. However, such shows represent only a small proportion (< 10%) of E/I programs. In fact, nearly 60% of E/I shows target elementary school–aged children, with the remaining programs directed at teenagers (Jordan, 2000). Interestingly, it is during elementary school that general interest in E/I programs begins to wane. Prior to middle childhood, children enjoy watching both academic and prosocial E/I programs. In contrast, during middle childhood, girls prefer to watch prosocial E/I TV shows over academic ones, and boys prefer to watch general entertainment media, eschewing both academic and prosocial E/I programs altogether (Calvert & Kotler, 2003). Thus, the greatest number of E/I programs are geared toward youth who have begun to lose interest in televised educational content.

Effects of academic E/I programming across development
When evaluating the impact of E/I programming on youth, it is important to distinguish between skill-based and knowledge-based learning. The former refers to complex cognitive processes, such as reading, problem solving, and understanding mathematical reasoning. In contrast,

the latter refers to vocabulary words and retained snippets of information, such as the highest mountain in the world and the boiling point of water.

Infancy and toddlerhood   In order to learn from television content, infants and toddlers first need to pay attention to the programs being aired. Initial research suggested that infants and toddlers pay little attention to television programs, even if the show on screen was *Sesame Street*. In fact, according to these early studies, it is not until 30 months of age that toddlers sit facing the TV (Anderson & Levin, 1976). In contrast, newer investigations have found that, starting around 12 months of age, programs aimed at a very young audience easily grab the attention of infants (Anderson & Pempek, 2005). In general, youth attend to television the most when the content being aired is easily within their level of understanding, a finding that occurs throughout the early childhood years. For instance, infants prefer programs with lively music and bright colors; toddlers prefer simple themes; and preschoolers prefer slightly more difficult content, such as that found in animated stories with easy-to-follow plot lines. Not surprisingly, young children pay little attention to programs with adult-oriented content and themes (Valkenburg & Vroone, 2004).

Research on the effects of educational media on infants and toddlers has primarily assessed knowledge-based learning, such as word acquisition, imitation of behaviors, and retrieval of hidden objects (Troseth, Saylor, & Archer, 2006). Although there is limited research in this area, infants and young toddlers (i.e., those younger than 16 months of age) *do not* appear to benefit from educational DVDs. Recent research even suggests that the language development of very young children may be negatively affected by it. For instance, Zimmerman and Christakis (2007) found that for infants and toddlers between 8 and 16 months of age, receptive vocabulary (i.e., words understood) was lower for youth watching "educational" DVDs daily, in comparison to those without such exposure. In fact, for every hour per day spent watching educational DVDs, infants understood six to eight words less than their non-watching same-aged counterparts.

Although educational DVDs may negatively impact youth under 16 months of age, such DVDs do not appear to have the same effect on toddlers between 17 and 24 months of age (Zimmerman & Christakis, 2007). In fact, some research suggests that toddlers can improve their vocabularies by consuming this type of media (Naigles & Kako, 1993). Beyond vocabulary development, other studies indicate that youth can begin to learn from televised educational media as early as 12 months of age. For instance, 12- to 15-month-old infants can imitate simple behaviors (such as taking off a mitten), observed on TV, 24 hours later (Barr & Hayne, 1999). By 2 years of age, toddlers can find the position of a hidden object in a room after seeing its location on video (Anderson & Pempek, 2005).

For toddlers, the *ease* of learning, as a result of viewing televised media, pales in comparison to the effortless way in which toddlers learn information during face-to-face interactions with parents, teachers, and so on. For instance, toddlers learn object labels better from a person face-to-face than from a video of that very same person (Krcmar, Grela, & Lin, 2007). Additional research has shown that when told the location of a hidden toy in person, 77% of 2-year-olds successfully retrieved the object. In contrast, when toddlers received the same information from a video, only 27% could find the toy (Troseth et al., 2006). Taken together, these findings suggest that during the infant and the toddler years, televised educational content does not appear to be a good substitute for real-life interactions with parents, grandparents, day care providers, and siblings.

The finding that infants and toddlers learn better from real-life people than from equivalent television experiences is referred to as the *video deficit effect* (Anderson & Pempek, 2005). The video deficit effect has puzzled researchers for years. Regardless of whether the information is relayed to youth on TV or in person, the message is the same; only the mode of presentation differs. But why does learning in infancy and toddlerhood depend so much on the presence of a real-live person? Echoing Vygotsky's (1978) contention that all learning takes place in the context of social interactions, Troseth et al. (2006) suggested that infants and toddlers are primarily attuned to *socially relevant* information. *Socially relevant information* refers to information presented by a social partner accompanied by appropriate social cues that focus on a mutually shared environmental stimulus. Examples of social cues include contingent responding, eye gaze, and pointing.

Although television shows geared for young children impart information through a quasi-social presentation (e.g., on-screen characters talk to the audience as if they are in the room), the information is relayed without appropriate social cues. That is, there is no back-and-forth exchange of information between the child and the televised character. Troseth and colleagues contended that over the course of time, young children learn that the behavior of televised characters is unrelated to what they are doing (i.e., noncontingent responding) and that televised characters are unresponsive to their needs. As such, infants relegate televised information as relatively unimportant, thus hindering learning.

Even shows such as *Blue's Clues*, which contain some appropriate social cues (e.g., asking questions about a shared referent), do not afford children the opportunity to direct the flow of information, a process that even very young children are quite accustomed to. Thus, for infants and toddlers, the absence of a two-way exchange of information appears to impair learning. However, learning from television does improve with repetitive viewing (Anderson & Pempek, 2005). Thus, even in the very young, knowledge can be gained in the absence of relevant social cues. Nevertheless, the presence of socially relevant cues increases the efficiency of learning, which ultimately benefits infants and toddlers, whose cognitive capabilities are limited.

Early childhood   The impact of educational media on youth during early childhood has been researched for over 35 years. During that time, the vast majority of the hundreds of empirical studies conducted have focused on the educational impact of one show, *Sesame Street*. By focusing on academic learning and social skill development (collectively referred to as *school readiness*), *Sesame Street* aims to help preschool-aged children prepare for elementary school. Other educational shows with a similar agenda include *Blue's Clues*, *Barney & Friends*, *Allegra's Window*, and *Gullah, Gullah Island*. Across the board, such educational programs do appear to benefit young viewers in many academic-related domains.

Educational media can teach young children knowledge-based facts. Whether it is learning body parts, counting to 40, identifying colors and shapes, or learning the alphabet, heavy viewers of educational media demonstrate advantages over nonviewers and light viewers. Educational television can augment children's understanding of previously learned words and even teach them new ones. Importantly, such beneficial effects remain after taking into consideration the influence of parents' level of education and preschool attendance. Moreover, in terms of school readiness, youth from disadvantaged backgrounds tend to benefit the most from viewing educational media (Fisch, 2002).

Viewing educational media during early childhood appears to benefit youth years later. For instance, in comparison to preschoolers who did not watch *Sesame Street*, viewers of Big Bird, Cookie Monster, and the like had better vocabularies, were better at reading during the first few years of elementary school, and were subsequently less likely to require remedial academic help (Wright et al., 2001; Zill, Davies, & Daly, 1994). Such benefits appear the strongest for youth exposed to educational media between 2 and 3 years of age (Wright et al.). Notably, Anderson and colleagues (2001) found that after statistically removing the influence of parental education, birth order, and school location, academic success in high school was still positively linked with viewing educational television at age 5 (Anderson et al., 2001).

Although knowledge-based learning appears to uniformly improve as a result of educational media, the data on skill-based learning are more mixed. Educational media does appear to help young viewers think flexibly (e.g., taking another's perspective), develop problem-solving skills (e.g., try multiple approaches), understand relational concepts, and solve simple riddles (Fisch, 2002). However, multiple studies have shown that educational media does not benefit the grammar of young viewers (Naigles & Mayeux, 2001). Remember that television lacks socially relevant cues. Even though the cognitive abilities of preschoolers may have advanced to the point that many facts and skills can be gained *without* a two-way shared focus of attention, grammar does not appear to be one of them. After all, from infancy through middle childhood, active participation in conversation is an extremely important element in the acquisition and development of language (DeHart, Sroufe, & Cooper, 2004).

Childhood During middle childhood, the influence of educational media on skill-based and knowledge-based learning has been primarily assessed within the confines of elementary school walls. In these studies, the following educational areas were evaluated: sight reading fluency, reading comprehension, letter naming, mathematical abilities and problem solving, and attitudes toward learning and scientific thinking (Wright et al., 2001). Across these differing educational domains, the findings have been consistent: E/I programming improves academic performance. In one of the largest pretest–posttest educational studies conducted, Ball and Bogatz (1973) assessed the impact of watching *The Electric Company* on the reading-related outcomes of 8,000 first through fourth grade students. The results of this school-based study found that numerous reading skills (e.g., reading consonant blends and reading for meaning) improved for all youth, but especially for first and second graders. Taken together, these findings suggest that E/I programming can augment a standard educational curriculum to enhance learning during middle childhood. However, none of the aforementioned studies assessed the video deficit hypothesis. It is quite possible that if teachers taught the content of educational videos during class (in addition to their regular curriculum), youth would have shown even greater academic improvements, relative to those resulting from educational media exposure. Thus, future research needs to address whether augmenting classroom content with educational media or additional instruction produces equivalent outcomes.

It is important to keep in mind that there may be limits to the benefits of academic media. For instance, Linebarger and colleagues (Linebarger, Kosanic, Greenwood, & Doku, 2004) found that kindergarteners at risk for reading problems did not benefit from E/I programming that focused on emergent literacy (e.g., *Between the Lions*). Moreover, in contrast to the findings for preschoolers, school-ready kindergarteners did not show academic improvement after watching *Sesame Street* (Fisch, 2002). Thus, for children at risk for academic problems, and for children with already well-developed skills (Ball & Bogatz, 1973), the benefits of educational media appear to be limited.

Finally, during middle childhood, there is some research to suggest that televised educational media impacts knowledge-based learning to a greater extent than skill-based learning. This makes sense given that skill-based learning often requires hands-on practice, which is something that traditional educational media (i.e., television) does not provide. Learning skills is difficult enough, but applying them to novel situations is even harder. Not surprisingly, the lessons learned from educational media are transferred to new areas with great difficulty (Peel, Rockwell, Esty, & Gonzer, 1987). In contrast to skill-based learning, knowledge-based learning is more easily enhanced following educational media exposure. Why? Repetition increases memory for facts, and in the studies mentioned above, children were repeatedly exposed to educational content. A recent study supports the contention that it is the repetition of information that leads to knowledge-based learning. Michel and colleagues (Michel, Roebers, & Schneider, 2007) found that, in comparison to youth watching a scientific film only once, children watching the film twice, as well as youth receiving a school lesson in addition to the film (resulting in a double exposure to content), performed better on tests of the educational content, in including memory for factual details.

Adolescence   Nearly a decade before the commercial availability of TV, numerous studies assessed the educational impact of film on learning. Typically, youth in middle school and high school were shown educational films during the school day, and their knowledge regarding the subject matter was subsequently tested days or months later. On some occasions, the film shown to youth (e.g., *Tableware*) was followed by a related lesson given by the teacher, whereas at other times, the film was the lesson. Regardless, there was uniformity in the findings, in that adolescents exposed to films learned more information about a topic than youth lacking such exposure. Moreover, knowledge-based learning was the strongest when films were paired with complementary lessons (Hansen, 1933). Some 65 years later, similar research found that adolescents watching a 10-minute news program during the school day (i.e., *Channel One*) knew more about current events than youth not exposed to the program (Anderman & Johnston, 1998).

Computer-Assisted Instruction

As a teaching tool, one of the primary limitations of televised educational media is that the flow of interaction is unidirectional (i.e., from the media to the child), making it difficult for the viewer to actively control the learning process. As a result, skill-based learning suffers. That problem can be overcome with computer-assisted instruction (CAI). During CAI, not only do children and adolescents view educational content, but also they respond to questions and receive feedback based upon their answers. In effect, CAI is designed to hone in on a child's area of learning potential, or, as Vygotsky (1978) put it, the child's zone of proximal development. The complexity of CAI varies from simple drilling of facts to instructional lessons involving simulations (e.g., dissecting a virtual pig). Moreover, CAI allows youth to engage in difficult problem-solving activities that require the application of previously learned material. Frequently, CAI takes place in the context of games. For instance, in the computer game *Typing of the Dead*, users are required to type the words appearing on the bodies of zombies in order to kill them. The faster you type correctly, the quicker the attacking hordes of the undead and assorted demonic creatures are destroyed.

Initial research on the effectiveness of CAI on educational achievement was mixed. Although some studies found that CAI improved learning, others found that it actually hindered it. For instance, during middle childhood, children exposed to CAI involving repetitive math *drills* had lower scores on tests of math achievement, in comparison to youth completing math-related CAI *simulations* and *games* (Wenglinsky, 1998). Across development, whether the focus of research was on reading, math, or science, traditional instruction (i.e., a live teacher) typically resulted in better outcomes than those produced by CAI (Christmann, Badgett, & Lucking, 1997). In contrast, and as the review below will illustrate, recent research clearly demonstrates that CAI can have a positive impact on educational achievement.

Infancy and early childhood
Infants, toddlers, and preschoolers are exposed to educational software on both computers and handheld devices, such as the *V-Tech Leapster*. Although educational software is found in many preschool-based programs, for infants and toddlers "educational software" is a product that is typically found at home. Similar to the educational DVD market, commercial educational software claims to benefit youth on a variety of cognitive abilities, such as reading readiness (e.g., letter recognition), math (e.g., counting and addition), language (e.g., vocabulary), and pattern recognition. One software program claims to teach "over 50 skills" to toddlers, whereas another states that 3- to 5-year-olds should use this program to "keep kids on target with preschool skills" (Garrison & Christakis, 2005). The inference from such advertising is clear: Parents who want their children to succeed in elementary school (which is only a few years away) *need* to expose their child to educational software now.

So, what does current research tell us about the benefits or hazards of educational software use from infancy through the preschool years? Unfortunately, during infancy and the toddler years there is no empirical research on the topic. However, CAI does provide relevant feedback in a turn-taking manner: The computer asks a question, the child provides an answer, and the computer evaluates the child's response. Moreover, the interactions between the computer and the child attempt to approximate the nature of real-life interactions involving socially relevant information. As such, it is expected that the benefits of CAI should be equal to, if not greater than, the effects of televised educational media and DVDs.

Although there is no direct research testing the specific claims made by the purveyors of educational software aimed at infants and young children, there is research addressing the benefits of CAI during early childhood. Similar to televised media, CAI appears to benefit youth in areas important for school readiness. For instance, in comparison to control groups, preschool children exposed to CAI showed greater improvements on two key components of reading success: phonological sensitivity (i.e., the ability to detect and manipulate sounds in language) and phonological composition (i.e., the ability to create and recognize words; Lonigan et al., 2003; Reitsma & Wesseling, 1998). Similarly, Din and Calao (2001) found that youth utilizing CAI scored higher on assessments of spelling and reading decoding than youth not exposed to the computerized experimental manipulation. However, whether or not CAI can impact grammar is unclear. As of yet, CAI has been unable to provide the type of *realistic* socially relevant cues that are needed for grammar acquisition during childhood. In the future, CAI involving virtual reality may be able to provide youth with "teachers" capable of engaging in socially relevant interactions that have a high degree of realism. Will computer-generated educators in virtual reality environments be as helpful in teaching grammar to youth as teachers made out of flesh and bone? Only time, and more research, will tell.

Although several studies have found that mathematical abilities improve as a result of CAI (e.g., Elliot & Hall, 1997), other studies have failed to demonstrate this effect. The inconsistent findings for math have led some to suggest that early childhood youth lack the cognitive maturity necessary to benefit from CAI (Vernadakis, Avegerinos, Tsitskari, & Zachopoulou, 2005). However, Fletcher-Flinn and Gravatt (1995) found that CAI actually improved mathematical abilities *better* than traditional instruction. Thus, rather than cognitive immaturity, it may be that variations in software between programs accounted for these differences. For instance, Luik (2006) found that the effectiveness of CAI differed depending upon the manner of feedback given. Whereas immediate and simple feedback (such as marking and erasing answers) fostered learning, competition and grouping questions by difficulty impeded it.

Middle childhood

As discussed above, CAI has been shown to help children *prepare* to read during early childhood. As youth age, CAI exposure continues to be beneficial to *beginning* readers. For instance, Bauserman and colleagues (Bauserman, Cassady, Smith, & Stroud, 2005) found that computer software programs help kindergarten youth develop phonological awareness (e.g., phone blending and segmenting), print concepts (i.e., understanding how print works), and listening comprehension skills beyond those of their classmates, who were not exposed to CAI.

For math, the findings have been more mixed. For youth in late middle childhood (i.e., fourth grade and above), exposure to CAI involving math simulations and applications (e.g., part of a math game) was associated with higher math achievement scores. In contrast, computer programs emphasizing the drilling of math facts were associated with lower math achievement scores (Wenglinsky, 1998). However, beyond these studies, there is little research on the effects of CAI in the areas of reading, math, and science.

Interestingly, there is a great deal of research on the effects of CAI on middle childhood youth who have learning disabilities or are otherwise at risk for falling behind their grade level. Here, the evidence is clear: CAI benefits reading decoding and reading comprehension (Hall, Hughes, & Filbert, 2000). Youth with learning disabilities need substantially more practice in reading-based skills than their "normal reading" counterparts, and practice is exactly what CAI can best provide. Moreover, CAI can provide instructional information, thus helping youth learn new skills in addition to advancing those already present. Similarly, research on youth with math disabilities has shown that youth exposed to CAI, relative to a control group, show greater improvements in tests of general math achievement across middle childhood (Hasselbring, Goin, & Bransford, 1988). However, a more recent study that assessed specific mathematical abilities during the first grade found that CAI led to improvements in addition, but not in subtraction or arithmetic story problems (Fuchs et al., 2006).

Given the paucity of research mentioned above, can the findings from children with learning disabilities be applied to normative youth? The answer is an unequivocal no, at least not without corroborative evidence. Just because CAI works for at-risk youth does not guarantee that the effects will carry over to normative youth. For instance, Macaruso (2006) found that CAI led to improved reading skills for low-performing first graders, but not for youth demonstrating grade-level reading abilities. It may be that current CAI programs can help bring youth "up to speed" but have more difficulty in advancing youth beyond grade-level abilities.

Adolescence

During adolescence, there is little research to support the contention that CAI improves reading or spelling. In fact, Brooks and colleagues (Brooks, Miles, Torgerson, & Torgerson, 2006) found that 11- to 12-year-olds exposed to CAI performed worse on tests of reading than youth not completing the computerized tasks. From Britain to Israel, CAI has consistently failed to improve reading and spelling achievement during adolescence (Angrist & Lavy, 2002). For math, in contrast, the limited amount of research conducted suggests that CAI can lead to greater problem-solving ability throughout adolescence (Chang, Sung, & Lin, 2006; Harskamp & Suhre, 2006). One recent study found that for early adolescents struggling with math, *personalized* CAI (which takes into consideration the adolescent's interests when creating word problems) leads to better performance on tests of mathematical problem solving than *nonpersonalized* CAI (Ku, Harter, Liu, Thompson, & Cheng, 2007).

The findings for science have also been generally positive, with CAI improving performance in a variety of domains, such as biology, physics, and chemistry. Notably, improvements were shown for both knowledge-based and skill-based learning, such as application of material and problem solving (Çepni, Taş, & Köse, 2006; Ozmen, 2007). On a bright note for animal lovers and activists, girls participating in a virtual pig dissection scored higher on practical and objective tests used to measure knowledge acquisition, relative to girls conducting a real dissection (boys were not assessed in this study; Maloney, 2005). A limiting factor related to the assessment of CAI on science, however, is that the research has been primarily conducted with late adolescents (i.e., junior and senior high school students). Thus, it is unclear whether CAI is effective for youth in early and middle adolescence.

Music and Academic Achievement: Myth or Reality?

With federal funds tied to the academic performance of youth and increasingly tight budgets taxing the fiscal welfare of schools, music programs (and arts programs in general) are being either cut from school curricula or scaled back. To buttress the case *for* the continuation of arts-related programs, supporters (e.g., SchoolMusicMatters.com) have taken an *effects orientation*. In this type of approach, scientific research is used to show the social, psychological, and academic benefits of participating in school-based music programs. But just what is the evidence? Moreover, for those lacking in musical talent, are there academic benefits associated with simply listening to music? Does music impact youth differently across development? With baton in hand, let us look at the score of evidence.

Specific to the issue of academic achievement, there are three distinct lines of research that address the potential cognitive and academic benefits of music: (a) the effects of focused music listening on task performance, (b) the benefits of music instruction, and (c) the impact of doing academic work with background music playing. The first line of research, more commonly referred to as the *Mozart effect*, addresses whether listening to music prior to completing a task (such as a test) can actually improve performance. Based on experimental research using adult participants, in which spatial abilities increased following exposure to classical music (Rauscher, Shaw, & Ky, 1993), it was once thought that playing Mozart for infants increased their intellectual capabilities. In fact, not only did this belief result in classical music CDs and DVDs being directly marketed to the parents of infants (e.g., *Baby Mozart* and *Baby Einstein*), but also the State of Georgia actually required that newborns be sent home from the hospital with a Mozart CD. But, as it turns out, the Mozart effect has yet to be demonstrated in infants. Although preschoolers do perform better on tests of cognitive abilities after listening to Mozart, children's tests scores also improve after listening to any type of music that they like, even if it is pop music (Schellenberg, 2005). It follows, then, that when youth dislike classical music, listening to Justin Timberlake may be better for their cognitive abilities than listening to Mozart. Moreover, the same cognitive benefits attributed to listening to recordings of Mozart are observed after listening to stories about Mozart sans music (Schellenberg). Thus, the Mozart effect is more myth than reality, as it cannot be reliably demonstrated at any age across development. To date, only three studies involving child or adolescent samples have directly assessed the impact of classical music on subsequent task performance, and not a single one of them has provided evidence that supports the Mozart effect (Črnčec, Wilson, & Prior, 2006).

At the heart of the "music matters" movement is the supposed benefits of music instruction on academic performance; after all, multiple correlational studies have demonstrated a positive association between the two. For instance, reading level, spatiotemporal reasoning skills (e.g., mentally rotating objects, and visualizing and recognizing objects in space), and intelligence are all positively correlated with music instruction. A recent quasi-experimental design even found that elementary and middle school students with a high-quality music program scored better on standardized tests of English and mathematical achievement than youth at schools with poor-quality music instruction or none at all (Johnson & Memmott, 2006). Nevertheless, given the possibility that unassessed third variables (e.g., parent education and SES) were responsible for the observed music–academic performance associations, causal claims cannot be made. To date, few experimental studies have demonstrated that music lessons during childhood or adolescence lead to gains in traditional academic areas, such as math and English. However, music lessons during childhood, and in particular early childhood, do appear to benefit spatiotemporal-reasoning skills. Unfortunately, this spatiotemporal-reasoning advantage disappears after 2 years (Hetland, 2000).

Research on the potential academic benefits of background music has been conducted since the late 1940s. As a result of nearly 60 years of research, it can be stated that in regular classroom settings, academic performance does not appear to increase when background music is playing. In contrast, for youth in special education programs, background music leads to improved academic performance in math as well as in overall levels of concentration. Črnčec and colleagues (2006) contended that soothing background music may help reduce high baseline arousal levels in special needs youth, thereby improving their academic performance, at least in the short term. Thus, certain types of music may help youth enter an arousal state that is optimal for learning. Not surprisingly, for normative youth, no benefits are gained from the presence of background music, as their baseline levels of arousal are already low enough to effectively allow learning to take place.

Developmental Points of Interest

During the first 2 years of life, youth are exposed to educational media on television, DVDs, and computer software. Now, more than ever,

Table 3.2 Sample Claims of Educational Videos (DVD/VHS)

Series	Age Range	Educational Claims: "This DVD teaches ..."
Baby Nick Jr: Curious Buddies	3–18 months	... cause and effect, colors, and matching
Baby Einstein: Baby Shakespeare	12 months +	... vocabulary "through the beauty of poetry, music, and nature"
Baby Einstein: Left Brain	6–36 months	... language, logic, patterns, and sequencing
Bilingual Baby	1–5 years	... a second language
Leap Frog: Match Circus	3–6 years	... numbers, counting, addition, and subtraction

parents are buying these types of educational media. In fact, the commercial educational DVD market is nearing $10 billion, in part because of the educational claims made by the "baby video" industry. Claims targeting specific educational outcomes such as "teaches language and geography skills," and vague educational claims like "can help stimulate cognitive development," appear on the jackets of most DVDs marketed to infants and toddlers. Unfortunately, there is little evidence to back up these claims or those stated on the packaging of educational software for children younger than preschool age. (See Table 3.2 for examples of claims made by manufacturers.)

Although preschoolers do appear to benefit from educational media, there are limits to what youth in early childhood can learn from academic programs. But more than that, in comparison to learning from preschool teachers and parents, the relative benefits of viewing E/I shows are unknown. In fact, there is little video deficit research beyond the toddler years. Thus, a key component in the understanding of the benefits of educational media has gone largely unexplored. It is one thing to suggest that youth benefit from E/I programs; it is quite another to suggest that the benefits are equivalent to, or surpass those of, real-life experiences. Despite the fact that over 90% of E/I programming is aimed at children over the age of 6, there is relatively little research on the effects of academic E/I programs on youth in middle childhood. The studies that have been conducted, however, suggest that, in terms of both knowledge-based and skill-based learning, educational television is beneficial for academic success. Research on educational software has corroborated these findings.

Currently, there is little if any research on the impact of televised and film-based educational media on skill-based learning in middle school and high school. Thus, we know very little about the effectiveness of televised E/I programming across adolescence. Given the cognitive advances associated with development, it is possible that E/I programming becomes more effective with increasing age, especially for knowledge-based learning. After all, children tend to comprehend television content better with age (Huston & Wright, 1998). But do the skills displayed in educational media transfer to real life? As there is no research on the topic, an empirical answer is clearly in need.

4

The Medical and Social Benefits of Media Use

Slap! As the stinging feeling in my face began to diminish, and after fighting off the urge to take away a year's worth of privileges, I politely asked my then first grade–bound son why he had just slapped me. He responded, "Dad, that's what they do on TV to get someone to stop freaking out." Apparently, and contrary to my expectations, the wacky faces I had been making at him were not nearly as entertaining as I thought they would be. Instead, my son had viewed them as a grave cause for concern and acted accordingly. After this event, a commercial for a 2004 Lexus RX 330 came on the air, and as I sat there staring at the TV, the pain in my face began to subside. Based on this anecdote, two conclusions can be made: First, television had taught my son that it is important to act prosocially when others are in psychological need. Thank you, *Three Stooges*. And, second, media consumption can affect the perception of pain. Anecdotes are great fun, but they are not a substitute for research. With that in mind, let us see what the real research has to say about the medical and social benefits of media consumption.

Pain Reduction Through Media-Based Distraction

Managing pain is a critical component of any medical treatment involving youth. Pain, and the subsequent anticipation of pain during procedures, can cause anxiety and fear in children and adolescents. For instance, following vaccinations, infants have been shown to associate nurses with pain, and subsequently cry at the site of a nurse in uniform. From needle insertion to dental work, procedural-based pain can cause youth to avoid treatment or struggle during procedures, thereby risking their current and/or future health. In addition, pain-inducing procedures are frightening, anxiety provoking, and, at times, a cause of psychological trauma. Thus, reducing the amount of pain experienced during medical procedures has become a standard part of medical care. Moreover, because anesthetic drugs have unwanted side effects, non-pharmacological techniques that influence the perception of pain have been investigated for decades.

Pain perception is a subjective process whereby the level of attention paid to painful sensory input moderates the level of pain experienced (Gold, Kim, Kant, Joseph, & Rizzo, 2006). As such, during painful medical procedures, activities that *attract* the attention of youth, and therefore distract them from focusing on their pain, have the potential to reduce the unpleasantness of the experience. Deep breathing, air blowing, and conversations with loved ones are all techniques of deflection that have been successfully used to reduce pain in children and adolescents (Noguchi, 2006). More recently, researchers have turned to video games, television, and music to distract youth during painful procedures.

Research on Infants

Unlike children and adolescents, infants are unable to talk about, rate, or otherwise communicate the amount of pain they are currently experiencing. As such, physiological and behavioral indicators of stress, such as increased heart rate, decreased oxygen saturation, and facial expressions, are used to identify the presence of pain (Bo & Callaghan, 2000). To date, only a handful of experiments with an infant population have been conducted, and all of them involved musical distracters. The type of music played during these experiments varied from one study to the next: Infants were exposed to classical music, a cappella singing, and music containing intrauterine sounds (such as the rhythmic pulsing of blood through an umbilical cord). Regardless of the type of music played, the findings were remarkably consistent: Listening to music during painful procedures reduced infants' pain-related stress responses. Moreover, the effectiveness of music for pain reduction was enhanced when it was used in concert with other nonpharmacological treatments, such as nonnutritive sucking (i.e., using a pacifier; Cignacco et al., 2007). Given these findings, future research should investigate whether other electronic media designed to attract the attention of infants, through sounds *and* images, would be even more effective at reducing pain than music alone.

Research on Toddlers and Preschoolers

To date, no studies have looked at the analgesic effects of media during the toddler years. In addition, the research conducted on preschoolers has failed to support the contention that media distracters *alone* can effectively reduce the perception of pain during dental work or immunizations (Atkin, Smith, Roberto, Fediuk, & Wagner, 2002; Noguchi, 2006). Unfortunately, the studies that have demonstrated a palliative effect of media on early childhood youth typically included samples with large age ranges (e.g., 1 to 7 years; MacLaren & Cohen, 2005). Moreover, in each of these studies, there were a greater number of older children than younger children. Because previous research has shown that younger children experience more distress during painful procedures than older children (MacLaren & Cohen), the possibility exists that the observed effect was driven by the older children. In fact, it appears that preschoolers are so distressed when in pain that they lack the necessary resources to divert their attention, by themselves, to a media distracter. In support of this contention, Cohen and colleagues (Cohen, Blount, & Panopoulos, 1997) found that watching cartoons during a medical procedure did reduce preschoolers' perception of pain, as long as it was accompanied by constant reminders from an adult to focus on the television content in front of them (Cohen et al., 1997). Taken together, these findings suggest that during early childhood, the combination of media distracters and coaching may lead to a reduction in the perception of pain.

Research on Youth in Middle Childhood and Adolescence

Across childhood and adolescence, numerous studies have demonstrated the benefits of watching TV, listening to music, and playing video games on both observed and self-reported pain perception. For instance, in 8- to 12-year-olds, the perception of pain resulting from the placement of an IV was reduced as a result of playing a *virtual reality* video game (Gold et al., 2006). Of note, in contrast to traditional video games, virtual reality allows youth to interact with game characters in an immersive, highly visual, three-dimensional environment involving stereoscopic displays. Thus, in virtual reality, the player *experiences* moving through a virtual environment, rather than *watching* a computerized character do the same thing. Another study showed that for youth between the ages of 7 and 12, the subjective experience of pain was lessened while watching cartoons (Bellieni et al., 2006). Media-based distraction seems to be particularly effective at reducing the pain and anxiety associated with needle sticks during venipuncture and vaccinations. However, media appears to be ineffective at reducing pain during medical procedures in which the pain is more severe or long lasting, such as in wound debridement (Landold, Marti, Widmer, & Meuli, 2002). In order for media to be an effective distracter during such cases, it may be necessary for youth to enter a media-induced altered state of consciousness.

Distraction Through Absorption and Flow

By definition, an altered state of consciousness is any state different from a normal waking state. Such states can be induced through hypnosis, meditation, drug use, or sleep. In general, when one is in an altered state of consciousness, conscious experiences such as pain can be effectively ignored. Media use and, in particular, video game play can lead to two different types of altered states: absorption and flow. When in a state of psychological absorption, there is a suspension in the typical integration of emotions, cognitions, and experiences. In other words, the real world is not processed, thought about, or experienced in the usual manner, and in effect, it goes largely unnoticed. Moreover, when absorbed in a task, the individual is intensely focused, less aware of his or her current emotional states (including those related to anxiety), and unaware of the passage of time. Flow is similar to absorption, in that attention is deeply focused on the task at hand and that the passage of time is distorted (e.g., it flies by). However, unlike absorption (in which negative emotions, such as frustration, can leak through into consciousness), individuals in a flow state experience intense feelings of joy and unparalleled success while completing a task. When in a state of flow, which is frequently referred to as being "in the zone," the physical and cognitive skills of the individual are maximized, and difficult challenges are met with relative ease (Funk, Chan, Brouwer, & Curtiss, 2006). In general, it is believed that it is more common for individuals to be in an absorbed state than in a flow state. Thus, for especially painful procedures, allowing youth sufficient time to become absorbed in a video game may be the most effective way to reduce the perception of pain through media use.

Table 4.1   Explaining Why Video Game Play Reduces Pain Perception

- Cognitive and motor requirements of game play demand attention.
- The difficulty of the game can be personalized to maximize user interest.
- Video games are appealing to most children and adolescents.
- Potential to induce an altered state of consciousness.

Pain and Video Games: A Prescription for Success?

As illustrated above, different types of media can successfully distract youth during painful procedures and, thus, lessen the perception of pain. But is there one particular media that works the best? Should doctors and dentists invest in DVDs, CDs, or video games? Currently, there is not enough research to answer this question. There is, however, plenty of theory to suggest that of the media currently available, video games, and in particular those involving virtual reality (because of its immersive qualities), may have the greatest impact on pain perception. As early as the late 1980s, researchers were touting the ameliorative effects of video game play on pain. Redd and colleagues (1987) suggested that the cognitive and motor requirements of video games demand attention, thereby leaving less attentional resources available to focus on pain. Additionally, video game play can be personalized to maximize user interest and attention. For instance, the level of game difficulty can be changed for novice and experienced players. Moreover, because video games appeal to most children and adolescents, the likelihood that the media-based distraction will be effective is enhanced. Finally, through absorption or flow, video game play affords the gamer the opportunity to enter an altered state of consciousness, where pain is no longer a focal point for attentional resources. (See Table 4.1.)

Additional Medical Benefits of Video Game Play and Virtual Reality

Griffiths (2003) described multiple studies in which video games were used to help children and adolescents deal with a variety of medical and psychological conditions. For instance, video game play was used as a form of physiotherapy to help a 13-year-old adolescent recover from an arm injury. Additional research demonstrated that the impulsivity of four adolescents improved following a month of video game play. Moreover, the use of a handheld video game system (e.g., *Nintendo DS*) was shown to prevent a boy from obsessively picking at his upper lip (Griffiths, 2003). Video game play during psychotherapy has been suggested to aid in the child–therapist relationship and provide insight into the child's problem-solving strategies (Gardner, 1991). Computer games have even helped asthmatic preschool children learn how to correctly use a spirometer (a device for measuring lung performance; Vilozni et al., 2005). More recently, Parsons and colleagues (Parsons, Leonard, & Mitchell, 2006) demonstrated the effectiveness of virtual reality in helping two adolescents with autistic spectrum disorder (ASD).

ASD refers to a variety of psychiatric disorders, such as autism, Rett syndrome, and Asperger's syndrome, that are characterized by significant deficits in social interaction and communication, often accompanied by highly repetitive behaviors (such as hand flapping and spinning). Specific to social situations, youth with ASD have difficulty initiating and sustaining interactions with others. Moreover, ASD youth frequently fail to understand emotional expressions, social cues, and social rules necessary for success in social situations. Such failures can lead to social isolation and anxiety. Some ASD researchers believe that through repetitive training, the social skills deficits associated with ASD can be improved upon; and that is where virtual reality comes in. Virtual reality allows ASD youth to interact with virtual others in three-dimensional environments that mimic real-life social settings. For instance, youth can attempt to join in on a conversation during lunch or while waiting in line for a bus. Such virtual environments allow ASD youth to repeatedly practice social skills in settings that would normally cause them trepidation and without the risk of real-life rejection. Moreover, therapeutic facilitators can sit next to ASD youth during their foray into a virtual world to discuss options for and outcomes associated with potential behaviors (Parsons et al., 2006).

Clearly, video game play and virtual reality offer unique opportunities for medical and psychological treatments beyond those offered in the real world. As technology improves, the application of video game play and virtual reality in medical and psychological settings will increase. However, at this point in time, the research supporting such video game–based interventions is limited. As interesting as the above findings were, with the exception of the spirometry research, the data were derived from case studies. Although case studies provide a great deal of information about the participants being studied, the findings lack sufficient generalizability to warrant widespread application of the findings to the population as a whole. For instance, virtual reality may help only a limited number of youth in the autistic spectrum, such as those who are high functioning and therefore already possess some basic social skills. Moreover, none of the research presented considered developmental status in their assessments. It may be that the effectiveness of different video game– and virtual reality–related techniques varies by age.

The Behavioral Benefits of Prosocial Media

Following the shooting and murder of 12 students at Columbine High School in 1999, newspapers throughout the country reported on the possible causes of this unspeakable tragedy. For a while, violent video games were considered to be a primary culprit. But when two high school students brought their school bus to a stop after the driver had a heart attack (suffering minor injuries in the process), and when an elementary school child did the same thing after his bus driver lost consciousness, not a single story addressed the positive contribution (if any) of media to these heroic acts. Is it possible that video games that simulate driving, like *Grand Tourismo* 4, helped these youth learn to handle stressful driving situations? Reporting on the impact of media on prosocial behavior is one thing, but demonstrating it through research is quite another.

As you recall from the previous chapter, youth are exposed to prosocial behavior on television through E/I programs, during which behaviors such as sharing, self-respect, and helping are modeled. For instance, in the Cartoon Network offering *Krypto the Superdog*, the importance of cooperation and helping your friends is illustrated during the trials and tribulations of a dog with superpowers. Other shows, such as *Tutenstein* and *Phil of the Future*, portray the day-to-day difficulties and dilemmas that children and adolescents (and, in the case of Tutenstein, mummies) face. At the same time, such shows also illustrate relevant coping and problem-solving behaviors. But before considering the impact of prosocial media across development, it is important to understand the cognitive requirements necessary to learn prosocial acts from television (and/or other media) models.

Cognitive Requirements Needed for Prosocial Learning

Developmentally, learning from prosocial media appears to be more difficult than learning from educational media. Educational shows, such as *Sesame Street* and *Bill Nye the Science Guy*, present academic materials in a magazine format involving simple, discrete vignettes. Academic materials are presented in a straightforward manner: Teach and learn if you will. In contrast, most prosocial media relays its message of beneficence in a narrative form, in which prosocial messages are imparted over time, with an integrated "take-home message" occurring near the end of the episode. Thus, in order to decode and understand such messages, children must be able to do the following: (a) Identify plot information relevant to the central theme of the story (e.g., it is wrong to hurt your friend's reputation in order to become class president), while at the same time ignoring incidental and peripheral program details (e.g., the campaign platform); (b) organize relevant central theme information into script form (e.g., detail the sequencing of events); (c) identify the character's feelings and motivations, some of which may need to be inferred from actions (e.g., a drooping head to indicate shame); and (d) integrate related, but disconnected, story elements into cause-and-effect sequences (e.g., the protagonist's shameless self-promotion alienated her best friend).

For age-appropriate shows, youth are able to successfully identify explicitly depicted central program content by 5 to 6 years of age. For instance, Rosenkoetter (1999) found that the majority of first and third graders understood a variety of moral themes depicted in an episode of *The Cosby Show*, including fighting, stealing, forgiving, and sharing. However, these same first graders were far less successful than third graders at deciphering the single moral theme depicted in an episode of *Full House*. It may be that youth entering middle childhood have yet to develop media-decoding skills sophisticated enough to consistently understand all plotlines, even if there is only one plotline central to the story. Additional research has shown that the ability to accurately detect central content themes improves markedly from the second to fifth grade (Collins, Wellman, Keniston, & Westby, 1978). Based on this finding, the inconsistency seen in the previous study is not too surprising. Similar improvements occur in the ability to correctly sequence central story themes between the first and third grade (which then remains stable throughout the rest of middle childhood). However, the ability to identify implicit content (i.e., inferred content associated with the central storyline that is not explicitly shown), such as emotional and motivational states, does not appear until age 10. Thus, with development, the ability to infer emotions and motivations from implicit and explicit content improves, as does the ability to understand more complicated plotlines (Calvert & Kotler, 2003).

If the behavior of children and adolescents is to be influenced by prosocial television, then, as described above, youth must both comprehend and remember televised prosocial content. However, such abilities, although necessary to impact behavior, are not sufficient to affect a behavioral predilection or cause a change in behavior, for when the opportunity arises, youth also need to be *motivated* to act prosocially (Bandura, 1986). In other words, knowing *how* to engage in prosocial actions does not necessarily cause youth to *behave* in a prosocial manner. Moreover, the cost of helping, sharing, and so on needs to be taken into consideration when deciding whether or not to engage in prosocial behaviors. For instance, the cost of sharing cookies with other children is that after completing this prosocial act, the child will have less food to consume in the future. Importantly, the rewards and punishments accompanying modeled behaviors are thought to directly impact children's motivation to engage in prosocial acts (Smith et al., 2006). Thus, when consuming media, children make note of not only the prosocial behaviors that were modeled but also the consequences resulting from them (both good and bad).

Research on Infants and Toddlers

True prosocial behavior does not appear until the second year of life. Toddlers, for instance, will react to the distress of their playmates with concern and prosocial acts, such as hugging or getting a teacher to help soothe the child. However, as Eisenberg and colleagues (Eisenberg, Fabes, & Spinrad, 2006) pointed out, there is relatively little research on prosocial behavior during infancy and toddlerhood. As such, it should come as no surprise that there is no research on the effects of television, or other media, on prosocial actions at these ages either. Given the amount of prosocial media available to infants and toddlers, the lack of research on this topic is surprising.

Research on Preschoolers

Over the past 3 decades, nearly 20 studies have assessed the impact of prosocial television programs on the prosocial behavior of 3- to 5-year-olds.

Typically, these studies utilized an experimental design in which children watched a prosocial television show followed by a period of unstructured "free play," during which children's behavior was observed. At times, the effects of prosocial media were compared against the effects of neutral content or no content (i.e., control). At other times, violent media was used for contrasting purposes. Regardless of the comparison, the results of these studies have been very similar: Prosocial media generally led to increases in positive interactions, sharing, and altruism, relative to youth observing other content (Mares & Woodard, 2007). For instance, Zielinska and Chambers (1995) found that after viewing prosocial video clips of *Sesame Street*, preschoolers were more likely to share, take turns, help, comfort, and act cooperatively with their playmates, in comparison to children who watched neutral segments from the same show.

Clearly, prosocial media can influence the behavior of preschoolers immediately following viewing. But that does not mean that the effects of prosocial media during early childhood are without limits. For example, although young children can mimic the exact types of prosocial behaviors seen on TV (e.g., helping out a friend), this media effect does not appear to generalize to other (nonviewed) types of prosocial acts (e.g., donating to charity; Friedrich & Stein, 1973). Moreover, the influence of prosocial media on children's behavior has primarily been assessed with less than a day's delay between media exposure and the assessment of outcomes (Mares & Woodard, 2007). Thus, because the impact of short-term prosocial media exposure on young children is likely to dissipate over time, the duration of the aforementioned prosocial effects are unknown. Moreover, the *long-term* impact of viewing prosocial media on youth has not been studied.

It is worth noting that not all prosocial media messages are beneficial to young children. In fact, depictions of cooperation and conflict in the same episode and prosocial-aggressive acts both tend to produce the opposite of the desired prosocial outcome. *Prosocial aggression* refers to acts of helping, sharing, protecting, and the like that are accomplished through the use of aggressive behavior. Superheroes frequently engage in this type of behavior. As an example, Batman is constantly saving the people of Gotham City from the criminals who inevitably escape from Arkham Asylum. During early childhood, research has demonstrated that viewing scenes containing prosocial aggression led to subsequent increases in aggressive behavior and/or reductions in prosocial actions.

For instance, the viewing of conflict and resolution on *Sesame Street* led to a decrease in cooperative behavior during a postviewing game of marbles (Silverman & Sprafkin, 1980). Similarly, after watching cartoon superheroes save the world via prosocial aggression, young children acted more aggressively and less prosocially than children watching programs that illustrated prosocial behaviors but without accompanying acts of aggression (Liss, Reinhardt, & Fredriksen, 1983).

Research on Youth in Middle Childhood and Adolescence

As children age, researchers rely less on free-play sessions and more on experimenter-controlled situations to assess prosocial behavior. When using a "free-play" paradigm, the researcher is at the whim of the nature of the play occurring, be it cooperative, competitive, or otherwise. As a result, the number of *chances* to engage in prosocial behavior varies from play session to play session. Some children listed as not acting prosocially may have engaged in prosocial behavior if given the chance, but their play did not afford that opportunity. Requiring all children to act (or not act) in specific ways forces the prosocial issue upon the child. This type of experiment guarantees that prosocial behavior will occur if, in fact, the child deems it *appropriate* to act in that manner. Typically, these types of experiments require youth to help or hinder another's performance. Such assessments use devices like the "help–hurt" machine, which ostensibly allows youth to increase or decrease the difficulty of a task being performed by another child by pushing a button (Collins & Getz, 1976).

During middle childhood and adolescence, studies using both free play and experimenter-created devices have shown that exposure to prosocial media leads to greater prosocial behavior than youth exposure to neutral media, aggressive media, or no media. For instance, Collins and Getz (1976) found that, in comparison to youth watching a wildlife documentary, fourth, seventh, and 10th graders watching an adult program edited to highlight prosocial content pushed the "help" button more often when viewing another child attempt to complete a task. However, the experimental findings during these later developmental periods are not as consistent as those during the preschool years, as proportionally more studies have failed to demonstrate that media exerts a positive impact on youthful prosocial behavior. Similar to these mixed experimental findings, correlational studies conducted using these age groups have demonstrated only weak associations between measures of prosocial behavior (e.g., teacher and peer nominations) and the consumption of prosocial television (Mares & Woodard, 2007). Clearly, with so few studies done in middle childhood and less than a handful involving adolescents, more research is needed before a true developmental assessment can take place.

The Psychological Benefits of the Internet

Adolescents spend more time surfing the Internet, instant messaging (IM), and chatting online with one another than do adults (Lenhart, Madden, & Hitlin, 2005). Do these types of interactions (which are devoid of face-to-face contact) influence adolescents' friendships, well-being, self-esteem, and identity formation? In addition, do the psychological benefits of the Internet vary across development? The answers to these questions are presented below.

Friendship

More so than for information seeking or for entertainment purposes, adolescents use the Internet for interpersonal communication. For instance, nearly 75% of adolescents use IM when online, and nearly 8 out of 10 IMs are directed at school-based friends (Gross, 2004; Lenhart et al., 2005). But does such extensive communication with others help or hinder *existing* relationships with real-life friends? According to the friendship reduction hypothesis, Internet use leads to a reduction in the perceived closeness to real-life friends. This outcome is posited to occur because the Internet encourages the creation of superficial friendships with strangers that take time away from real-life relationships. In contrast, the friendship stimulation hypothesis contends that Internet use enhances current real-life relationships because it affords youth the opportunity to more easily engage in behaviors that foster friendships, such as the disclosure of feelings and the sharing of intimate information (Valkenburg & Peter, 2007a).

So which is it, friendship reduction or stimulation? The answer to this question, in part, lies in the decade in which the research was conducted. Valkenburg and Peter reported that the empirical findings from the 1990s (which used only adult samples) pointed toward the reduction hypothesis. In contrast, research on both adults and adolescents conducted since the mid-2000s points toward the stimulation hypothesis. Interestingly, the cause of this cohort effect appears to be access to the Internet. A decade ago, few adolescents had Internet access at home, and as such, online contacts with real-life friends occurred infrequently. Thus, the more time adolescents spent with friends made online, the less time they spent with their offline friends. Today, home Internet access is so commonplace that most online friends are also offline friends.

Valkenburg and Peter reported that 61% of preadolescents (10 to 11 years of age) and 88% of adolescents (12 to 16 years of age) use the Internet with the primary intent of maintaining existing offline friendships. Moreover, for these youth, IMing online with their school-based friends leads to greater feelings of closeness toward those friends. The stimulation effect appears to be particularly strong for adolescents who are socially anxious (and, as a result, have great difficulty sharing intimate information in person). The reduced social and emotional cues on the Internet allow socially anxious youth to express their feelings in an environment that is perceived to be less threatening. However, Internet communication does not appear to help adolescents who describe themselves as *lonely* improve upon their existing, but limited, friendships. When lonely adolescents engage in chat, more often than not, they are communicating with strangers. As a result, the amount of time spent communicating with known others is reduced. Moreover, for both lonely and nonlonely youth, public chat does not appear to improve the quality of existing relationships. This finding is most likely due to the fact that most conversations in public chat rooms occur between strangers and not friends (Valkenburg & Peter, 2007a). Thus, the benefits of online interactions appear to be limited to communications with friends.

Well-Being and Social Self-Esteem

Adolescents who feel good about their lives (i.e., they are generally happy and satisfied with the way things are currently going) are said to have a sense of well-being (Diener, 1984). Social self-esteem, which is one of many contributors to well-being, refers to an individual's evaluation of the social self, involving peer and other relationships. Individuals with high social self-esteem feel good about their social relationships, whereas individuals with low social self- esteem feel poorly about them. The results from several recent studies suggest that, for teens, IM with friends appears to have a positive impact on well-being. Interestingly, the link from IM to well-being is not direct. Instead, IM appears to enhance friendships, which in turn contributes to an overall sense of well-being. In contrast, IM and chat with strangers appear to negatively impact adolescent well-being (Valkenburg & Peter, 2007a, 2007b). More so than youth who have a number of friends, youth in need of friends tend to talk more frequently with strangers on the Internet. Such online interactions reduce offline opportunities to inter-act with known individuals (to either create or enhance a friendship). In turn, the lack of real-life friends leads to lower levels of well-being. Of note, there is no research on the impact of IM and chat on social self-esteem. However, given that adolescents could receive both positive and negative reactions to their messages, the nature of the reaction to their posting could either enhance or hurt their social self.

In addition to investigating the influence of IM and chat on the afore-mentioned constructs, recent research has also focused on social net-working sites, such as MySpace and Facebook. Youth who participate in such sites post online personal profiles and invite others to comment on their postings. Profiles can include pictures, self-descriptors (e.g., likes, dislikes, and favorite things), music, video clips, and links to friends in their network. Profiles can be open to the general public to view or be restricted to a network of friends. Comments posted on these sites range from positive accolades to negative missives. Recent research suggests that most adolescents (78%) receive positive comments on their net-working site profiles. Not surprisingly, when adolescents receive good news about their postings, both self-esteem and well-being are enhanced. In contrast, negative feedback was associated with lower levels of these constructs. It is worth noting that the number of online friends on a net-work site appears to be unrelated to social self-esteem. Thus, it is the quality of the relationships (as measured by the tone of the feedback) and not the quantity of them that appear to impact how adolescents feel about their social selves (Valkenburg, Peter, & Schouten, 2006).

Identity Exploration

One of the primary tasks of adolescence is identity exploration, where *identity* refers to setting specific aspects of the self that interact with the environment (DeHart, Sroufe, & Cooper, 2004). Thus, identity provides the answer to the question "Who am I?" with the answer depending upon the setting in which the question was asked. For instance, a female adolescent can view herself as an outgoing cheerleader at school, a caring sister at home, and a responsible employee at work. During adolescence, identities are explored through interactions with others, thus affording the adolescent the opportunity to try out differing aspects of the self in different settings. The Internet allows youth to explore identities in ways not readily available in the real world. When online, youth can be old or young, male or female, rich or poor, nice or mean, helpful or selfish, smart or dumb, and so on; in other words, virtually any identity can be tried out (and more than one identity can be tried out at the same time). Moreover, the relative anonymity of the Web (such as in public chat rooms) allows youth to try out identities with little concern about real-life negative social consequences. Outlets for such exploration include IM, chat, social-networking sites, and blogs.

Developmental Points of Interest

Currently, there is little research on media-related pain reduction during the toddler years. When toddlers did participate in empirical studies, they were typically included as part of a nondevelopmental study of preschool children (e.g., MacLaren & Cohen, 2005). But development is a crucial factor in the perception and experience of pain. Over the course of toddler and preschool years, even the youngest of children make marked improvements in their ability to focus and attend to stimuli (DeHart et al., 2004). Thus, the possibility exists that media distracters may be increasingly effective for older children, as focused and sustained attention on the media distracter improves with age. As children get older, physiological and behavioral assessments of pain are accompanied by self-report measures of pain perception. Such assessments are important because they provide insight into the cognitive, and very subjective, experience of pain. For instance, it is possible that two children may express similar facial grimaces in response to a vaccination shot (and consequently be rated by an observer as experiencing the same level of pain) but report very different levels of felt pain. Moreover, the subjective experience of pain may differ with development as well. However, such developmental variability has yet to be tested empirically.

Across development, the best distracter from pain for any child is the one that is most likely to grab that child's attention. For infants and young children, and for those with limited video game skills, preferred TV shows and music may be the best choice for distraction. But what if the preferred distracter is a violent video game or a violent TV show? Isn't it like trading one evil (pain) for another (violent behavior)? Simply put, no. For most youth, the traumatic consequences associated with painful medical procedures have more potential to harm than does exposure to violent media. Be it violent or nonviolent, future research should investigate more thoroughly the impact of preferred versus nonpreferred media distracters on pain reduction, across development.

In comparison to the research conducted in early childhood, there are far fewer studies (< 10) on the impact of prosocial media on the prosocial behavior of youth between the ages of 6 and 16, with only a couple of studies using an adolescent sample. Unlike the E/I stimuli shown to preschoolers, research using child and adolescent samples has used network programs to illustrate prosocial behavior. Of note, the TV programs used in these studies included comedies (e.g., *I Love Lucy* and *Gilligan's Island*) and dramas (e.g., *The Mod Squad* and *Lassie*). Whether or not comedic or dramatic presentations of prosocial behavior impact youth is unclear, as there are too few studies (using children of similar ages) to make an effective comparison. Moreover, television shows meant for young children specifically target prosocial themes for each episode, whereas the primary intent of shows meant for an older audience is to entertain. Thus, younger and older children may be getting different "doses" of prosocial behavior per episode. As a result, it becomes difficult to compare the relative effectiveness of prosocial media across development.

Research on the potential benefits of prosocial media on youth has been languishing for decades. In fact, no new experimental studies involving television, or video games for that matter, have been conducted on youth of any age since the late 1980s. Incidentally, the lone experimental study involving prosocial video game play and prosocial behavior failed to produce a significant effect. Apparently, the helping-out video game *Smurfs* does not translate into helping classmates sharpen pencils or increase the amount of money donated to charity (Chambers & Ascione, 1987). Similarly, few studies have assessed the impact of prosocial media on youth from a correlational perspective (Ostrov, Gentile, & Crick, 2006; Rosenkoetter, 1999).

As you might expect, with so little developmental research in this area, there are many questions left unanswered. In addition to those questions mentioned above, consider the following: First, does the medium matter for the prosocial message to have an effect? Although prosocial TV can impact behavior, past research has failed to illustrate the benefits of video game play on youth. But what about the behavioral influence of newer, more realistic video games and virtual reality? Will the increased realism translate into increased impact? Second, do the physical characteristics of the prosocial model matter? That is, are youth more likely to imitate and learn prosocial behaviors from characters of the same age, race, and gender or from those of a different age, race, and gender? In addition, research is needed to address the changing influence of these types of media-based characteristics on youth across development. Finally, are children and adolescents who frequently engage in prosocial behaviors affected by prosocial media to a greater or lesser extent than other youth? Although theory can provide potential answers to each and every question mentioned above, theoretical answers are no substitute for empirical ones. Of course, there are many other questions in need of answering, and they will remain unanswered unless media researchers start to more systematically address the benefits of prosocial media on youth.

Currently, there are no studies on the impact of the Internet on the friendships, well-being, self-esteem, and identity exploration of children during middle childhood or younger. However, by the end of middle childhood, nearly 61% of children frequently use the Internet to communicate with friends (Valkenburg & Peter, 2007a). Therefore, it is very likely that children younger than age 10 are also communicating online with friends and strangers. After all, entertainment sites catering to younger children, such as Club Penguin and Runescape, allow players to chat during game play. Unfortunately, the impact of online communication on offline friendships, well-being, and so on during these younger age periods is unknown.

In the service of identity exploration, adolescents have presented themselves as older, more macho, prettier, the opposite gender, someone they know, or a fantasy person. In general, early adolescents (72%) engage in such identity exploration on the Internet to a greater extent than middle adolescents (53%) or late adolescents (28%) (Valkenburg, Schouten, & Peter, 2005). Such a result is not surprising, given that from a developmental perspective, identity exploration starts in early adolescence. When youth enter adolescence, newfound cognitive abilities allow them to more easily engage in self-reflection and abstract thought, and, as a result, consider who they are at a deeper level than when younger. The physical, emotional, and social changes accompanying adolescence allow the self to be defined in ways that could never before be done. After several years of exploration, however, youth have begun to settle on a core set of identities, thus limiting the need to experiment with their identity on the Internet or elsewhere. However, you can have too much of a good thing. The more often that youth present fake identities on the Internet, the more likely they are to have low self-esteem, social anxiety, and poor social skills (Harman, Hansen, Cochran, & Lindsey, 2005). Harman and colleagues suggested that rather than coming to terms with who they are or who they will become, excessive fakers become absorbed in an idealized self, a self that in reality they can never attain. As a result, such youth become disappointed and frustrated with who they really are in the real world.

5

Advertising, Consumer Behavior, and Youth

Children of all ages receive presents for their birthdays, gifts during the holiday season, and "I love you" knickknacks throughout the year. A quick search on Amazon.com reveals that there are more than 500,000 toys, games, books, and video games to choose from, virtually an endless sea of possibilities. With so many choices, how are well-meaning parents and grandparents supposed to find gifts that are not only suitable for their youthful recipients but desired by them as well? With my own kids, I can either ask them directly or check the "acceptable gifts" list taped onto the refrigerator or the duplicate electronic copy sent to me via e-mail. Simple enough, but then again, how do children and adolescents actually know what they want in the first place? That is where advertising comes in. When done well, advertisements have the power to influence the objects that youth think about, desire, and ultimately purchase.

Children and adolescents have not always been the targets of television commercials. During the 1950s, most advertisements focused on the individuals perceived to have the greatest purchasing power, namely, adults. However, that belief soon changed. By the 1960s, advertisers realized the potential influence that children and adolescents had in family-related consumer purchases and started directing commercials at them. Youth were identified not only as independent consumers with their own money to spend, but also as important influencers in family purchases (Johnson & Young, 2003). Advertisers still target youth, and with good reason: Brand loyalty has the potential to start during early childhood and last well into adulthood (Moschis & Moore, 1982). With future purchases in mind, it is not surprising that advertisers want young children to recognize their particular brand of products (i.e., brand awareness), even if they are too young to purchase them (or influence purchases) at the moment. For instance, in 2003, Ford Motor Company sent preschools free alphabet-style posters that illustrated safety tips. Many other preschool settings used supplies and instructional materials provided by corporate sponsors, such as Care Bear worksheets and the Pizza Hut reading program (Mayer, 2003). But more than for future consumption, the current purchasing power of today's children and adolescents is staggering. Annually, children under 12 years of age spend nearly $40 billion on their own, tweens spend around $30 billion, and adolescents spend close to $160 billion. Beyond these independent purchases, youth influence an additional $600 billion in family spending (Chang, 2007). We are not just talking about snacks, cereals, and toys, for youth also influence high-ticket purchases as well, such as electronics, vacation destinations, and choice of vehicle (Valkenburg & Cantor, 2001).

Consumer Behavior Across Development

Unlike adults, infants have no understanding of important consumer concepts, such as "sale" items, buy-one-get-one-free promotions, and comparison shopping. In other words, consumers are not born; they are made. Through the process of consumer socialization, children learn the knowledge, skills, and attitudes needed to become an effective consumer. According to Valkenburg and Cantor (2001), there are several aspects of consumer behavior that can vary across development: (a) desires and preferences, (b) the search to fulfill desires and preferences, (c) final decision and purchase, and (d) product evaluation. Based on mastery of these tasks, the authors identified four stages of consumer behavior; with each new stage characterized by the emergence of one of the aforementioned tasks. The stages are as follows: feeling wants and preferences, nagging and negotiations, adventure and the first purchase, and conformity and fastidiousness (see Table 5.1).

Feeling Wants and Preferences

The first stage of consumer behavior, *feeling wants and preferences*, occurs during infancy and toddlerhood. Obviously, the cognitive and language limitations of these developmental periods limit consumer behavior to the first task. As early as the first few months of life, infants feel desires and display preferences for certain types of tastes (e.g., sweet), odors

Table 5.1   Stages of Consumer Behavior

- Feeling wants and preferences
- Nagging and negotiations
- Adventure and the first purchase
- Conformity and fastidiousness
- Adolescent skepticism

(e.g., pleasant), images (e.g., high in contrast), colors (e.g., bright), and sounds (e.g., human voices). Of course, retailers make sure that there are plenty of food choices, toys, and games to match these preferences. But aside from grunting at or reaching out to an object placed on a nearby shelf, infants have yet to develop the communication skills necessary to convey any product-related desires that they may have. That soon changes, and between 18 and 24 months, many toddlers (about 40%) not only are capable of asking for products by name but also can recognize products in the store that they had previously seen on TV. In fact, one study found that 2-year-olds made an average of 18 product requests during a mere 25 minutes of shopping (Holdren, 2003). Still, more often than not, product requests by infants and toddlers are in response to seeing an object in front of them, rather than a conscious goal-directed request made in the product's absence. Nevertheless, such requests can have a powerful impact on parental buying decisions. Many a parent has reinforced a toddler's tantrum in the grocery story by buying the child the desired object.

Nagging and Negotiations

Nagging and negotiations, the second stage of consumer behavior, occurs during the preschool years. By this age, children not only have developed a sense of *general* likes and dislikes, but also show preferences for *specific* brands of products. So powerful are these preferences that they can even influence preschoolers' evaluation of related stimuli. For instance, Robinson and colleagues (Robinson, Borzekowski, Matheson, & Kraemer, 2007) demonstrated that healthy foods (i.e., carrots and milk) tasted better to preschoolers when they came wrapped in McDonald's packaging in comparison to when they did not.

In addition to being aware of their own desires and preferences, preschoolers are now actively trying to fulfill them. Moreover, they will use any means necessary to do so, including whining, throwing a tantrum, crying, and, of course, nagging and negotiating. In fact, parent–child conflict during store visits peaks during this stage of consumer behavior, with 70% of parents of 5-year-olds reporting conflicts while shopping. In contrast, only 41% of parents of 2-year-olds and 58% of parents of 8-year-olds report such events. Such conflicts are part of the reason that these young children complete the first major consumer milestone during this stage: making a "pseudo-independent purchase." In the presence of a parent, more than half of 4-year-olds have purchased an item at a grocery or department store (Valkenburg & Cantor, 2001). In doing so, children are accomplishing the third task in the development of consumer behavior: making a decision and purchase.

Tremendous improvements in children's memory (85% of 4-year-olds now recognize products in stores) and communicative ability occur during the preschool years. However, Valkenburg and Cantor (2001) pointed out several cognitive and emotional limitations of early childhood that result in the tumultuous manner in which preschoolers try to fulfill their perceived needs. First, preschool-aged children often perceive commercials as either short, entertaining programs or helpful sources of information about toys, cereals, and the like. The persuasive intent of advertisements is generally lost on these young children. Thus, from a preschooler's perspective, products like Chia Pets and *Star Wars* action figures *must* bring joy and merriment to all, because that is what the commercial communicates. Preschoolers fail to realize that commercials do not necessarily have their best interests in mind (Kunkel, 2001). In fact, less than one third of preschoolers understand that commercials are trying to get children to buy the products being advertised (Wilson & Weiss, 1992).

Second, preschool children's maturation as consumers is limited due to centration, which restricts their ability to make proper evaluations and/or comparison of products. Centration is the tendency to direct one's focus to a singular, prominent feature of an object at the expense of other features (DeHart, Sroufe, & Cooper, 2004). For instance, Acuff (1997) found that when given a choice of three dolls, preschool-aged girls based their selection on the presence or absence of one visually salient characteristic (i.e., a large sequined heart) and ignored other important aspects of the dolls, such as the cost, realism, beauty, and workmanship. Style over substance rules the world of products for preschoolers, and parents' admonitions regarding the quality and utility of the product (or lack thereof) have the potential to fall on deaf ears. Thus, the stage is set for parent–child conflict.

Finally, a general lack of impulse control and limitations in the ability to delay gratification result in those three little words that many parents come to fear: "I want that!" *Delay of gratification* refers to the ability to hold out for a better reward later by forgoing an immediate, lesser reward. When faced with an attractive object (e.g., a toy, cookie, or book), preschoolers have great difficulty resisting the temptation before them. They will act impulsively and put all their efforts into getting the desired object. Moreover, promises of greater riches later (e.g., ice cream) for good behavior now (e.g., stop the tantrum) may not necessarily result in the outcome desired by parents. Rarely do preschoolers initiate techniques that will help themselves delay gratification. Thus, when faced with resistance from parents, preschoolers will impulsively resist back.

Adventure and the First Purchase

Taking place during the early elementary school years (ages 5–8), *adventure and the first purchase* is the third stage in the development of the child as a consumer. Like their younger counterparts, children still display centration, have impulse control and delay of gratification issues, and have difficulty understanding the persuasive intent of commercials, although to a much lesser extent than before. For instance, the percentage of youth who comprehend the persuasive intent of advertisements more than doubles from the preschool years to age 8, by which point nearly three quarters of youth understand that commercials are really tools of persuasion (Wilson & Weiss, 1992). As children progress through this stage, there is a preferential shift from slow-paced programs with friendly characters (e.g., *Barney*) to programs with a faster pace and more complicated plots (e.g., *Scooby Doo*). Not surprisingly, the pace of commercials directed at 5- to 8-year-olds picks up as well (Jennings & Wartella, 2007).

During this stage, children make their first true independent purchases. According to Valkenburg and Cantor (2001), 21% of 5-year-olds have walked into a store on their own and bought an item or two. By age 8, nearly 50% of children have made an independent purchase. Nevertheless, parental nagging is still prevalent, with the greatest success occurring for food-related requests (e.g., restaurants and grocery items). Development plays a role here as well. Whereas 5-year-olds nag parents more often for products than older children, children 7 years of age and older are more likely to have their requests met (Bridges & Briesch, 2006). Taken together, the combination of making independent purchases, effective nagging of parents, and a limited awareness of persuasive intent seems to make younger children in this stage especially vulnerable to marketing campaigns. However, as Buijzen and Valkenburg (2000) pointed out, advertisements do in fact appear to impact children under 8 years of age to a greater extent than older children and adolescents.

Conformity and Fastidiousness

Conformity and fastidiousness is the final stage in Valkenburg and Cantor's (2001) theory of consumer development. Between 8 and 12 years of age, tweens begin to consider value in their purchases. A dramatic drop in centration allows tweens to think about more than one detail at a time, resulting in the appreciation of quality products. Moreover, their ever-improving eye for detail allows youth to amass items as true collectors, purchasing items based on their unique qualities, such as the ultimate cards for *Yu-Gi-Oh* battles. In contrast, younger children tend to accumulate items, collecting for the sake of collecting. For example, when my son was 5, he was set on having a "collection of collections." Additionally, tweens' increasing cognitive abilities allow them to compare and contrast the qualities of different items available for purchase. In doing so, they have completed the fourth and final task in consumer development.

Despite the fact that they are perceived as entertaining, advertisements are viewed negatively during this stage of development (John, 1999). In contrast to younger children, tweens understand that commercials attempt to convince the viewer to make specific product purchases. However, knowledge is not always power, for even when youth know that an attempt is being made to persuade them, they can still become persuaded. Research has shown that viewing commercials increases tweens' desires for advertised products and that repeated exposure to the same commercial increases the desire even more (Gorn & Goldberg, 1978). Additionally, children and adolescents watching the greatest number of commercials tend to request advertised products from parents more often than other youth (Buijzen & Valkenburg, 2003).

The roles of peers

From the later elementary school years on, peers play an increasingly important role in the lives of youth. In an attempt to "fit in," most children will try to follow the norms of their peer group (DeHart et al., 2004). For instance, when my daughter was 9, she received an e-mail from a friend in a different state bemoaning the "stupid" fact that all fourth grade girls were wearing bras. Despite her disgust, my daughter's friend then mentioned that she too was wearing a bra. Thus, during this stage youth start to become attuned to clothes, products, and so on that are considered by their peers to be "cool" or "in." It is not uncommon for tweens to seek out and flaunt such products in front of their peers (Lindstrom, 2003). As such, advertisers attempt to provide products meeting tweens' perceived needs. Of note, tweens are especially interested in television shows and commercials depicting adolescents older than they are. This was recently evidenced by the incredible popularity among tweens for *Disney's High School Musical* and *Hannah Montana*, each of which relays the trials and tribulations of youth in high school. Tweens also start avoiding shows meant for younger audiences. Apparently watching *Bob the Builder* is not considered "cool" by the peers of 10-year-olds.

Consumer Behavior During Adolescence

Although Valkenburg and Cantor's (2001) stage theory of consumer development ends around age 12, consumer behavior continues to develop across adolescence. Adolescents show marked improvements in all four stages mentioned above. Newly found cognitive abilities (such as introspection and formal logic) allow adolescents to more effectively scrutinize their own wants and preferences, negotiate more effectively for material goods, and evaluate the quality of the products they are thinking of buying. As youth become less dependent on their parents for transportation and money (e.g., they can earn their own), they increasingly become independent consumers with their own money to spend. However, they also add to their existing consumer skills a healthy dose of skepticism (Jennings & Wartella, 2007). John (1999) pointed out that not only do teens question the veracity of advertisements, but also they are able to identify specific tactics that advertisers use to deceive consumers, such as the use of exaggerations and disclaimers. Along with advertisements, personal experience with products increasingly influences consumer behavior. Moreover, peers continue to play an important role in determining which products adolescents buy, with commercials frequently being used as a source of information regarding current trends in fashion, music, and so on to discuss with their friends (Gunter, Oates, & Blades, 2005).

Consumer Behavior and the Moderating Effect of Materialism

During childhood and adolescence, consumer behavior is influenced by more than just peers and commercials. In fact, one of the key factors that moderates (i.e., influences the strength of a relationship with) the effect of advertisements on consumer behavior is materialism. *Materialism* refers to the importance that people place on their possessions, either for self-enhancement or in an effort to define themselves (Chaplin & John, 2007). According to one study, youth high in materialism value toys over friends (Goldberg & Gorn, 1978). Highly materialistic youth are an advertiser's dream. They not only purchase more material goods but also are more likely to be influenced by marketing promotions (Chaplin & John).

In addition to being a moderator of consumer behavior, materialism is also considered to be an unintended effect of viewing advertising. The intended effects of advertising are increasing brand awareness, creating positive brand attitudes, and influencing purchasing requests and behavior (each of which is discussed in greater detail below). Thus, *unintended effects* refer to outcomes (which are typically negative) that do not impact any of the three intended effects mentioned above. For instance, across development, parent–child conflict does appear to slightly increase following exposure to televised commercials (Buijzen & Valkenburg, 2003).

Numerous correlational and experimental studies have shown that youth become increasingly materialistic as they watch more and more advertisements. For instance, Greenberg and Brand (1993) found that adolescents attending schools in which students were required to watch Channel One were more materialistic than students attending schools without the program. Channel One presents video features and news programming that target youth, including advertisements. Schools broadcast the channel for their own gain, as participating schools get free TVs, DVD players, and access to a video library. The effects of advertisements on materialism remain, even after removing the influence of important moderator variables, such as SES, and parent and peer communication about consumption. Thus, frequent viewing of advertisements does appear to increase the likelihood that children and adolescents will desire objects that they would not have otherwise wanted and helps create a mind-set that material possessions are of extreme importance to the self.

Developmentally, materialism has been observed in children as young as 6 years of age (Atkin, 1975). It then appears to increase through middle childhood and peak between ages 12 and 13. Though materialism decreases thereafter, the levels of materialism found during middle and late adolescence are still greater than those seen in children younger than age 10 (Chaplin & John, 2007). So, how do children change from sharing and caring preschoolers to materialistic, product-absorbed children? In comparison to less materialistic youth, materialistic children and adolescents tend to have materialistic parents, ineffective parent–child communication, and greater levels of communication with their peers. They also tend to watch more television, and therefore are exposed to more commercials, than their less materialistic peers (Chaplin & John).

Advertising, materialism, and self-esteem

Interestingly, Chaplin and John (2007) have recently demonstrated that the developmental apex of materialism corresponds to the developmental bottoming out of self-esteem, both of which occur during early adolescence. Many researchers believe that in an attempt to compensate for insecurities and a poor sense of self, youth purchase material goods. In essence, youth procure objects of significant value in a veiled attempt to view the self as having significant value. It is like saying, "I'm worth a lot because my coat, bag, and shoes are worth a lot." In order for materialistic goods to impact self-esteem, children need to (a) understand the social significance of certain products and possessions, (b) incorporate such items into their sense of self, and (c) recognize how their possessions influence the way their peers perceive them and the impressions they make on others. Although the first two requirements develop over the course of middle childhood, the third requirement does not appear until early adolescence. Thus, it is not surprising that materialism peaks during this age range, as it is during this developmental stage that the importance of material goods to self-esteem is first discovered. As children progress through middle and late adolescence, their sense of self improves and the use of materialistic goods as a coping strategy is reduced. Rather than bolstering self-esteem through "retail therapy," older adolescents have learned more effective means of handling issues related to the self, such as valuing activities, accomplishments, and their current network of friends (Chaplin & John). Taken together, these findings suggest that for youth with low self-esteem, early adolescence may be a time of increased susceptibility to the effects of advertising.

Advertisements That Target Youth

Each year, companies spend billions of dollars advertising products to children and adolescents. For instance, promotions for food and beverages alone cost companies $1.6 billion in 2006 (see Figure 5.1). Nearly half of all advertisements that youth encounter are on television (Federal Trade Commission, 2008). However, determining the exact number of commercials that children and adolescents are exposed to is a difficult task. Most estimates are based on simple multiplication procedures in which the average number of commercials aired per hour is multiplied by the average number of hours that youth watch TV each week (Jennings & Wartella, 2007). However, the broadcasting of a commercial does not necessarily guarantee that the commercial was viewed by the target audience. During commercials, youth will flip channels, talk with their friends, grab a snack, go to the bathroom, and so on. Please keep this caveat in mind when considering the following data. Because 30% of the television programming viewed by children is ad-free (e.g., PBS), youth between the ages of 2 and 7 see around 14,000 commercials each year. As children age, ad-free TV is replaced with ad-supported programming. As such, the number of commercials viewed annually by 8- to 12-year-olds and 13- to 17-year-olds is more than double that viewed by young children (to 28,655 and 30,155, respectively). Each day, young children see a total of 17 minutes worth of advertising, whereas older children and adolescents view commercials for 35 to 37 minutes (Desrochers & Holt, 2007; Gantz, Schwartz, Angelini, & Rideout, 2007). Predictably, junk food (candy, snacks, and sodas), cereals, toys and games, and fast-food restaurants are advertised to children the most (Jennings & Wartella). In contrast, advertisers primarily target

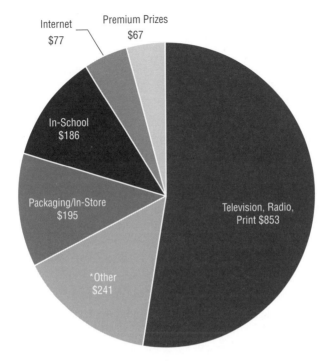

Figure 5.1   Cost of advertising food and beverages to youth (in millions).
* *Other* includes monies spent on product placements; movie theater, video, and video game advertising; character or cross-promotion license fees; athletic sponsorships; celebrity endorsement fees; and other miscellaneous expenditures.
Source: Data adapted from Federal Trade Commission (2008).

adolescents with commercials for music, videos, and other electronic media (Buijzen & Valkenburg, 2002).

Characteristics of Advertisements Targeting Youth

In an attempt to persuade youth to purchase products, advertisers make use of a variety of techniques, including celebrity endorsements, premium prizes, exaggeration, on-package marketing, cobranding, and advergames.

Celebrity endorsements
Movie and television stars, musicians, professional athletes, and other celebrities are frequently used to advertise material goods. Endorsements

by cartoon characters, such as Fred Flintstone or Mickey Mouse, fit in this category as well. Advertisers believe that positive attitudes toward celebrities are transferred to the products they are endorsing. Moreover, the product and the celebrity are thought to become linked in children's minds, thus increasing the likelihood that they will buy those products when the opportunity arises. For instance, during the 1990s advertisers used the catch phrase "Be like Mike!" to promote Gatorade. "Mike" was Michael Jordan, arguably the greatest basketball player of his era. Across development, celebrity-endorsed products receive more favorable evaluations than the same product advertised without celebrity endorsement (Ross et al., 1984). Moreover, older children and early adolescents appear to be influenced by celebrity endorsements to a greater extent than younger children and older adolescents (Desmond & Carveth, 2007).

Premium prizes

Premium prizes are objects given away for free with the purchase of a specified product. For instance, McDonald's Happy Meals typically include a toy as the premium prize. Growing up in the 1970s, I purchased Cracker Jacks whenever I could just to get the premium prize included at the bottom of the box. My own experience has been verified by research. Several studies have found that across development, the availability of premium prizes increases children's and adolescents' desire and request for the advertised product (e.g., Atkin, 1975). Interestingly, many premium prizes are gender stereotyped, with "toys for boys" being action oriented (often in red, green, or blue) and "toys for girls" being a doll of some sort (and in a pastel color).

Exaggeration

As a little boy, I was mesmerized by Sea-Monkeys, which according to the advertisements were pink, smiling, seahorse-like creatures that wore crowns on their heads. Just by adding water, Sea-Monkeys would emerge from their state of hibernation and bring merriment to all who were fortunate enough to be near. Some 30 years later, with the advertisement clearly in mind, I purchased my daughter a family of Sea-Monkeys. The experience was completely disappointing as the seamonkeys were neither pink nor smiling, and they did not wear crowns on their microscopic-sized heads. Apparently, I had fallen for the common advertising ploy of exaggeration. Through animation, special effects, and misleading statements (e.g., "the best"), advertisers mislead the child consumer into thinking that the advertised product offers more excitement, fun, ways of playing with it, and so on than it can in reality. Across development, the ability to detect exaggeration improves. For instance, Wilson and Weiss (1992) found that 80% of preschoolers believed that commercials always "tell the truth" but that by age 7 that percentage has dropped to less than 30%, and by 9 years of age less than 10% believed in the veracity of commercials. To offset such exaggerations, commercials come with disclaimers (e.g., "Some assembly required," and "Each part sold separately"). However, children under 8 years of age have difficulty understanding what the disclaimers actually mean (Liebert, Sprafkin, Liebert, & Rubinstein, 1977). Surprisingly, there is too little research on children's and adolescent's comprehension of disclaimers to assess differences across development.

On-package marketing

Advertisers use every trick they know to promote their products, including creating a "look" that appeals to children, a process referred to as *on-package marketing*. A fun-looking, colorful package is thought to grab the attention of children, increasing the likelihood that they will ask their parents to buy it for them at the point of sale. In addition, branded characters and mascots, like the Trix Rabbit, frequently appear on packages in an attempt to sway children's choices. Each year, over $3 billion is spent creating packaging that directly appeals to youth (Palmer & Carpenter, 2006). Clearly, the advertising industry views product packaging as an extremely important marketing tool.

Cobranding

In addition to branded characters and mascots, advertisers are increasingly using cobranding to promote toys, food, and the like to youth. Cobranding is the advertising technique in which two companies work together to cross-promote products or services. A popular cobranding technique is to adorn the packaging of food products with popular cartoon and movie characters. Recent examples include *Spiderman* Pop-Tarts and *Veggie Tales* Fruit Snacks, with the cobranding intent of improving television ratings and product sales, Nickelodeon has allowed a number of its cartoon characters to appear on product packages, such as *SpongeBob Squarepants* Macaroni 'n' Cheese and *Dora the Explorer* crackers (Batada & Wootan, 2007).

Table 5.2   Examples of Advergames on the Internet

Product	Website
Capri Sun	www.kraftfoods.com/caprisun/
Chuck E. Cheese Restaurants	chuckecheese.com
Kellogg's Cereals	kelloggsfunktown.com
Lego Toys	www.lego.com
Wonka Candy	wonka.com

Advergames

Advergames, which blur the line between advertisement and entertainment, are web-based games that incorporate the product brand and/or brand character into the game itself. For instance, at CartoonNetwork.com children can play a variety of games involving characters from shows airing on the network. Rather than providing stand-alone games, some websites create a virtual world for children to explore. One such website, Millsberry.com (which is operated by General Mills Cereals), allows children to read books, shop at stores, earn virtual money, play games, and watch videos. Of course, General Mills products are found throughout this virtual community. Advergames are thought to create a high level of interest and engagement in children and adolescents, grabbing the attention of youth to a far greater extent than can be done in 30-second television commercials. Moreover, advergames make use of *viral advertising* to promote products. Viral advertising is a marketing technique in which advertisers rely on preexisting social networks (e.g., blogs, e-mail, etc.) to promote products by encouraging users to voluntarily pass along web links, video clips, Flash games, and so on. The extent to which youth do this, however, is unclear. See Table 5.2 for a list of some advergame websites.

Advertisements That Are Not Supposed to Target Youth but Most Likely Do

A quick sampling of the commercials aired on Nickelodeon, Cartoon Network, and the Disney Channel reveals commercials that directly target age-appropriate products at youth. But children and adolescents also watch television on channels that cater to adults, and they watch at all hours of the day and night. As such, youth will view commercials for material goods and services that target adult consumers and are, therefore, not age appropriate. For instance, preschoolers need neither Aflac supplemental insurance nor Geico car insurance. However, it is a good bet that many preschoolers can recognize both the Aflac duck and the Geico lizard. In fact, a recent study found that 2- to 3-year-olds recognized 8 of 12 brand logos (e.g., McDonald's, Mercedes, Shell Gas, Nike, and Cheetos) presented to them by matching the logo with the product. By age 8, recognition of these logos was 100%. It is worth noting that 50% of the logos were for material goods whose advertisements typically target adults (Valkenburg & Buijzen, 2005).

As it turns out, many "adult-oriented" commercials appear to be designed to attract the attention of a younger audience, in addition to their older target audience. Remember that brand awareness during childhood has the potential to turn into consumer behavior years later. Advertisements for beer (with their talking lizards, croaking frogs, and horses that play football), in particular, are entertaining enough to keep individuals who are 10 to 15 years under the legal drinking age attuned. Brand awareness resulting from such ads appears to be intact weeks and months later. For instance, Lieber (1996) found that 9- to 11-year-old children are better able to recognize the Budweiser frogs (73%) than Tony the Tiger (57%). More recently, Collins, Ellickson, McCaffrey, and Hambarsoomians (2005) found that 66% of fourth graders and 92% of ninth graders correctly identified the ferret mascot of Budweiser beer.

Creating advertisements for adult-oriented products that youth finding entertaining has been going on for decades. For instance, during the 1960s, not only was *The Flintstones* sponsored by Winston cigarettes, but also Fred and Wilma Flintstone were actually shown smoking a Winston during commercials. Gerbner (1990) contended that such ads are the result of a willful attempt on the part of the advertiser to attract new consumers for adult-oriented products, even if the consumers are underage. Once again, the advertisements for the tobacco industry exemplify this point. According to an internal memo from the R. J. Reynolds Tobacco Company, approximately one half of men and one third of women begin smoking prior to age 18, with brand selection occurring around age 18 as well (Tredennick, 1974). Thus, one of the primary goals of cigarette advertising is to attract smokers before they start smoking. Because TV commercials for cigarettes were banned in 1971, R. J. Reynolds shifted their advertising dollars from television to magazines and billboards, with the cartoon-like character Old Joe Camel leading the way. By 1991, 30% of 3-year-olds and 91% of 6-year-olds correctly associated Old Joe Camel with cigarettes (Fischer, Schwart, Richards, Goldstein, & Rojas, 1991). Today, around half of all cigarette advertisements are placed in magazines that are popular with adolescents, such as *People* and *Sports Illustrated* (King, Siegel, Celebucki, & Connolly, 1998).

Development and the intended effects of advertising
As mentioned above, there are three primary intended effects of advertising: (a) increasing brand awareness, (b) creating positive brand attitudes, and (c) influencing purchasing requests and behavior. In studying these intended effects, researchers have divided the more than 50 empirical findings conducted into three broad areas: cognitions, emotions, and behaviors.

Research on Intended Cognitions

Research on the impact of advertising on cognitions has primarily focused on brand awareness, with special attention paid to brand recall and brand recognition. Whereas brand recognition involves matching a brand logo or character to the appropriate product (which is presented along with related but incorrect products), brand recall involves naming the product upon seeing the brand logo or character without any additional stimuli. Brand recognition experiments are meant to approximate the real-life experience that children and adolescents have in a store, in which the target brand and various alternatives are placed alongside one another on a shelf. Brand recall experiments, on the other hand, are meant to assess children's ability to remember a product in the absence of stimuli. For instance, when writing a letter to Santa Claus, children are often required to list a series of toys they would like, without the images of the toys being present. Brand recognition and brand recall are both thought to be important aspects of consumer behavior (Valkenburg, 2004).

Brand recognition develops quickly, as children are able to identify an array of products with high accuracy by age 8, even if the products are adult oriented in nature. Of course, children do not recognize all brand logos and characters advertised on television, and their performance on experimental tests is a function of the popularity of the logo presented. Generally, the greater number of logos presented to children during testing, the worse performance gets. For instance, Dubow (1995) found that adolescents under 18 recognized only 52% of the 80 logos presented to them. To put this finding in perspective, however, adults in their mid-20s recognized 42% of the logos, and adults in their mid-30s recognized 38%, with the percentages continuing to drop with increasing age. Thus, even though adolescents recognized only about half of the logos, they still outperformed adults.

Brand recall develops a bit more slowly than brand recognition. This makes sense given that brand recall is a two-step process, requiring youth to mentally create their own list of possible logo–product matches, and then choose the correct ones. Though improvements in brand recall occur over the course of early and middle childhood, Valkenburg and Buijzen (2005) found that 8-year-olds could recall only 42% of brand logos and characters presented to them. Considering that children were asked to identify logos and characters immediately after exposure, their recall on the task was quite poor. Additional research on adolescents has shown that teens recall around 70% of commercials presented to them immediately after viewing. However, recall for logos drops to around 34% when testing occurs the next day (Dubow, 1995). Interestingly, adolescents' recall for brand logos and characters was still better than that of adults.

Even though children and teens do not show tremendous brand recall the day after testing, it is important to remember that such studies involve a one-time showing of commercials to youth. In reality, children and adolescents see the same commercials on multiple occasions. With each viewing, their ability to recall and recognize the brand should improve. In fact, numerous studies have shown that the more TV commercials children watch, the greater their brand awareness becomes, at least when assessed through tests of brand recognition (Valkenburg & Buijzen, 2005). Moreover, youth probably remember more brand logos and characters for products that they desire than for products that they do not. For instance, Valkenburg and Buijzen found that boys recognized the logos for Mercedes and Shell Oil better than girls. This finding may reflect a gender-typed preference for toys related to automobiles, resulting in better brand awareness for boys than girls. Additionally, brand awareness research is limited in that children may recognize and recall plenty of brand logos and characters, but the ones they remember were not presented to them during the experiment. Finally, brand awareness does not necessarily turn into requests for the advertised products. For instance, Pine and Nash (2002) found that, when writing letters to Santa Claus, children between the ages of 3 and 7 requested few toys by product name. In fact, only 10% of the toys being advertised on TV prior to the buildup to Christmas were mentioned in the letters.

Research on Intended Emotions

One Saturday afternoon several years ago, my 5-year-old son could be heard shouting, "Dad come quick, you GOTTA see this ... you can jump on the bed and the wine glass won't move!" As he looked at the NASA-endorsed mattress on TV, my son was smiling from ear to ear. He clearly had enjoyed the commercial and the association with astronauts. In addition to creating brand awareness, the second intended outcome of advertisements is to create a liking for the brand. Doing so, however, appears to get more and more difficult with age, for with development, children like commercials less and less. One study found that whereas 69% of first graders liked commercials, only 25% of children in the fifth grade did (Rossiter & Robertson, 1974). John (1999) suggested that children have positive attitudes toward commercials only up to age 7. At that point they start to view commercials more negatively, and by age 11 they become increasingly skeptical of them. In fact, as children make their way through middle childhood, commercials are increasingly described as boring, annoying, and irritating. Of course, not all commercials are disliked. Children and adolescents tend to prefer commercials that are entertaining and funny, and portray social interactions among children (Jennings & Wartella, 2007). Importantly, when children like the commercial they tend to like the brand as well, especially in the case of children under age 7 (Valkenburg, 2004).

Though children and adolescents state their general dislike for commercials, advertisements can, in fact, help create positive brand- and product-related attitudes across development, though the overall impact of advertisements is quite small ($r = .15$ on average; Desmond & Carveth, 2007). But with children seeing thousands of commercials in their lifetimes, why is the effect so small? In addition to advertisements, there are other factors that influence children's liking of products, such as peer and family preferences, and their own personal experiences with the products. Nevertheless, even viewing an advertisement just once can increase children's liking of the product (Gorn & Goldberg, 1978). At the very least, most commercials do not create negative product-related attitudes that dissuade youth from requesting the advertised products. In fact, children and adolescents tend to request branded products. When given the choice between brand-named toys (e.g., Barbie doll) and similar toys without an associated brand name (e.g., "Betty" doll), preschool children consistently choose (68% of the time) the branded products. The more children watch television, the more they tend to desire such brand-named products. This latter effect, however, seems to wane during adolescence and may be replaced by peer-endorsed brands (Jennings & Wartella, 2007).

Research on Intended Behavior

Although brand recognition and positive attitudes toward products are important intended outcomes of advertisements, the ultimate goal of commercial messages is to affect product purchases. After all, high brand recognition and appealing advertisements do not guarantee sales to youth. In addition, the development of brand loyalty and preference is the ultimate outcome of advertising, for it helps assure both current and future purchases. Though economic independence increases with development, children and adolescents typically have far less of it than adults. As such, youth must rely on their parents and others to purchase most of the products that they desire. Thus, when assessing the impact of advertisements on consumer behavior across development, researchers assess both purchasing behavior and product requests from parents (with the assumption being that parents will buy what their children want).

Experimental research

In a typical experiment, youth watch an age-appropriate television program with the advertisements embedded within. Afterward, children are presented with an array of products, some of which appeared in the advertisements and some of which did not, and are asked to pick one. In general, such experiments find that youth choose the advertised products more so than the ones for which there were no commercials. For instance, in one laboratory experiment, Gorn and Goldberg (1980) found that children in middle childhood chose to eat a brand of ice cream advertised during a television show in comparison to a variety of brands that were not. These findings were replicated for a variety of foods and beverages in a sample of 5- and 8-year-old children attending summer camp (Gorn & Goldberg, 1982). Although there are few studies with adolescent participants, developmental differences have yet to be identified in this type of research. Regardless of age, youth tend to choose advertised products over nonadvertised ones.

Based on these studies, one could conclude that advertising causes children to pick particular products, at least when they are free. However, it would be inappropriate to conclude that commercials cause children to buy particular items, for none of the aforementioned studies assessed actual purchasing behavior. Thus, such experimental assessments are limited because they measure product choice and not product purchase. It may be that children and adolescents are more willing to try out advertised products that are free in a laboratory setting rather than purchasing the product in a store with their own money (or their parents'; Gunter et al., 2005). Gunter and colleagues have levied several other criticisms against laboratory research, all of which call into question the ecological validity of the studies. First, laboratory experiments require children to pick an object immediately after viewing a television show, something that typically does not occur in real life. Second, children watch television in the home and in the laboratory differently. For example, unlike in experimental studies, at home youth interact with others and multitask when watching TV. Finally, experimental studies limit the influence of product choice to the advertisements shown. In real life, parents, peers, and commercials for competing products all influence the purchasing behavior of children and adolescents.

Correlational research
Correlational research has traditionally focused on the relationship between the *amount of advertising* youth are exposed to and the *number of requests* made for advertised products (actual purchasing behavior is not assessed). In general, studies with children and early adolescents find positive correlations (of medium strength) between these two variables (majority $r = .30$). Valkenburg (2004) interpreted these data to mean that heavy viewers of commercials will, on average, ask for advertised products 30% more often than light viewers of commercials (65% vs. 35%, respectively). Developmentally, advertisements result in the most product requests from younger children, relative to older children and early adolescents. There is no research on product requests for youth in either middle or late adolescence.

Developmental Points of Interest

Although cause-and-effect relationships cannot be determined with correlational analyses, such assessments offer something that experimental research in advertising cannot: specifically, the relative contribution of advertising to purchasing requests in the context of other environmental factors. For instance, peers not only talk about commercials they have seen on TV but also discuss the nature of advertising itself (e.g., what makes a good commercial). In addition, parents frequently socialize their children to be wary of commercial messages (Gunter et al., 2005). Unfortunately, too few studies have been conducted in this area to draw any strong conclusions. However, an intriguing study by De Bens and Vandenbruane (1992) found that children's product preferences and purchases were more likely to be impacted by peers and direct experience with the toy at the point of purchase than by television advertisements. Nevertheless, changes across development in the relative importance of such factors require additional investigation.

To date, the vast majority of advertising research has focused on the impact of television commercials on youth. However, recent advertising trends suggest that the Internet may offer advertisers the best way to increase children's and adolescent's brand awareness and create positive brand attitudes, with the ultimate goal of influencing their purchasing requests and behavior (Moore, 2006). Of note, I am not talking about those annoying popup ads that appear on-screen, or the easily ignored banners placed across the tops or sides of webpages. Instead, I am referring to the more sophisticated advergames.

Given that around 64% of children under the age of 15 access the Internet to play games (U.S. Department of Education, 2003), advergames tap into a wide-open market. In fact, Moore (2006) reported that during a 3-month period more than 12 million children (under age 12) visited one of the 107 product-related websites assessed in her study. Although it is difficult to determine if youth attend to commercials aired on television, advertisers can not only track the number of times individuals access specific websites but also assess the length of time spent per visit. Given that most advergames require children to state their gender and age, advertisers can easily determine if their target audience is playing the game (and thus being exposed to the product). Currently, there is very limited public research on the effectiveness of advergames to influence brand awareness, attitudes, and purchases in children and adolescents (though such research probably exists to a far greater extent in the private sector, e.g., marketing firms). The public research conducted to date has failed to show that advergames influence the intent to request products in children. However, one study did find that 8-year-olds playing advergames showed an increased preference for the branded product in the game (Mallinckrodt & Mizerski, 2007). Given the increasing frequency with which youth are accessing product-related websites and playing advergames, additional assessments in this area are clearly warranted.

6

Media and Stereotyping

Growing up in the 1970s, I was treated to many advertisements on television that are now considered classics. Some 3 decades after seeing them, commercials for Wendy's ("Where's the beef?"), Life cereal ("Give it to Mikey—he won't eat it, he hates everything"), and Coke ("I'd like to buy the world a Coke ...") have iconic power. One of my favorite advertisements was actually a public service announcement (PSA) paid for by the nonprofit organization Keep America Beautiful. In this classic antipollution PSA, a stately older Native American (dressed in traditional attire) is shown canoeing through a contaminated lake and breathing toxic air. The PSA culminates with trash being thrown at the feet of the now saddened Native American, a lone tear resting on his cheek. Although the "Crying Indian" PSA (as it was called) was intended to reduce pollution, it in fact endorsed and promoted the stereotype of Native Americans as being one with the environment and victims of its abuse. (See Table 6.1 for links to some of these classic ads.)

The Nature of Stereotypes

Stereotypes are generalized and/or assumed conceptualizations about a group of individuals. Being either positive or negative, stereotypes relay a simplified view of others that typically centers on a limited number of characteristics. Moreover, stereotypes create the impression of homogeneity among a group of individuals. Most everyone in the group is perceived to have the same characteristics. Stereotypes create biased expectations for what others should look like and how they

Table 6.1   Links to Classic Commercials of the 1970s and 1980s

"Where's the beef?" (Wendy's)	http://www.youtube.com/watch?v=Ug75diEyiA0
"Give it to Mikey" (Life cereal)	http://www.youtube.com/watch?v=vYEXzx-TINc
"I'd like to buy the world a Coke" (Coca-Cola)	http://www.youtube.com/watch?v=Q8H5263jCGg
"Jimmy is my Jewish friend" (PSA)	http://www.youtube.com/watch?v=JpwamoXgb3U
Crying Native American (PSA)	http://www.youtube.com/watch?v=X3QKvEy0Alk

Table 6.2   Traits Characterized as Traditionally Masculine and Feminine

Masculine	Feminine
Adventurous	Affectionate
Aggressive	Emotionally expressive
Argumentative	Impetuous
Assertive	Nurturing
Competitive	Panicky
Decisive	Passive
Risk taker	Tender
Self-reliant	Understanding

should think, feel, and act. Stereotypes influence not only the manner in which other people are viewed and treated but also the ways in which we view and treat ourselves (Aronson, Wilson, & Akert, 2004). In support of this contention, consider the following example: A common gender-related stereotype is that boys are better at math then girls. Parents holding this stereotype believe their daughters to be worse at math than their sons, and girls adopting this stereotype view themselves as having poor math skills, even when they do not (Rowley, Kurtz-Costes, Mistry, & Feagans, 2007). Once created, stereotypes are thought to be resistant to change. Although parents, peers, friends, and siblings can influence stereotype formation, the current chapter focuses on the unique contribution of media to gender- and race-related stereotypes across development. Table 6.2 presents personality characteristics typically associated with being masculine or feminine, and Table 6.3 points out some common race-related stereotypes.

Table 6.3   Some Common Racial Stereotypes

African American	Asian	Latino	Native American
Athletic	Compliant	Drug dealer	Alcoholic
Criminal	Humble	Illegal immigrant	Brave
Poor	Model minority	Low-status jobs	Lazy
Rhythmical and musical	Smart	Uneducated	Spiritual
Unintelligent	Wealthy	Very religious	Wild

Stereotypes in the Media That Youth Consume

Just how stereotyped is the media that children and adolescents take in? In order to investigate this issue, researchers have made use of the procedure known as *content analysis*. Rather than detailing the intent of media-based content or even the effect of that content on viewers, a content analysis is study of the message itself (Kassarjian, 1977). Across a variety of dimensions, content analyses describe both the qualitative and quantitative aspects of media-based words, images, and sounds. For instance, Evans and Davies (2000) identified not only eight masculine and eight feminine traits in elementary school textbooks (i.e., a qualitative attribute) but also the proportion in which each trait appeared (i.e., a quantitative feature). Through counting and categorization, a content analysis organizes words, images, and sounds into a common set of characteristics. However, the findings of this type of labor-intensive assessment are moot if the media chosen for inclusion in the study does not reflect the media that children and adolescents typically consume. Moreover, content analyses can quickly become outdated, potentially rendering the findings irrelevant for today's youth.

Stereotypes in Literature

Content analyses of books for children in infancy, toddlerhood, and early childhood
Before they can even read, infants and young children are exposed to literature in the form of picture books, many of which have such an enduring quality that they are read from one generation to the next. For instance, Beatrix Potter's *The Tale of Peter Rabbit*, originally published in

1902, remains popular today. Over the course of 100 years, the book has sold more than 150 million copies worldwide (Copyrights Group, 2008). Given the long-lasting nature of picture books, it is important to place gender and race representations in their proper historical context, for even picture books over 100 years old are still available in stores and in school libraries.

Gender representations   Prior to the 1970s, picture books were heavily stereotyped, with depictions of males and females frequently demonstrating gender-specific behaviors (e.g., aggressive males and nurturant females), personality characteristics (e.g., independent males and dependent females), and occupations (e.g., male doctors and female nurses). Moreover, males appeared more often than females as both main and ancillary characters (Tepper & Cassidy, 1999). In contrast, contemporary picture books portray males and females as alike on a variety of personality characteristics (Oskamp, Kaufman, & Wolterbeek, 1996). For instance, Gooden and Gooden (2001) found that males and females were equally likely to be described as being cooperative, imitative, competitive, and persistent. Similarly, Tepper and Cassidy (1999) reported that there were no differences in the types of emotional words (e.g., angry and shy) associated with male and female characters. In an assessment of more than 200 picture books (published between 1995 and 2001), Hamilton and colleagues (Hamilton, Anderson, Broaddus, & Young, 2006) found that male and female characters engaged in rescue behaviors, were rescued themselves, and acted aggressively, passively, and assertively to a similar extent.

Despite this equality, gender differences are still apparent in modern picture books. Gooden and Gooden (2001) found that newer story lines depicted male characters alone more often than female characters. Similarly, Hamilton and colleagues (2006) demonstrated that there were 53% more illustrations of males than females and nearly twice as many male main characters as female main characters. Moreover, males were more likely to be portrayed as independent and creative than females, while at the same time, males were rarely depicted doing household chores or caring for children. In contrast, females were characterized more often as dependent and submissive than males. Gender-role occupations in picture books were highly stereotyped as well, with males and females appearing in 9 to 10 times more traditional occupations than nontraditional ones. For instance, female characters were frequently portrayed as teachers, nannies, librarians, nurses, and dancers. Additionally, females were more likely than males to not hold a job (Gooden & Gooden; Hamilton et al.; Oskamp et al., 1996).

Race representations   Prior to the mid-1960s, minorities rarely appeared in picture books, and when they did, they were portrayed less positively than Whites. For instance, Whites were more likely than African Americans, Asians, or Latinos to be characterized as smart. Additionally, non-White characters were almost universally ancillary to the main story line (Edmonds, 1986). However, by the early 1990s, 20–30% of all picture books, and 30–50% of picture books with human characters, contained at least one African American character; with a significant number of these stories with African American main characters (Pescosolido, Grauerholz, & Milkie, 1997).

Though the increasing level of diversity in picture books is promising, more work needs to be done. At the same time that African Americans were appearing more frequently in picture books, other ethnic groups, such as Asians, Latinos, and Native Americans, appeared as main characters less than 10% of the time (Mosely, 1997). On the bright side, Mosely found little evidence of racial stereotyping in more than 140 modern picture books at a local elementary school. That is not to say that stereotypes were absent from picture books. For instance, Edmonds (1986) demonstrated that stories about Native Americans stereotypically involved folklore that emphasized the bravery of the main characters. Likewise, Asians were stereotypically portrayed in picture books as being reserved. It may be that schools simply refrain from purchasing picture books laden with such stereotypes for their libraries.

Interestingly, depictions of race in picture books have differed between award-winning and non-award-winning books. For instance, recipients of the Caldecott Award (given yearly to outstanding picture books) depicted at least one African American character two times more often than non-award-winning books (e.g., books in the Little Golden Books series). Additionally, nearly 20% of Caldecott Award books involved an entirely Black cast of characters (though they primarily depicted Blacks in Africa). Similarly, Latinos and Asians were portrayed in Caldecott Award books nearly 10 times more often than in non-award-winning books (Nilsson, 2005; Pescosolido et al., 1997).

Interestingly, picture books have historically depicted few intimate interracial relationships. Instead, such relationships have involved acquaintance-like contact, as found on playgrounds and in classrooms (Pescosolido et al., 1997). Moreover, there are few stories with African American adults as central characters. Beyond these studies, little is known about the presence or absence of racial stereotypes in picture books. Finally, no study has assessed either gender or race representations in picture books published after the year 2001. Thus, additional research is necessary to accurately determine just how prevalent gender and racial stereotyping are in picture books today.

Content analyses of books for children in middle childhood

By the time children enter middle childhood, chapter books have begun to replace picture books. Reading, however, is not limited to children's literature, for children are also required to read textbooks and basal readers in school. Basal readers, which help teach reading skills to children, contain short stories that are organized around a central theme. Basal readers also come with teacher manuals that provide theme-related topics for discussion and classroom activities. Although reviews are limited in number, several studies have assessed gender and racial stereotyping in elementary school–aged reading materials.

Gender representations   Due to the vast number of chapter books available to youth, the percentage of male and female characters in stories has yet to be adequately assessed. However, like picture books, numerous studies sampling the vast panoply of books on the market indicate that chapter books have historically presented both males and females in a stereotyped fashion (Kortenhaus & Demarest, 1993). At times, such stereotypes manifest themselves in the form of benevolent sexism, defined by the presence of at least one of the following: (a) Women in traditional female roles are idealized, (b) women are viewed as "delicate creatures" requiring protection, and (c) women are portrayed as overly romantic (Diekman & Murnen, 2004). Benevolent sexism is a common theme in many fairy tales, in which a prince falls in love with a beautiful woman who happily cooks, cleans, sews, and so on (traditional role idealization); rescues her from those who would do her harm (delicate creature requiring protection); and, after a brief but intense courtship, lives happily ever after with his bride (overly romantic). Such findings lead publishers and researchers to create a list of nonsexist books for children to read. Popular chapter books recommended as nonsexist include *Alice in Wonderland*, *Where the Lilies Bloom*, and *Harriet the Spy* (Diekman & Murnen, 2004). But just how "nonsexist" are these books?

Just as "the road to hell is paved with good intentions," so too may the road to gender stereotyping be paved with books that attempt gender neutrality. In an assessment of mid-elementary-school novels, Diekman and Murnen (2004) found that "nonsexist" books still portrayed female characters as having stereotypically female personalities and engaging in leisure activities and domestic chores that were also stereotypically female. Moreover, the amount of stereotyping in nonsexist books was equal to that of books deemed to be sexist. However, nonsexist books did portray female characters as adopting more male-stereotypic characteristics and roles than sexist books. Interestingly, there was no evidence of gender equality for males, as both sexist and nonsexist books failed to show male characters adopting many stereotypical female characteristics and roles.

Gender representations in *textbooks* and *basal readers* have been assessed for both the frequency with which male and female characters appear and the manner of those appearances. Studies of basal readers from the 1970s to 1990s consistently found that male characters outnumbered female characters, males held a greater variety of job occupations than females, and stereotypical portrayals of males and females were prevalent. For instance, males were portrayed as brave, intelligent, industrious, and active, whereas girls were presented as passive, mindless, and domestic (Hunter & Chick, 2005).

A recent study established that little has changed in the ensuing decade. In an assessment of over 700 basal reader stories, Hunter and Chick (2005) found that males were more likely to appear in illustrations than females and that adult human males appeared as main characters in stories four times more often than adult human females. In contrast, no such differences in gender representation were evident for child and animal characters. Some additional improvements over previous decades were found in the area of gender-role depiction, as males and females held many of the same occupations. However, females were still more likely than males to be an unsalaried house person and males were overwhelmingly shown as cow hands, farmers, laborers, and astronauts. Similarly, Evans and Davies (2000) found that males, more so than females, were characterized as aggressive, argumentative, and competitive. In fact, male characters in basal readers rarely show feminine traits, such as being emotionally expressive, nurturing, tender, and understanding. Females, in contrast, have been depicted as having both masculine and feminine traits since the 1990s (Witt, 1996).

Race representations   Precious little research has investigated race representations in chapter books and elementary school reading materials. The literature that does exist suggests that, similar to picture books, the content of literature and textbooks during the elementary school years has primarily related stories of White characters. For instance, during the 1980s less than 1% of children's books involved African American characters, and an even smaller percentage portrayed Latinos, Asians, and Native Americans. By 1990, the number of books with African American main characters had doubled to 2% (Reimer, 1992). Once again, award-winning books had greater percentages of minorities than non-award-winning books. For instance, between 1922 and 1994, Latino characters appeared in books receiving the prestigious Newbery Medal (awarded to the author of an outstanding children's book) 10% of the time. However, the winning of an award did not necessarily guarantee that the portrayal of minority characters was positive. In an assessment of award-winning children's books from 1963 to 1983, Gary (1984) found that the characters' physical descriptors, language, and community status negatively stereotyped African Americans.

Research on minority representation in basal readers during the 1990s mirrors that of chapter books, in that the main characters of basal readers tended to be White. However, the percentage of minorities in elementary reading texts was far greater than that of chapter books. Reimer (1992) noted that nearly 40% of the main characters in basal readers involved minority characters. Interestingly, teacher manuals accompanying basal readers provided few discussions of racial and cultural differences. Such omissions were particularly glaring when the reading selection involved racial alienation, discord, or prejudice (McDermott, 1997). Unfortunately, no new assessments of race representations and stereotypes in chapter books or basal readers have occurred in the last decade, so current trends cannot be assessed.

Content analyses of books for children during adolescence
Gender representations   Gender representation and stereotyping in literature and textbooks for teens have been completely overlooked.

I could find no research on the topic. However, a quick review of popular books for teens reveals the presence of traditional stereotypes for both adolescent boys and girls. Consider, for example, the tween targeting book *The Big Book of Girl Stuff* (King & Kallis, 2006), in which girls can learn "how to shop," "why boys smell so bad," and "how to deal with a killer crush!" The book also covers "important topics" like "friends, cliques, secrets, and gossip"; "dance"; "etiquette"; and "beauty." And in *Hatchet* (Paulsen, 2007), a 13-year-old boy must endure the physical trials of being lost in the wilderness for 54 days with only a hatchet for comfort, while at the same time dealing with the emotional consequences of his parents' divorce. Do such stereotypes abound in literature for teens? Currently, that question remains unanswered.

Race representations   A limited number of studies have assessed race representations in books for adolescents. In the most comprehensive of these studies, Klein (1998) reviewed the presence of multicultural characters in over 600 books recommended for students in high school in 1964 and in 1995. Not surprisingly, White characters were the majority, although the percentage of characters dropped from 85% in 1964 to 68% in 1995. Nearly 17% of recommended books in 1995 involved African Americans, more than four times that of the 1964 level. Asian and Native American characters appeared in books around 6% of the time in both assessment periods. Although the roles (e.g., professionals, sportsmen, romantic figures, etc.) minorities played in these books were not overtly stereotypical, the number of roles available to minority characters were not as varied as those for White characters.

Stereotypes in Newspaper Comics

One of my favorite childhood nonelectronic activities was reading the comics in the daily newspaper. *The Far Side*, *Calvin & Hobbes*, and the timeless *Peanuts* were among my favorites. Though little is known about the numbers of children and adolescents who read comics today, what is clear is that when youth read newspaper comics, they are rarely exposed to minorities and frequently exposed to gender stereotypes. In fact, over the past 2 decades, few improvements in racial diversity and gender stereotyping have occurred in newspaper comics.

Gender representations

In an assessment of more than 50 popular newspaper comic strips involving more than 1,070 characters, Glascock and Preston-Schreck (2004) found that male characters outnumbered female characters 6:1. With regard to stereotypes, female characters were two times more likely than males to be married or to be shown with children. When child care, household chores, and serving food were depicted, females engaged in these activities more than males. Females were also more likely to be verbally aggressive than males, with a great number of these acts directed at their husbands (i.e., the "nagging housewife" stereotype). In contrast, males were more likely than females to be associated with a job, do yard work, and act physically aggressive.

Race representations

Glascock and Preston-Schreck (2004) found little evidence of racial diversity in comic strips. In fact, 96% of comic strip characters were White, with 2.5% being African American and the remaining 1.5% comprised of Asians, Latinos, and Native Americans. Overt negative stereotypes of minorities were generally absent, but minorities were less likely than Whites to hold professional jobs and more likely to be blue-collar workers.

Stereotypes in Cartoons

Once thought of as Saturday morning and after-school fare, cartoons are now available for viewing 24 hours a day (e.g., on the Cartoon Network). In addition, youth can consume "classic cartoons" from the 1960s onward on the Boomerang channel, and view cartoons and animated films on DVDs from the early beginnings of animated film in the 1930s. As such, viewers of cartoons and animated films are exposed to gender and race representations from over 70 years worth of animation.

Gender representations

Ostensibly, little has changed in gender representations in cartoons over the past 70 years. Across decades, numerous studies have found that male characters, which far outnumbered female characters, were more likely to be portrayed as leaders, emotionally restrained, heroic, and physically aggressive than females. In contrast, females, which tended to be minor characters, were portrayed in a manner characteristic with benevolent sexism (Streicher, 1974; Thompson & Zerbinos, 1995; Towbin, Haddock, Zimmerman, Lund, & Tanner, 2003). But appearances are not always what they seem. Recent assessments have found that gender stereotyping varies by cartoon genre.

Leaper and colleagues (Leaper, Breed, Hoffman, & Perlman, 2002) noted that males outnumbered females only in traditional adventure cartoons (which have male main characters; e.g., *Johnny Quest*) and comedy cartoons, but not in educational and family or nontraditional adventure (involving at least one female main character; e.g., *The Powerpuff Girls*) genres. Moreover, whereas males were more physically aggressive than females in traditional adventure cartoons, no such differences were evident in nontraditional cartoons. Similarly, Baker and Raney (2007) found that male and female cartoon superheroes were alike on 44 of 51 variables traditionally associated with gender stereotyping. Notable differences were that male superheroes outnumbered female superheroes two to one, and that female superheroes were characteristically more emotional, attractive, and concerned about physical appearance than male superheroes. These findings are consistent with those of Leaper and colleagues (2002), who found that regardless of cartoon genre, females were more likely than males to show fear and act romantic, polite, and supportive.

Race representations
Historically, minorities have rarely appeared in short cartoons (20 minutes or less) as either major or minor characters (Klein & Shiffman, 2006). Between 1930 and the late 1960s, the number of minority characters in short cartoons decreased from 16% to a little over 4%. However, during the 30 years following the civil rights movement, the overall percentage of minority characters increased to 20–30%. Still, by the mid-1990s, the majority of minority characters in short cartoons appeared only in supportive roles. Overall, Asian (1.7%), Latino (2.4%), and Native American (1.5%) cartoon characters appeared slightly less often than African American characters (3%). However, most minority characters (10%) were represented as people of color, without an identifiable race.

Although overt racism in short cartoons (e.g., Native Americans saying, "How!") occurred in approximately 10% of short cartoons between 1930 and 1960, few if any instances of overt racism occurred between 1965 and 1996. In fact, people of color were portrayed similarly on most physical, social, and psychological dimensions. Some positive race-related characteristics emerged. Most notably, African Americans engaged in more prosocial acts and fewer antisocial acts than members of other races. Nevertheless, a few stereotypes were present. First, African American characters were more likely than any other race to sing, dance, or otherwise entertain those around them. Second, African Americans engaged in nearly twice as many leisure activities as members of other races. Finally, Latinos were less likely than other races to be shown working (Klein & Shiffman, 2006).

Little is known about the percentage of minorities in feature-length films, such as those released by the Disney and Dreamworks studios. However, in an assessment of 26 Disney films dating back to *Snow White and the Seven Dwarfs*, Towbin and colleagues (2003) established the fact that marginalized racial groups have been primarily portrayed in negative and stereotypical ways. For instance, the hyenas in *The Lion King* have been criticized for mimicking negative stereotypes of inner-city minorities, whereas the crows in *Dumbo* and the apes in *The Jungle Book* were thought to portray a racist view of African Americans. In comparison to older Disney animated features, *some* newer films, such as *Mulan* and *Pocahontas*, have less ethnic stereotyping. Nevertheless, much more research is needed to assess race representations in feature-length animated films that children frequently view across development.

Stereotypes in Educational Television and Computer Software

Few studies have assessed stereotyping in media designed to educate youth. The research that has been conducted, however, consistently shows that males outnumber females on E/I television programs and in education software for youth of all ages (Calvert, Kotler, Zehnder, & Shockey, 2003; Sheldon, 2004). Moreover, research on E/I programming suggests that male characters were more likely than female characters to speak, engage in a wide range of behaviors, and be central to the story line (Barner, 1999). On E/I television programming, both genders tended to be presented in a stereotypical manner, with males displaying traits like aggression and dominance and females acting dependent and nurturant. Similarly, portrayals have been shown for educational computer software. However, females were more likely than males to engage in counterstereotypical behavior (i.e., behaviors, attitudes, and emotions that go against traditional expectations for females). There was one notable exception: Females were more gender stereotyped in appearance than males (Sheldon, 2004). To date, no research has assessed race representations and stereotyping in E/I programming or educational computer software.

Stereotypes in Television Commercials

Gender representations

When products are marketed to children, males have consistently appeared more often than females for over 30 years. In comparison to females, males not only were more likely to take a major role in commercials but also were portrayed in more varied roles (Davis, 2003; Stern & Mastro, 2004). For products marketed to adolescents, however, males and females have recently appeared in similar proportions (Stern & Mastro, 2004). Additionally, males and females have advertised different types of products (Jennings & Wartella, 2007). For instance, boys have consistently appeared in advertisements for toys related to independence and competition, such as war toys (e.g., toy guns, swords). In contrast, girls were likely to be shown in commercials for products related to emotions (e.g., diaries), relationships (e.g., dolls), and domestic settings (e.g., kitchens). Given this fact, it should come as no surprise that the activities and activity level depicted within commercials differed by gender as well. Davis found that whereas females engaged in either passive (e.g., sitting and talking) or domestic activities, males were shown to be active participants with their surroundings. Moreover, the personality traits displayed by male and females in commercials for children and adolescents have tended to fall along gender-stereotypical lines. Not only have males and females been portrayed differently in commercials, but also the composition of the advertisements varied by the gender of the targeted consumer. Products marketed to boys contained loud music, energetic activities, and quick shifts from one scene to the next. In comparison, advertisements that were female oriented used soft music, slow pacing, and gentleness (Gunter, Oates, & Blades, 2005).

Of note, children's play behavior does in fact mirror the types of products advertised to them. Preference for sex-typed toys begins during the toddler period, with boys preferring cars, swords, guns, and action figures, and girls preferring teddy bears, dolls, and other objects that can be nurtured (Singer & Singer, 1990). In general, throughout childhood boys tend to prefer toys and activities that allow a great deal of active play, and girls tend to choose more sedate activities. Interestingly, for toys marketed to both boys and girls, the commercials tend to use boy actors. The reason? Although girls will purchase products advertised with boy actors, boys will not do the same for toys marketed with girl actors (Gunter et al., 2005).

Race representations
Over the last 30 years, racial minorities have increasingly appeared in commercials aimed at children. In fact, Li-Vollmer (2002) found that African Americans appeared in 19% of the nearly 1,500 commercials evaluated, exceeding the percentage of African Americans (13%) in the United States (Children Now, 2004). However, Asians (2%), Latinos (2.4%), and Native Americans (0.2%) appeared less often in commercials than in the U.S. population (4%, 12.5%, and 1.5% respectively). In contrast to the limited number of racial minorities appearing in advertisements for commercially available products, 65% of government-funded PSAs involved minority characters (45% African American and 20% other races).

More troubling than the lack of racial diversity in advertisements (not including PSAs) is the manner in which race is portrayed. For instance, during racially integrated commercials Whites (86%) were the primary speakers more often than all other racial minorities combined, and characters of color were primarily seen as background members in a crowd of White characters. Moreover, Whites were 55 times more likely to be a product spokesperson than African Americans, and no members of any other racial group were even cast as spokespersons. In addition to appearing in a greater variety of roles than racial minorities, Whites were also more likely to be portrayed as go-getters and problem solvers. African Americans, in contrast, were more likely than Whites and other minorities to be cast as athletes and musicians. Asians rarely appeared in commercials, and when they did they tended to show up in commercials for technology products, such as computers and video games. Latinos were almost entirely limited to advertisements for restaurants; in fact, 95% of Latinos appearing in commercials were found in such ads. Moreover, African Americans and Latinos were virtually absent from commercials promoting hygiene products.

Stereotypes in Live-Action Television Programming

In the last 30 years, no research has assessed gender and race representations in children's entertainment programming involving live-action characters (i.e., people, not cartoons or puppets). There is, however, research on gender and race representations during "prime time" (8 p.m. to 11 p.m.), which, coincidentally, is the period of the evening during which children have traditionally watched live-action shows with their families.

Gender representations

The most recent evaluation of prime-time television, which assessed shows aired during the fall of 2003, indicated that there were more male characters (65%) and more male main characters (59%) than female characters (35%) and female main characters (41%). Both of these findings represent increases from the prior 2 decades, when the percentage of females on television was much lower. Similar to the findings from previous research, male characters spoke more often and were more physically aggressive than female characters. In contrast to previous findings, male and female characters appeared in a wide range of occupations. However, males were more likely than females to be doctors, lawyers, elected officials, firefighters, law enforcement officers, and CEOs. In comparison to males, female characters were more likely to work in low-status jobs, engage in domestic responsibilities, and show more verbal aggression. In general, women were more likely to be cast in traditional and stereotypical roles than males (Children Now, 2004; Signorelli, 2001).

In addition to prime-time television, masculine characteristics are often highlighted during sports programming. One study found that boys were five times more likely to watch sports programming than girls. Moreover, the messages that consumers of sports programming received were more extreme versions of the stereotypes depicted on prime-time television. According to sports programming, a real man is strong, tough, and aggressive. Weakness is not shown, pain to be ignored, and, above all else, a real man is a winner (Children Now, 1999).

Race representations

In addition to gender representation, Children Now (2004) assessed the racial makeup of prime-time television shows. Similar to the findings from previous studies, Whites (74%) continued to far outnumber other races. When racial minorities were shown, African Americans (18%) were depicted more often than Asians (1%), Latinos (6%), or others (1%). However, a similar percentage of White characters (34%), African American characters (33%), and Latino characters (38%) played roles that were integral to the story line. In contrast, Asians were nearly 4 times as likely to play a minor role (39%) than a major one (11%).

Although adolescents frequently stay up to 11 p.m., younger children go to bed somewhere in the middle of prime time. For instance, 8-year-olds typically go to bed around 9 p.m. (National Network for Child Care, 2007). Not surprisingly, children are more likely to watch primetime shows between 8 and 9 p.m. than at any other time period. Unfortunately, shows during this time period, as well as during the 9 o'clock hour, have historically shown little diversity. In contrast, shows airing from 10 to 11 p.m. have depicted the most racial diversity (Children Now, 2004).

In general, people of color have been portrayed more negatively than Whites during prime time. For instance, African Americans appeared more provocatively dressed and involved in the criminal justice system than Whites. Similarly, Latinos were most often cast in roles related to crime such as police officers or criminals, or as domestic workers (Children Now, 2004; Greenberg et al., 2002). In fact, in comparison to other races, Latinos were least likely to be cast in high-status professional occupations (Children Now, 2004). However, it is interesting to note that contrary to previous decades, 26% of African Americans and 37% of Asians appeared in high-status professions at levels similar to those of Whites (32%).

Stereotypes in Video Games

Gender representations

Several studies have assessed gender and race representations in video games, without consideration for the age appropriateness of the video game. The first of such studies, conducted by Braun and Giroux (1989), assessed the content of popular arcade games during the late 1980s. The findings indicated that male characters outnumbered female characters 30 to 1. Studies that have considered ratings have produced similar findings, with males outnumbering females as both main and ancillary characters (Smith, 2006). However, it is worth noting that females representation in video games has increased dramatically since the 1980s. For instance, Haninger and Thompson (2004) reported that 89% of video games contained playable male characters and 52% of the video games had playable female characters. However, throughout video game play, females are still in the minority, as they comprise less than 20% of all characters experienced during game play (Beasley & Standley, 2002; Children Now, 2001). Across studies, female characters tended to be presented as props, bystanders, damsels in distress, and victims of violence (Smith, 2006). Other research has shown that female characters were twice as likely to share and four times as likely to be nurturing as male characters (Children Now, 2001). Moreover, when cross-gender behavior occurred, it was females who took on masculine traits rather than the other way around; male characters tend to be exclusively aggressive and violent (Smith).

Race representations
With regard to race, characters in video games have been over-whelmingly White (60–70%; Children Now, 2001; Jansz & Martis, 2007). Additional studies have shown that African Americans comprised a little over 20% of characters, with between 7% and 9% being Asian, and 2–3% having Latino origins. Native Americans were virtually absent from video games. Moreover, when minorities were included in video games, they tended to be portrayed as athletes, street thugs, victims, and criminals. In contrast, most video game heroes were White (Children Now, 2001; Jansz & Martis).

Stereotypes on the Internet

Even though children and adolescents spend countless hours on the Internet visiting websites, blogs, and chat rooms, little is known about the prevalence of stereotyping available for online consumption by minors. What is known, however, is that 13- to 18-year-old adolescents report being exposed to negative stereotypes and racial prejudice when communicating with others on the Internet. Nonetheless, teens also reported learning about cultural practices and beliefs, as well as the consequences of racial prejudice, from online acquaintances and friends (Tynes, 2007). Still, if youth are looking for sexist, racist, or other hate sites online, they are easily found, as more than 7,000 extremist websites, newsgroups, blogs, chat rooms, and online clubs exist and are easily accessible (Simon Wiesenthal Center, 2007).

Effects of Stereotypes in the Media on Youth

As the previous review illustrated, media directed at children and adolescents is limited in diversity and filled with both gender and racial stereotypes. But do such messages actually impact the stereotypes and attitudes of youth?

Stereotyped Media and Gender

When investigating the impact of media-based gender stereotyping on youth, researchers have primarily assessed two gender-related constructs: gender stereotyping and gender-role attitudes. Whereas *gender stereotyping* refers to the expectations that children and adolescents have regarding how males and females should look, act, think, feel, and so on, *gender-role attitudes* refer to youths' beliefs about the appropriateness of those stereotypes for males and females. Highly stereotyped youth expect males and females to espouse traditional masculine and feminine characteristics and hold traditional gender-specific occupations. Traditional gender-role attitudes reflect the acceptance of stereotypes regarding the work, appearance, and behaviors deemed appropriate for males and females. For instance, youth with traditional gender-role attitudes agree with contention that males should be the "breadwinners" of the family and that females should engage in homemaking and child-rearing activities.

Gender stereotyping

Research on the development of gender stereotyping has assessed the degree to which television consumption causes youth to view males and females along stereotypical lines. Correlational studies involving children and adolescents have produced similar findings; each has found that higher levels of television viewing are associated with traditional expectations of gender-related activities, occupations, and traits (Oppliger, 2007; Ward & Harrison, 2005).

However, a careful rereading of the previous paragraph reveals that correlational research has assessed the influence of general television consumption on youth, and not the consumption of stereotyped content. Although television shows present stereotypical portrayals of men and women, counterstereotypes are also prevalent. Because scientists operate on fact and not conjecture, we should not assume that higher levels of television consumption correspond with the viewing of significant amounts of stereotyped programming. Given the directionality and third-variable problems associated with correlation, the aforementioned findings should be described, at best, as weak evidence that media-based stereotypes impact youth. For instance, the correlation between television viewing and high levels of stereotyping may result because stereotyped youth consume more television than nonstereotyped children and adolescents (directionality) that confirms the stereotypes presented to them by their parents (third variable).

Nevertheless, a limited number of laboratory experiments conducted with children and adolescents have shown that the presentation of stereotyped material may increase gender stereotyping (e.g., O'Bryant & Corder-Bolz, 1978). Conversely, the viewing of nontraditional programming has been shown to decrease stereotyping (e.g., Nathanson, Wilson, McGee, & Sebastian, 2002). Thus, stereotyped media content may in fact be able to influence gender stereotyping in youth. However, the majority of research was conducted more than 20 years ago, and only a handful involved experimental designs. Much more research is needed to provide a convincing argument that stereotyped media content influences modern youth.

Gender-role attitudes

Numerous correlational studies have shown that higher levels of general television viewing are associated with increasingly traditional gender-role attitudes across middle childhood (e.g., Frueh & McGhee, 1975) and adolescence (e.g., Morgan, 1987). There is no research on preschoolers (Rivadeneyra & Ward, 2005). However, because previous research assessed general television viewing rather than the consumption of stereotyped programming, the possibility exists that something other than stereotyped content produced the observed outcomes. As such, this type of research should be interpreted with caution. On the other hand, a recent study by Aubrey and Harrison (2004) did assess the association between stereotyped content in children's favorite cartoons and gender-role attitudes in the first and second grades. However, the results were far from impressive. For boys only, watching cartoons replete with male stereotypes was associated with only two of eight gender-role attitudes associated with being male. The two characteristics that were significant, *telling good jokes* and *being hardworking*, rarely appear in lists of characteristics associated with being stereotypically male. Additionally, the study failed to find significant effects for girls. Unfortunately, experimental research cannot clear up these muddled findings, as the few studies in this area have produced contradictory findings (Ward & Harrison, 2005).

The influence of media-based stereotypes on gender-role attitudes across development may differ not only for adult- and child-oriented behaviors and characteristics, but also by the gender of the child. Boys' gender-role attitudes may be influenced the most by media-based gender stereotypes involving children, whereas girls' gender-role attitudes may be primarily affected by media-based gender stereotypes involving adults. The following findings support this contention: Whereas nontraditional images of adults lead to less stereotyped attitudes toward adult females for girls (but not boys; Geis, Brown, Walstedt, & Porter, 1984), stereotyped commercials for toys lead boys (more so than girls) to be more accepting of the belief that toys marketed to boys should be used only by boys in real life (Pike & Jennings, 2005). However, much more research is needed to evaluate the proposed interaction involving the child's gender and the adult–child nature of the stereotype.

Racial Stereotypes

Despite concerns that the lack of diversity in media can negatively affect racial stereotyping in children and adolescents (Children Now, 2004), there is absolutely no research on the topic. This is not to say, however, that the impact of race on television has been ignored; far from it. Research has shown that minority children generally feel better about their own race after seeing cartoons and commercials with same-race characters. Similarly, positive portrayals of minorities on television shows, such as *Sesame Street*, can lead to positive views of minorities by White children (Bogatz & Ball, 1971). Other studies indicate that children are better able to retain the message of a television program when it is delivered by a member of their own race (Graves, 1999). Nevertheless, the role of media-based racial stereotypes on racial stereotype formation and prejudice throughout development is in dire need of assessment.

Developmental Points of Interest

Some might argue that the rising numbers of minority characters in books, television, and the like demonstrate real progress in the racial diversification of media directed at youth. There are several reasons, however, to suggest that this is not the case. First, although some researchers have implied that the percentage of minority characters in media should be consistent with that of the general population (Children Now, 2004; Li-Vollmer, 2002), the end result for many racial minorities is still few media offerings. For instance, Asians and Native Americans would encounter their races in media less than 5% and 2% of the time, respectively. Second, racial diversity is more than just equitable representation in media. Rather, racial diversity involves the presentation of minorities in a variety of roles. Unfortunately, at this time, the roles portrayed by racial minorities are fairly limited in scope. Finally, although some progress has been made in reducing the occurrence of racial stereotypes in children's media, many portrayals of minorities occur in a manner consistent with their associated stereotypes.

In comparison to children of the 1970s and 1980s, today's youth are more frequently exposed to dads doing housework, moms in the workplace, and numerous other examples of counterstereotypes. Does media have the power to override the counterstereotypes personally experienced by children and adolescents of the 2000s? Only research can answer this question. Additionally, not all stereotypes are of equal value to children and adolescents. Previous research has shown that youth demonstrate fewer stereotypes for roles and characteristics associated with adults in comparison to same-aged peers (DeHart, Sroufe, & Cooper, 2004). Thus, future research needs to clarify and differentiate the impact of media-based stereotypes on children's and adolescents' views of others across development. Because boys are especially likely to be rebuked by parents and peers for cross-gender behavior, they may be more attuned than girls to stereotypes that could immediately impact their lives (Pike & Jennings, 2005). In contrast, girls are often encouraged to engage in cross-gender behaviors. As such, media stereotypes may affect boys more than girls, but only for child-centered gender-based characteristics and behavior. Moreover, the influence of media on youth has been primarily limited to television content. Less is known about the impact of other forms of media, such as books, video games, and the Internet, on gender stereotypes across development.

Historically, media has presented males and females in ways that reflect the socialization practices of the day. Boys were socialized to adopt an instrumental role, which was characterized by assertive, competitive, dominant, goal-oriented, and independent behavior. In contrast, girls were socialized to adopt an expressive role, reflecting behavior that was cooperative, kind, nurturing, and sensitive to the needs of others (Parsons, 1955). Little has changed in the last 50 years, as today's children are still socialized with instrumental and expressive roles in mind (DeHart et al., 2004). However, one change has occurred in gender-role behavior. In particular, females are increasingly socialized on many instrumental characteristics, such as having independent, goal-oriented behavior (Eagly & Diekman, 2003). Mainstream media offerings mirror real-life, as books, video games, and TV offer plenty of counterstereotypical fare involving females. Rarely seen, however, is media depicting males adopting expressive role characteristics. This, too, reflects real life. Boys are primarily socialized to show masculine traits and, as such, are less likely to engage in cross-gender behaviors than girls. The reason may be, again, one of self-preservation, for boys who engage in traditionally feminine activities are often chastised by their peers, siblings, and parents (Leaper & Friedman, 2007).

Research on the impact of E/I television programs on gender and race representations has been limited in developmental scope. Although the target audience of E/I programs has ranged from toddlers to adolescents, research has consistently failed to address stereotyping in relation to the programs' target audience. It may be that stereotyping is more likely to be shown during programs geared toward certain developmental periods than during others. Moreover, across development, youth prefer to consume different genres of media offerings. For instance, educational programming becomes less interesting to youth during middle childhood (Calvert & Kotler, 2003). Thus, the impact of media stereotypes may have the greatest impact during the developmental periods in which children are consuming that genre the most. Moreover, previous research has not distinguished between E/I programs that focus on prosocial development and those that emphasize academic content. In contrast to academic E/I programming, prosocial E/I programming emphasizes both prosocial behaviors and the acceptance of diversity. As such, gender and race representations during prosocial E/I programs may impact youth to a greater extent than similar content presented in academic E/I programs. Future research needs to more clearly distinguish stereotyping by genre and target audience in order to assess differential influences of stereotyped media across development.

Future studies investigating the influence of media on either gender or racial stereotyping and attitudes in children and adolescents need to address the following question: Which impacts youth more, the frequent viewing of stereotyped images (i.e., the "drip, drip" hypothesis; Reep & Dambrot, 1989) or the perceived importance of characters who act in a stereotyped fashion (i.e., the "drench" hypothesis; Reep & Dambrot)? According to the drip, drip hypothesis, media slowly shapes the attitudes and beliefs of the viewer. As a result, stereotypes are forged over time by the repeated viewing of media-based stereotypes, with heavy viewers showing the greatest level of stereotyping. In contrast, the drench hypothesis contends that the number of stereotype exposures is relatively unimportant for stereotype formation. Instead, it is the quality of the portrayal that matters. As such, characters who have an intense and powerful effect on the viewer are thought to influence stereotyping in youth the most. Although both hypotheses may influence youth, their impact may vary by developmental stage. For instance, because identity formation is such a critical component of early adolescence, teens (more so than youth of any other age) may latch on to one or more characters to emulate, thereby supporting the drench hypothesis. It may also be that individual differences exist. Whereas some youth may be primarily impacted by the cumulative viewing of stereotypes, others may be chiefly affected by specific characters in the media. Let the research begin.

7

Media Influences on Obesity, Body Image, and Eating Disorders

When you are ready, close your eyes and imagine the perfect female body: its height, weight, and shapeliness. Can you name a person who closely resembles the goddess-like form in your mind? Now do the same for males, paying careful consideration to muscle size and tone. At any point did you picture yourself as having the ideal body? Probably not, as the vast majority of females wish to weigh less and have a smaller body shape, and most males desire to have additional muscle mass and be leaner (Neighbors & Sobal, 2007). So, if you did not picture yourself, who did you picture? In all likelihood, the "perfect" body belonged to someone you saw on TV, in a movie, on the Internet, or in a magazine.

For centuries, media has influenced the "body ideal" for women. During the 1950s, the curvaceous Marilyn Monroe, and her size 14 physique, represented bodily perfection. A decade later, the model Twiggy and her thin stature were considered idyllic. But long before the advent of magazines, television, and movies, images of beauty in paintings, such as those by Rubens, Renoir, and Raphael, influenced cultural standards for the ultimate body. Rather than being physically fit, women of the 17th–19th centuries were painted as being plump and curvy. Today, the "ideal" body image for women can take many shapes; waif (e.g., Kate Moss), curvy (e.g., Jessica Simpson), or athletic (e.g., Lo Lo Jones). In fact, for many women, the combination of being curvaceous and thin is the ideal; small waist, small hips, and a medium-sized bust. But there is one thing that contemporary "ideal" body shapes have in common: They are definitely not Rubenesque (Derenne & Beresin, 2006).

But more than influencing the cultural standards for the ideal body, can media influence how children and adolescents view their own bodies? Do such views impact the psychological and physical well-being of

Table 7.1 BMI Percentile and Weight Status Category

BMI Score	Percentile Range	Weight Status Category
≤ 18.4	Less than 5th percentile	Underweight
18.5–24.9	5th to less than 85th percentile	Healthy weight
25–29.9	85th to less than 95th percentile	Overweight
≥ 30	95th to 100th percentile	Obese

youth? These important questions will be addressed below. First, however, the impact of media consumption on obesity, a health crisis affecting youth throughout the world, will be reviewed.

Media Consumption and Body Weight

Adiposity can be measured in numerous ways, including skinfold thickness, hydrostatic weighing, and dual energy X-ray absorptiometry. However, in most of the studies reviewed below, weight status was assessed using a measurement approach called *body mass index* (BMI). For children and adolescents, BMI is based on the child's height, weight, gender, and age. Youth are considered to be obese when their BMI score is greater than or equal to the 95th percentile for their gender and age (see Table 7.1). In a recent assessment of obesity in the United States (Ogden et al., 2006), BMI scores indicated that 14% of 2- to 5-year-olds, 19% of 6- to 11-year-olds, and 17% of 12- to 19-year-olds were considered obese. Worldwide, there are 155 million obese children (or 1 in 10) between the ages of 5 and 17. Nearly 25% of children in the European Union are at or above the 95th percentile in BMI. Even in developing countries (e.g., Brazil, China, and India), rates of childhood obesity are on the rise. In fact, 3.3% of children in developing countries under the age of 5 are now obese (WorldHeartFederation.org, 2007). Because significant physical (e.g., type II diabetes, metabolic syndrome, and cardiovascular disease) and psychological (e.g., victimization, stigma, and low self-esteem) health risks are associated with childhood obesity, scientists have set out to uncover its causes. In addition to diet and genetics, media consumption has been a frequent focus of obesity research across development. But media contains no calories, zero protein, and not a single trans fat. So how is it possible that its consumption could affect body weight?

Explaining Why Media Can Be Fattening

Three potential mechanisms have been forwarded to explain how media consumption can impact weight: (a) Sedentary behavior displaces physical activity, (b) the intake of nutritionally poor foods primarily occurs when using media, and (c) advertisements for food lead to poor eating habits in children and adolescents. Each will be discussed in turn.

Sedentary behavior displaces physical activity

With the exception of Dance Dance Revolution and an assortment of video games for the Wii, and in particular the Wii Fit, media consumption is primarily a sedentary activity. Couch potatoes and mouse potatoes alike burn few calories while surfing the Internet, watching TV, or playing video games. Some have argued that physically inactive media consumption displaces high-energy movement; and that when media is not available, children are outside running, jumping, or otherwise engaged in calorie-burning activities. It has been theorized that as a result of displacing physically active energetic pursuits with physically inactive behaviors, body fat increases (Gortmaker, Dietz, & Cheung, 1990). However, the extant body of research fails to support this contention. For instance, Janz and colleagues (2002) were unable to establish a link between vigorous physical activity and TV viewing in 4- to 6-year-olds. Jordan (2007) pointed out that throughout the day, youth have ample opportunity to both "chill out" with media and engage in vigorous activities; the two are not mutually exclusive. Thus, across development, media consumption does not appear to displace physically active behavior.

Regardless of the amount of time engaged in vigorous activity, youth still spend hours per day with media, and during that time they move relatively little and burn few calories. A decade ago, Bar-Or and colleagues (1998) stated that sedentary media consumption, such as TV viewing, is not only a likely cause of high body fatness, but a clinically significant one as well. This makes a great deal of intuitive sense. After all, it is hard to imagine getting rock-hard abs or a lean physique while reclining in a La-Z-Boy chair watching *The Biggest Loser* on TV. But, do long periods of media-related physical inactivity really influence adiposity? An additional decade's worth of research suggests that intuition is not always correct.

From early childhood through late adolescence, numerous studies have attempted to causally link obesity with television viewing, computer use, and video game play. Although several studies have found significant associations between media use and body fatness, the strength of these relationships is consistently weak (Jenvey, 2007; Marshall, Biddle, Gorely, Cameron, & Murdey, 2004). For instance, Wake and colleagues (Wake, Hesketh, & Walters, 2003) found that parental report of their children's television consumption accounted for only 1% of BMI scores during middle childhood and early adolescence. Other studies have failed to connect media use and BMI altogether (Jenvey). These mixed findings led Marshall and colleagues (2004) to conclude that, contrary to popular opinion, the impact of media use on obesity is "too small to be of clinical relevance."

The intake of nutritionally poor foods primarily occurs when using media
With the introduction of the first TV dinner in 1954 (SwansonMeals. com, 2008), Swanson Foods validated the notion that dining in front of the television was socially acceptable. It would be several decades before scholars expressed concern that eating while watching TV, playing video games, and the like increased body fatness in youth. The problem is not that children are consuming healthy foods while using media; rather, it is that media use leads to increased caloric intake of nutritionally poor foods. In support of this contention, Coon and colleagues (2001) demonstrated that families eating two or more meals per day in front of the TV consumed more meat, pizza, snacks, and soda, but ate fewer fruits and vegetables, than other families. But rather than TV causing youth to eat poorly, it may simply be that families who consume few healthy foods also tend to watch a lot of TV, including while they are eating.

In addition to traditional meals, children and adolescents periodically snack, and when snack foods are being eaten, media is often in use. In fact, snacks are more likely to be consumed in front of the TV than any other meal (Matheson, Killen, Wang, Varady, & Robinson, 2004). However, Matheson et al. found that, for third and fifth graders, whether the TV was on or off did not affect the total fat content and calories of the foods consumed. Similarly, eating in front of the TV did not impact preschoolers' total energy intake (Francis & Birch, 2006), and Carruth and colleagues (Carruth, Goldberg, & Skinner, 1991) found that for 10th–12th graders, the viewing of food commercials did not lead to an increase in concomitant snacking. Thus, snacking in front of the TV does not appear to displace the intake of nutritionally good foods for nutritionally poor ones. Moreover, such assessments may be moot, as Field and colleagues (2004) found that, irrespective of media consumption, snack food intake has no impact on BMI in children 9 to 14 years of age.

Food advertising leads to poor eating habits in children and adolescents post viewing

Recently, the United Kingdom banned television commercials for "junk foods" (defined as foods high in fat, salt, and sugar) aimed at children under the age of 16 (BBC.com, 2008). Concern that TV advertisements caused children to have poor eating habits (post viewing) led to this policy decision. But is this type of advertising censorship warranted?

The prevalence of food advertising   Each day children and adolescents are inundated with advertisements for food products. Nearly 50% of all television commercials targeting youth promote food (e.g., snacks, cereal, and candy) or food-related items (e.g., restaurants and ice cream makers). Gantz and colleagues (Gantz, Schwartz, Angelini, & Rideout, 2007) found that when food products are advertised, 9 out of 10 times they promote nutritionally poor provisions: 34% are for candy and snacks, 28% are for cereal, 10% are for fast food, 4% are for dairy products, and 1% are for fruit juices, but none are for fruits and vegetables. Even on the #1 cable network for children, Nickelodeon, 88% of food-related ads promote nutritionally poor foods (Batada & Wootan, 2007). This is particularly ironic, given that Nickelodeon sponsors several PSAs to address childhood obesity and allows show-related characters to appear on signs to promote fruits and vegetables.

Additionally, children and adolescents are exposed to unhealthy foodstuffs through product placements in movies, TV programs, and video games. It is no mere coincidence that the judges on *American Idol* drink from large cups emblazoned with the Coca-Cola logo. Product placements can impact the bottom line. During the early 1980s, for instance, sales of Reese's Pieces increased by 65% following its appearance in the blockbuster movie *ET* (Palmer & Carpenter, 2006). Food advertisements are everywhere, even in the sanctity of school. Seven out of 10 commercials aired on the in-school network Channel One were for nutritionally poor foods (e.g., candy, fast food, and soda; Horgen, Choate, & Brownell, 2001). This is particularly ironic given that children are taught about making healthy food choices during class.

On the Internet, hundreds of food-related websites (e.g., Kellogg's Fun K Town) allow children to interact with branded products (e.g., Yogos) and characters (e.g., Tony the Tiger). They can also watch commercials for foods and encounter product placements embedded during advergame play. More than 85% of the leading brands that target children with television ads also have interactive websites that promote food products, and 64% of these websites use viral advertising to persuade youth to e-mail their friends with a link to the website (Moore, 2006). Interestingly, some advergame websites, such as Kellogg's Fun K Town, have Flash messages that tell children to go outside and play for 15 minutes before accessing the website's interactive content. I wonder if any youth actually follow this advice.

Beyond electronic media, youth encounter food advertisements in print media, such as magazines, and on product packages. More often than not, those ads promote unhealthy foods. For instance, one study found that 76% of food products advertised in *Nickelodeon Magazine* were for foods of a nutritionally poor quality (Batada & Wootan, 2007). Additionally, when Nickelodeon characters appeared on the packaging of food products, 6 out of 10 times the food found within was unhealthy. Children can also read about food-related products, such as Skittles, Froot Loops, and Oreo Cookies, in books designed for young readers (Palmer & Carpenter, 2006). When my son was little, I read to him a counting book in which Cheerios could be placed in special locations on each page. Of course, after reading the book he ate the Cheerios.

FOOD ADVERTISING AND OBESITY RESEARCH   Over the past 30 years, obesity rates in the United States have doubled for preschool-aged children and adolescents, and tripled for children during middle childhood (Desrochers & Holt, 2007). Many researchers have suggested that this increase is a result of exposure to food advertising (especially on TV), which leads children to request, purchase, and ultimately eat foods of a nutritionally poor quality (World Health Organization, 2003). However, recent research has demonstrated that children's exposure to *televised* food advertisements has actually decreased over the past 3 decades, whereas exposure to foods of poor nutrition has remained at the same level (Desrochers & Holt).

Nevertheless, such macrolevel studies are problematic because they require broad generalizations in which all children are treated the same. But youth can be light or heavy viewers of TV, and, correspondingly, they will be exposed to few or many commercials for food products. It may also be that the impact of advertisements on youth varies across development. Consider this: Although the rates of obesity in preschoolers and adolescents have both doubled, preschoolers watch about one third fewer food commercials per day than adolescents Yet, middle childhood youth, who watch just four more food commercials per day than adolescents (Gantz et al., 2007), have seen their rates of obesity triple. These data suggest different degrees of vulnerability to food advertisements across development.

Correlational and experimental research on youth during early and middle childhood indicates that when given a choice, children prefer food products that they have seen advertised on TV, in comparison to those they had not (Gorn & Goldberg, 1980, 1982). Although most of this research was conducted more than 20 years ago, contemporary research continues to support the argument that advertising influences food preference. For instance, Borzekowski and Robinson (2001) recently found that preschoolers preferred peanut butter and juice brands advertised during a cartoon program more than nonadvertised brands. There is no research on the impact of advertising on older adolescents' food-related requests or purchases.

Research on the influence of advertisements on subsequent food intake has been consistently documented in experimental studies involving controlled settings (e.g., laboratories or classrooms) across early and middle childhood (there is no research on adolescents). For instance, Jeffrey and colleagues (Jeffrey, McLellarn, & Fox, 1982) demonstrated that commercials for nutritionally suspect foods led to greater energy intake in children between the ages of 4 and 9 than did commercials for healthy foods or toys. Some 22 years later, Halford and colleagues (Halford, Gillespie, Brown, Pontin, & Dovey, 2004) found that 9- to 11-year-olds ate more snack foods after watching food-related advertisements than non-food-related ads. Also, this effect was more pronounced in obese and overweight children in comparison to children of normal weight. Using a slightly younger sample, Halford and colleagues (Halford, Boyland, Hughes, Oliveira, & Dovey, 2007) found the viewing of food-related commercials led to a substantial increase in food intake during a snack period that followed television viewing for both normal weight (17% increase) and obese (14% increase) 5- to 7-year olds. Importantly, the junk foods eaten in this study were not the ones advertised during the television program. Thus, commercials for food stimulated eating in general, and not just the eating of foods seen on TV. Moreover, the food consumption occurred after the television was turned off, indicating that the commercials had a relatively long-lasting impact on the appetites of youth.

Parents, Media, and Obesity

It is important to remember that parents, and not media, are the biggest influence of eating patterns and food preferences during childhood. In general, parents influence kids through the modeling of healthy and unhealthy eating habits, with the purchasing of healthy and unhealthy foods, and by offering healthy and unhealthy food choices during meals and snack time (Jenvey, 2007). Research has also shown that the amount of food eaten and the nutritional quality of the food consumed are similar between parent and child. Thus, parents who eat a lot of nutritionally poor foods have kids who do the same (Grier, Mensinger, Huang, Kumanyika, & Stettler, 2007). Like their children, parents too are influenced by food advertising. In turn, this impact can affect the foods that parents purchase. For instance, in an assessment of parents of underprivileged youth in early and middle childhood, Grier and colleagues (2007) found that greater exposure to fast-food commercials was increasingly associated with the belief that eating fast food was a normative behavior. Of great significance, the more parents saw advertisements for McDonald's, Burger King, and the like, the more often their children ate fast food.

Media and Obesity Stigma

The *obesity stigma* refers to the negative attitudes, stereotypes, and discriminatory behavior directed at overweight youth. Across development, youth view their overweight peers to be more selfish, lazy, stupid, ugly, sloppy, and unlikeable than acquaintances of normal weight. Obese children are also less likely to be preferred as playmates, and experience high levels of social rejection, teasing, and bullying. Obesity stigma, which has been documented in children as young as 3, worsens over the course of development, only lessening during the college years. In addition, the more the child weighs, the worse the stigmatization (and associated bias, stereotyping, and prejudicial behavior). Parents and teachers can also convey statements and act in ways consistent with the obesity stigma. Parents have been shown not only to transmit negative stereotypes about obese children (e.g., laziness) but also to tease their own progeny about their weight. Classroom teachers view obese youth to be less tidy, less likely to succeed, and more emotional than youth of average weight. Similarly, physical education teachers have been shown to hold negatively biased weight attitudes (Puhl & Latner, 2007).

In addition to peers, parents, and teachers, media may also contribute to the prevalence of the obesity stigma. Consider Dudley Dursley from the *Harry Potter* series, and Augustus Gloop from *Willy Wonka and the Chocolate Factory*, as exemplars of media offerings that promulgate weight bias. Both are obese, both are gluttons, and both disregard admonitions from adults regarding inappropriate behavior. Research has assessed weight status in only one medium that children frequently watch: cartoons. In an analysis of more than 60 years worth of cartoons, Klein and Shiffman (2005) found that overweight characters were shown to be less intelligent, and more unhappy and unloved, relative to thinner cartoon characters. Additionally, overweight characters were depicted eating more junk food and behaving more physically and verbally aggressive than lighter characters. Similarly, in an assessment of the top 25 children's videos sold on Amazon.com (most of which were cartoons), Herbozo and colleagues (Herbozo, Tantleff-Dunn, Gokee-Larose, & Thompson, 2004) found that obesity was associated with negative traits 64% of the time.

Additionally, youth watching adult-oriented television shows frequently encounter weight bias. For instance, prime-time television shows tend to depict overweight and obese women to be less attractive and less likely to be involved in romantic relationships than thinner female characters (Greenberg, Eastin, Hofschire, Lachlan, & Brownell, 2003). Although such shows reinforce the obesity stigma, do they also actually impact weight bias in youth? Limited research does, in fact, suggest that media may influence the obesity stigma in children and adolescents. For instance, as television consumption increased, first through third grade boys viewed overweight girls (but not overweight boys) to be more greedy, unintelligent, dirty, and untruthful (Harrison, 2000). Recently, Latner and colleagues (Latner, Rosewall, & Simmonds, 2007) found that media use by 10- to 13-year-olds predicted greater dislike of obese boys and girls, as well as more negative attitudes, in general, toward obese children. Of the media assessed in this study (magazines, TV, and video games), the strongest predictor of weight bias came from magazine reading. Latner and colleagues (2007) contended that this finding is the result of airbrushed and manipulated images in magazines that present a more flawless presentation of the body than those seen on TV or in video games. It may also be that magazine reading, which is far less common than playing video games or watching TV, occurs more frequently for youth concerned about their body image than for those who are not. In turn, youth who value thinness may also espouse negative views of overweight and obese children (Davison & Birch, 2004).

Body Image and Media

Body image refers to the attitudes, feelings, and thoughts related to the appearance of one's body (Jung & Peterson, 2007). Youth can either be satisfied or dissatisfied with the way their body looks, in terms of its overall weight, shape, height, and muscle tone. As it turns out, a significant number of children and adolescents are dissatisfied with their bodies, a process that begins early in life. In fact, the desire for thinness appears to develop around age 5 or 6, becoming more pronounced thereafter (Lowes & Tiggemann, 2003). For instance, Collins (1991) found that 42% of 6- to 7-year-old girls and 30% of same-aged boys preferred silhouettes of bodies thinner than their own. From middle childhood onward, between 40% and 50% of all youth desire to be thinner (Clark & Tiggemann, 2006; Dohnt & Tiggemann, 2006). However, prior to age 8 the desire for thinness is not equivalent to body dissatisfaction. This will soon change, as Wood and colleagues (Wood, Becker, & Thompson, 1996) found that 55% of 8- to 10-year-old girls and 35% of same-aged boys were dissatisfied with the size of their bodies. As youth progress through middle childhood and into adolescence, body satisfaction continues its downward trend (Eisenberg, Fabes, & Sprinrad, 2006).

In general, body dissatisfaction for girls (regardless of age) centers on weight, whereas the lack of muscle mass is the most frequent source of a poor body image for adolescent boys. As a result, across childhood and adolescence, girls are more likely than boys to develop a desire to be thin. In contrast, boys are more likely than girls to strive for increased muscle mass and definition, that is, espouse a "drive for muscularity." However, during childhood, overweight boys wish to be thinner and not necessarily more muscular (Jung & Peterson, 2007). Across development, female body dissatisfaction appears to result, in part, from normative increases in adiposity. However, for girls, the negative body image, observed throughout childhood and adolescence, cannot be fully accounted for by BMI changes alone. Similarly, as adolescent boys enter puberty, they naturally put on more muscle mass. Yet, they too are not happy with normative gains in muscle. Clearly, additional factors are influencing the body image of both males and females.

A great deal of research has focused on the multitude of factors that lead to body dissatisfaction in children and adolescents. In addition to biological predispositions, peers, parents, and siblings, the role of mass media has come under frequent scrutiny. Rather than promoting a positive body image in youth, media critics contend that depictions of male and female bodies in magazines, television, video games, and so on are so unattainable in the real world that body dissatisfaction follows. As it turns out, this just may be the case.

Depictions of Body Image in the Media

Dolls and action figures

For nearly 40 years, Barbie's curvaceous measurements were estimated to be 39-18-33. If she were real, Barbie would weigh about 110 lbs. and stand between 6 and 7 feet tall. Like many celebrities of the 1990s, Barbie had plastic surgery and now sports measurements of 33-17-30. Other than Barbie, little is known about the representation of the female body in dolls. At 5'10", GI Joe's lean and hypermuscular body supports an 85-inch chest, 34-inch neck, and 65-inch waist (Baghurst, Carlston, Wood, & Wyatt, 2007). These numbers nearly double those of the average male physique and easily surpass the measurements of Issac Nesser, the world record holder for the largest chest (with a 74-inch chest, 23.5-inch neck, and 44-inch waist; see TrulyHuge.com, 2008). Beyond GI Joe, other action figures, such as Superman, Batman, and the Hulk, have become leaner and more muscular over the past 25 years. Since 1980, the arms, chests, necks, forearms, thighs, and calves of the aforementioned action figures have increased in size between 50% and 60% (Baghurst et al., 2007).

Magazines

Magazines targeting adolescent girls present females in near physical perfection, with virtually all blemishes and "problem areas" removed or altered into an idealized form (Labre & Walsh-Childers, 2003). For decades, magazines have depicted the female body to be tall and thin, standing 5'10" and weighing 110 lbs. – so thin, in fact, that pictured models have an average BMI of 15.8, classifying them as underweight and making them skinnier than 98% of American women (Levine & Smolak, 1996). Images of the female body, however, have changed in the past few years. Bessenoff and Del Priore (2007) found that although the estimated BMIs of models in magazines like *Glamour*, *Seventeen*, and *YM* (BMI 20.7) were lower than that of the typical reader (BMI = 24.3), they were still well within the normal range for weight status.

Beyond images, magazine articles can convey messages about the ideal female body. Davalos and colleagues (Davalos, Davalos, & Layton, 2007) found that 15% of magazine headlines viewed by young women (e.g., *Seventeen* and *Teen Vogue*) focused on diet and body image. Ballentine and Ogle (2005) found that the articles within *Seventeen* describe the ultimate body (i.e., the über body) to be smooth, trim, toned, and lean, with abs and legs "of steel." A slim body is touted as being a "well-managed" body, reflective of a person who is in control of her life. Readers are given advice to reduce "nasties": areas of fat deposit around the body (which are normal for adolescent girls to have). At the same time that *Seventeen* idealized the über body, they were also telling readers to resist the notion of the "thin ideal" and be happy with who they are. Incidentally, online versions of teen magazines provide the following messages: (a) Girls' bodies can easily "get out of control," (b) every body part should be perfect, (c) beauty requires physical perfection, and (d) girls are not OK as they are (Labre & Walsh-Childers, 2003).

Little is known about the portrayal of men's bodies in magazines read by children and adolescents. In general, however, images of male bodies have become leaner and more muscular over the last 3 decades. Men's magazines promote six-pack abs, perfect pectorals, bulging biceps, and low body fat as representative of the ideal male body. Healthy bodies limited in muscularity are rarely shown. The primary message in men's magazines is that achieving a lean, muscular physical appearance is of the utmost importance (Labre, 2005).

Video games
Females in video games are typically depicted with a curvaceous body, distinguished by large breasts and a tiny waist. Lara Croft of the *Tomb Raider* series and Rayne from the *Blood Rayne* series exemplify this body

type. Beasley and Standley (2002) found that 7 out of 10 women in M-rated games (i.e., games recommended for individuals 17 and up) and nearly half of women in T-rated games (i.e., games recommended for youth 13 and up) had unrealistically large breasts. Surprisingly, nearly a third of female characters in E-rated (i.e., games recommended for youth 6 and up) were characterized as voluptuous. Slightly less in occurrence were extremely thin body types, such as the scantily clad Casey Lynch from *Guitar Hero III*. In contrast, the physiques of male characters were more in line with a healthy male body type. Still, more than a third of male characters were depicted with a hypermuscularized body type (Children Now, 2001).

Television and movies

Few investigations exist on the representation of the female body during programs typically viewed by children and adolescents. Research on cartoons from the 1930 to the 1990s found that 88% of animated characters were of normal weight (Klein & Shiffman, 2005). However, an assessment of popular movies purchased on Amazon.com during 2003 revealed that 60% of the movies (cartoons and live action) depicted female main characters who were slender (Herbozo et al., 2004). In contrast, only 33% of main female characters in televised situation comedies (e.g., *Friends* and *Home Improvement*) popular with youth (aged 10 to 16) were below average in weight (60% were average; Fouts & Burggraf, 1999). Comparatively, 69% of female characters on TV were rated as "thin" in 1986 (Silverstein, Perdue, Peterson, & Kelly, 1986). Historically, movies, prime-time television shows, and soap operas have presented female characters who were thinner than the average person (Tiggemann & Pickering, 1996). However, the most recent content analysis of TV shows and movies viewed by youth was conducted nearly a decade ago. As the Fouts and Burggraf (1999) study indicated, the average weight of TV characters increased between 1980 and 1990. Has this trend continued into the new millennium? Only more research will tell.

In popular children's movies, male characters rated as attractive have typically been portrayed as thin and/or muscular (Herbozo et al., 2004). Other than this limited study, little is known about the representation of the male body on television or in movies directed at a young audience. However, for more than a decade, one trend that has remained constant is for male television actors appearing in commercials or on prime-time television to be lean and muscular (Gunter, Oates, & Blades, 2005; Levine & Smolak, 1996). Such V-shaped men have broad shoulders, well-developed arm and chest muscles, and a slim waist. Nowhere is this more evident than in professional sports (e.g., Tom Brady) and in the nonsport of professional wrestling (e.g., Triple H). In fact, the bodies of men in professional wresting go well beyond the lean muscular look by presenting the hypermale body as ideal. Such Adonis-like bodies are big, muscular, and strong, which, incidentally, is a physique that very few males can ever hope to achieve.

Of note, children and adolescents are also exposed to underweight women and overmuscled men in magazine advertisements and TV commercials for weight-loss products. Helping to propel this $40 billion a year market along (Dolson, 2003) are beautifully thin and toned actors, each of which is more than happy to promote the weight-loss benefits of meal replacements (e.g., Weight Watchers), diet supplements (e.g., Hoodia 850), creams (e.g., Body Sculp Cellulite Cream), wraps (e.g., Wrap Yourself Slim), and exercise equipment (e.g., *Melt It Off! With Mitch Gaylord*). Regardless of the product being advertised, the same message is almost always being sent: "Beauty is thin-deep." Currently, little is known about children and adolescents' overall exposure to such weight-loss ads. What is known, however, is that idealized depictions of male and female bodies in the media do in fact influence the body image of youth (Groesz, Levine, & Murnen, 2001).

Body Image Research

Three theories have been forwarded to explain why idealized media images may lead to body dissatisfaction in children and adolescents: thin- or muscular-ideal internalization, social comparison, and contingent self-worth. First, it has been postulated that the extent to which females cognitively internalize society's doctrine for thinness and males internalize muscularity standards leads to greater body dissatisfaction in youth failing to meet those standards. Media is thought to help create and reinforce the "idealized body" internalized by youth. Second, children and adolescents engage in social comparison processes in which they evaluate their own bodies against those presented in the media. Youth unable to measure up to the thin or muscular bodies in the media become dissatisfied with their own bodies. Finally, contingent self-worth theory contends that societal standards for appearance suggest to youth that their value is determined by their appearance. As such, youth unable to meet the thin or muscular ideal feel bad about themselves, which in turn leads to body dissatisfaction and concern with other people's perception of their bodies (Strahan et al., 2008).

Research during early childhood

By the time children are 3 years old, they have already begun to receive messages from their parents regarding the ideal body, with mothers emphasizing thinness to girls and muscle mass to boys. Many preschool-aged boys and girls are aware of not only the appearance of their hair and clothes, but the size of their bodies as well. Despite these findings, during early childhood, there is no research on the effect of *media* on body satisfaction, the internalization of the thin ideal, and the drive for muscularity (McCabe et al., 2007).

Research during middle childhood

Media and body image in girls   Demonstrating that media exposure influences body image during the elementary school years has proven problematic. Not a single study conducted in the last decade has found that viewing thin women on television or in magazines affects *current* levels of *body dissatisfaction* in 5- to 12-year-old girls (e.g., Clark & Tiggemann, 2006; Dohnt & Tiggemann, 2006; Harrison, 2000, Sands & Wardle, 2003). Interestingly, one study did find that television exposure in prepubescent girls predicted what the girls reported they wanted to look like in the *future*, after they "grew up" (Harrison & Herner, 2006). Unfortunately, this study assessed the total amount of television consumption rather than the frequency of viewing programs with thin actors. As such, it is difficult to know if girls' reported desire to be thin in the future truly stemmed from seeing underweight females on TV. In terms of television and magazine exposure influencing the *internalization of the thin ideal* during childhood, the limited research has been mixed. Only two studies have been conducted, with just one finding that TV viewing was related to the internalization of the thin ideal (Clark & Tiggemann, 2006; Harrison, 2000).

Does the much maligned Barbie doll really influence the body image of young girls? The answer is a qualified yes. In the lone experimental study conducted, Dittmar and Halliwell (2006) showed 5- to 8-year-old girls images of either a Barbie doll or an Emme doll (which has a more realistic shape to it, as it is based on the liked-name full-figured supermodel). After seeing images of Barbie, but not Emme, girls between the ages of 5 and 7 reported increased levels of current body dissatisfaction and a greater desire to be thinner as an adult. In contrast, 8-year-old girls' current and future idealized body was unaffected by Barbie. Contrary to expectations, exposure to Emme images resulted in older girls wishing to be thinner when they grew up (current levels of body dissatisfaction were unaffected). For younger girls, Dittmar and colleagues contended that body image changes are the direct result of exposure to environmental stimuli (e.g., Barbie), rather than the internalization of the thin ideal. The authors also suggested that by age 8, girls have established concept of the thin ideal. Thus, for older girls, the Emme doll may have elicited concern about how they will look as adults themselves. In other words, by 8 years of age, girls believe that it is more acceptable to be heavier (but not fat) during childhood than adulthood, and react accordingly to images that correspond with that belief.

Media and body image in boys   With regard to the influence of media on boys' pursuit of lean muscularity during middle childhood, only two studies have been conducted. Both studies failed to link frequent exposure to different health and fitness, fashion, and sports magazines with the body image of boys (Harrison & Bond, 2007; Murnen, Wright, & Kaluzny, 2002). However, Harrison and Bond found that the frequency of reading *video game magazines* at the start of the study was associated with a greater desire to increase muscle mass and definition in White boys, but not African American boys, one year later. The authors suggested that boys are most likely to identify with same-race characters, and as video games characters are primarily White, African American boys were unaffected by hypermuscular images in gaming magazines. However, because the authors failed to assess additional environmental factors that have been shown to influence body image (Sands & Wardle, 2002), it is possible that the reported association was caused by something other than exposure to gaming magazines. For instance, White youth tend to view their bodies more negatively than African American youth (Jones, Fries, & Danish, 2007). As a result, White children, more so than African American children, may try to avoid the uncomfortable feelings associated with these negative perceptions by escaping into the world of media, which includes the reading of video game magazines.

Research during adolescence

Media and body image in girls   From early to late adolescence, *laboratory exposure* to thin women in magazines or on television has consistently resulted in heightened negative body image among girls (Clay, Vignoles, & Dittmar, 2005; Hargreaves & Tiggemann, 2004). For instance, Bell and colleagues (Bell, Lawton, & Dittmar, 2007) found that body dissatisfaction during late adolescence increased after watching music videos of thin female singing groups, such as the Pussycat Dolls and Sugarbabes. More than a decade earlier, Shaw (1995) documented the negative impact of photos of ultrathin adult and teenage fashion models on 14-year-old girls' level of body dissatisfaction. Interestingly, body dissatisfaction increased to a greater extent after viewing images of adult fashion models, in comparison to teenage ones. It may be that adolescents view adult fashion models as possessing the ideal body type post adolescence and post puberty (a time of increasing adiposity). In comparing their current body to the ideal body of the future, adolescents may be concerned about the attainability of their final, and idealized, adult form. Although viewing thin teenage models negatively impacts current body satisfaction, adolescents may also realize that their own body, which is currently in flux, has not reached its final form, thereby lessening (but not eliminating) the impact of seeing similar-aged models.

The results from experimental studies suggest that media can influence adolescents' current views of their body, at least in the short term. How long such effects last, however, has yet to be determined. In an effort to assess the long-term impact of media exposure to the thin ideal on body image, researchers have relied on *correlational studies*, many of which involved a longitudinal design. However, the findings from these studies, which attempt to link the frequency of television viewing in the home with body image, have been mixed. Studies relating total viewing time (regardless of content) with levels of body satisfaction have generally produced nonsignificant associations (e.g., Borzekowski, Thomas, Robinson, & Killen, 2000; McCabe & Ricciardelli, 2003; Tiggemann, 2005). This is not surprising given that watching more television does not necessarily equate to the increased viewing of ideal body forms. In relation to body image, it is far more important to know the content of media consumed and the adolescents' motivation for consumption, more so than simply knowing how much time is being spent in front of the TV.

It may very well be that certain television genres influence body image to a greater extent than others. For instance, viewing soap operas has frequently and positively been associated with the drive for thinness in adolescent girls (e.g., Tiggemann, 2005; Tiggemann & Pickering, 1996). The serial nature and slow plot development of soap operas allow the adolescent time to develop emotional connections to on-screen characters. Because many adolescent girls report using television to learn about life, including what one should look like (Tiggemann), the trials and tribulations of soap opera characters may impact body image to a greater extent than other media. Moreover, the intensity with which adolescent girls watch soap operas can lead to the development of parasocial relationships. As you recall from Chapter 1, parasocial relationships are one-way relationships in which the individual feels an emotional, even intimate, connection toward a media character. Recently, Maltby and colleagues (Maltby, Giles, Barber, & McCutcheon, 2005) found that middle adolescent girls experiencing intense celebrity worship (where they keep their parasocial relationship secret from friends) had poorer body image than girls without fantasy relationships.

In contrast, the watching of music videos has proven to be an inconsistent predictor of body image (Borzekowski et al., 2000; Tiggemann, 2005), with only one study finding a significant association between the two (Tiggemann & Pickering, 1996). The lack of association between music videos and body image may simply reflect the fact that assessments of total viewing time fail to measure the frequency with which girls are exposed to the thin ideal in music videos; watching more music videos does not necessarily equate to seeing more images of the thin ideal.

As you recall, the negative influence of television on body image is predicated on the idea that youth are exposed to the thin ideal over the airwaves. However, shows with predominantly African American casts (e.g., *The Bernie Mac Show* and *Girlfriends*) tend to present a wider range of female body types than shows with primarily White characters (Tirodkar & Jain, 2003). Research on college-aged women has demonstrated two important findings related to body image: (a) Same-race television characters influence White and African American females, more so than cross-race media models; and (b) viewing same-race television characters produces the opposite effects for White and African American. For White women, watching White characters on TV was associated with a negative body image. In contrast, for African American women, viewing programs with African American casts was linked with a healthy body image (Schooler, Ward, Merriwether, & Caruthers, 2004). Additional research is needed to see if similar findings occur for children and adolescents. For Latina adolescents, the picture may be more complex. Whereas the frequent viewing of shows with women of color (with varied body types) was associated with greater body satisfaction over a 2-year period, the viewing of mainstream television shows, with mostly White casts (with primarily thin body types), was linked with decreases in body image over time (Schooler, 2008). Taken together, these findings suggest that body image is influenced by both factors endogenous to the individual (e.g., race, and reasons for consuming media) and characteristics of the media consumed (e.g., the race and physical appearance of media-based models).

Media and body image in boys   The extent to which images of lean muscularity influence adolescent boys' body image is unclear, as the findings from both correlational and experimental studies have been mixed. For instance, Farquhar and Wasylkiw (2007) found that images of muscular male models in *Sports Illustrated* negatively influenced how sixth through ninth grade boys perceived their bodies. Moreover, Tiggemann (2005) found that the viewing of soap operas and music videos predicted the drive for muscularity in 14-year-olds. In contrast, television commercials portraying the muscular ideal failed to impact their level of body satisfaction (Hargreaves & Tiggemann, 2004). Another study found that adolescent males' use of muscle-enhancing products was unrelated to the total amount of media consumed (Field et al., 2005).

Researchers have also examined the *perceived* importance of media on adolescents' body image. It would make sense that adolescents perceiving greater media influence would have a higher drive for muscularity than youth without this perception; and recent research has supported this contention (Smolak & Stein, 2006). However, perceived media influence failed to predict body satisfaction or satisfaction with muscle size in adolescent 12- to 14-year-old boys (Stanford & McCabe, 2005). Given these data, no conclusive statement regarding the impact of media on adolescent boys' body image can be made.

Thin-Ideal Media and Eating Disorders in Females

As previously demonstrated, media-based representations of the thin ideal have the potential to negatively influence the body image of female adolescents. Because body dissatisfaction has consistently proven to be a significant risk factor for disordered eating (Haines & Neumark-Sztainer, 2006), researchers have posed the following question: Can adolescents' virtually insatiable media appetite influence the development of eating disorders, such as anorexia nervosa and bulimia nervosa? Anorexia nervosa is typified by self-starvation and marked weight loss. Techniques to maintain extremely low levels of body fat include compulsive exercise and the use of laxatives, diuretics, and enemas. Bulimia nervosa is characterized by frequent binge eating, followed by the elimination of the food through self-induced vomiting, laxatives, and so on. A common feature for both types of eating disorders is the presence of a distorted body image. Eating disorders are relatively rare, occurring in less than 5% of the adolescent population, and require extensive evaluation by a medical staff for an official diagnosis. As such, in media effects research, investigators have focused on the broader category of eating disorder symptomatology, which is composed of behaviors that are consistent with the classification of an eating disorder (such as purging, using laxatives, etc.) but are not diagnostic of one (Lapinski, 2006).

Numerous studies have demonstrated that greater exposure to the thin ideal in magazines is associated with increased eating disorder symptomatology for adolescent females (Neumark-Sztainer et al., 2007; Vaughn & Fouts, 2003). Beyond the images depicted within, many youth look to magazines for "helpful" information on how to lose weight. The more they do this, the more likely they are to engage in unhealthy weight control behaviors, such as taking diet pills, using laxatives, and inducing vomiting (van den Berg, Neumark-Sztainer, Hannan, & Haines, 2007). Recent research suggests that although television viewing, in general, is not associated with disordered eating in female adolescents (Neumark-Sztainer et al.), exposure to television programs exhibiting the thin ideal is associated with these habits (Harrison, 2001). Once again, such studies illustrate the importance of knowing specifically what youth are watching and not simply recording how much television they consume.

Additional studies have shown that adolescents who want to look like celebrities or who report feeling that the media pressures them to be thin tend to exercise more (Taveras et al., 2004), are more concerned about their weight (Field et al., 2001), and engage in unhealthy weight control behaviors more so than other youth (Peterson, Paulson, & Williams, 2007). Although eating disorders are not typically diagnosed until adolescence, media exposure has been linked to eating disorder symptomatology in preadolescents (Harrison & Hefner, 2006). Such data are consistent with the finding that eating disorders do not just suddenly appear out of nowhere during adolescence; rather, there may have been predictive markers present prior to puberty (Haines & Neumark-Sztainer, 2006).

The question arises as to which comes first: Is it that thin-ideal media causes disordered eating in youth? Or is that those with disordered eating search out thin-ideal media, in order to reinforce their already established pathological patterns of eating and weight control behaviors? In actuality, both effects are present: Youth with disordered eating seek out thin-ideal media while at the same time being influenced by the thin-ideal media that they consume. In turn, a feedback loop develops (a downward spiral), in which thin-ideal media reinforces and exacerbates eating disordered symptomatology, and disordered eating increases interest in thin-ideal media. The proliferation of more than 500 websites promoting eating disorders on the Internet supports this contention (Wilson, Peebles, & Hardy, 2006).

Pro-eating disorder (pro-ED) websites are generally classified into two types: pro-ana, which promotes anorexia nervosa; and pro-mia, which endorses the bulimic way of life. Rather than viewing eating disorders as an illness, pro-ED websites laud disordered eating and weight control practices as an acceptable *lifestyle* choice. Through message boards and blogs, pro-ED websites provide users with weight loss tips (e.g., fasting and drinking lots of water), methods for avoiding detection by health care workers and family (e.g., exercise at night when no one can see you), and "supportive statements" ("Be strong and you will be better than everyone else"; Lapinski, 2006, p. 250). In fact, 9 out of 10 pro-ED websites have motivational content, the most provocative of which is called "thinspiration," which depict images of ultrathin women. Thinspiring images include rib-exposing pictures of actresses and models, such as Angelina Jolie, Mary-Kate Olsen, Kate Moss, and Mischa Barton, as well as members of the pro-ED online community (Harper, Sperry, & Thompson, 2008; Wilson et al., 2006). Currently, no data exist on the number of adolescent females accessing pro-ED sites. However, a recent study of adolescent girls diagnosed with an actual eating disorder revealed that by visiting pro-ED websites, they learned new techniques to maintain their unhealthy weight status (Wilson et al., 2006). Clearly, such sights may contribute to the downward spiral of disordered eating.

Lean Muscularity and Muscle Dysmorphia in Males

Even though the connection between viewing Adonis-like images in the media and the drive for muscularity in adolescent males is tenuous, it is possible that such images are particularly powerful for youth at risk for muscle dysmorphia. Muscle dysmorphia is a psychological disorder characterized by a preoccupation with, and the pursuit of, muscle mass. Recent research on muscle dysmorphia symptomatology suggests that a downward spiral model may be influencing adolescent males' drive for muscularity in the same way that it influences adolescent females' pursuit of thinness. Adolescent boys perceiving the media to influence their desire to build muscles are more likely to use supplements than boys without this perception, and they were also more likely to have symptoms of muscle dysmorphia. Moreover, the reading of health and fitness magazines or men's fashion magazines has also been linked with the use of products to increase strength (Cafri, van den Berg, & Thompson, 2006; Field et al., 2005). With 1 in 25 boys using diet pills and 10% of adolescent boys reporting the use of one or more muscle-enhancing drugs in their lifetime (Cafri et al., 2006; Chao et al., 2008), the search for risk factors associated with muscle dysmorphia, and the specific role of the media in its development, is of paramount importance.

Developmental Points of Interest

Despite the concern that media consumption affects the waistline across development, there is little evidence that media use displaces physically active behavior. Nor does eating in front of the TV guarantee that youth will consume copious amounts of calories at the same time. However, food intake does appear to increase post media consumption. It may be that food cues in advertisements stimulate postviewing overeating in viewers. Recent research suggests that food cravings can, in fact, be elicited by exposure to food cues (Sobik, Hutchison, & Craighead, 2005). Not surprisingly, food-related commercials (or magazine ads, etc.), with their vivid imagery, provide strong food cues. It appears that commercials lead to cravings, which then stimulate eating, which in turn can result in overeating for those with little impulse control (Nederkoorn, Braet, Van Eijs, Tanghe, & Jansen, 2006). Future research needs to determine if the increased food consumption observed in the laboratory carries over to the home. If it does, then children with unlimited access to nutritionally poor foods would be at the greatest risk for adiposity as a result of the frequent viewing of food commercials. Additionally, future research needs to identify just how long the desire to eat lasts after viewing food advertisements, across development. Such information will be helpful in developing interventions to help youth ward off the desire to overeat after advertisement exposure. It appears, then, that the United Kingdom made a prudent decision in banning advertisements to youth. But, as the previous findings reviewed, advertisements directed at parents are still being aired, and therefore continue to influence the eating habits of children.

Regardless of the extent to which media impacts obesity, one thing is certain: Obese children and adolescents are heavily stigmatized. Besides, parents, teachers, and peers, the media may contribute to the development of weight bias. For instance, cartoons portray heavy characters in a manner consistent with the obesity stigma. Are such representations common in all children's media? That question remains unanswered as no research has assessed the characterization of weight status in live-action television shows, video games, or magazines that target youth. Nor has this been assessed from a developmental perspective. As an example, are overweight teen characters stigmatized more than overweight child characters? Nevertheless, the consumption of media does appear to influence the extent to which youth espouse attitudes along the lines of the obesity stigma.

Rather than being mutually exclusive, each theory accounting for body dissatisfaction in youth (thin- or muscular-ideal internalization, social comparison, and contingent self-worth) could play a role across development. The internalization of societal norms occurs before children are even 3 years old. The social comparison process begins in earnest during the elementary school years. By the time children are in first grade, physical appearance has already become a component of self-esteem. Self-esteem peaks during the preschool years, then gradually declines during childhood. During adolescence, self-esteem continues to drop (especially for girls) and becomes more differentiated, with body image becoming increasingly important to the self-esteem of youth (Robins & Trzesniewski, 2005). Taken together, these data suggest that body image can be affected by media at any age; however, adolescence appears to be a time of greatest vulnerability.

8

The Role of Media in Alcohol, Tobacco, and Drug Use

Candies with drug-inspired names, such as Kronic Kandy, Purple Haze, and Pot Suckers, brazenly state that their marijuana-flavored products "Taste like the real 'Deal'!" and "are a favorite among people who enjoy smoking blunts/cigars." Despite being FDA approved, legislators in Georgia, such as Senator Doug Stoner (D-Smyrna), expressed serious concern that marijuana-flavored products promoted drug use in youth. In fact, in the summer of 2008, the State of Georgia banned the sale of marijuana-flavored candy to minors (WSBTV.com, 2008). Ironically, the State of Georgia (which conservatively generates $100–200 million annually in tobacco sales; UGA.edu, 2008) does allow the sale of candy cigarettes to children and adolescents. Inconsistent policy aside, whether or not candy versions of marijuana and cigarettes promote drug use and smoking in youth is an empirical question that will be answered below. Moreover, in the following pages, the broader impact of media depictions of cigarettes, alcohol, and illicit drugs (CAD) on the attitudes and behavior of youth will be evaluated. But first, the prevalence of CAD use across development will be explored.

Prevalence of Cigarette, Alcohol, and Drug (CAD) Use Across Development

According to recent statistics, 61% of cigarette smokers start before the age of 18, 89% of recent alcohol initiates were under the legal drinking age of 21, and 58% of new illicit drug users were not old enough to vote. Each day, close to 3,800 adolescents smoke their first joint, nearly 11,000 teens take their first alcoholic drink, and 1,300 youth between the ages of 12 and 17 start smoking (Substance Abuse and Mental Health Services Administration, 2006).

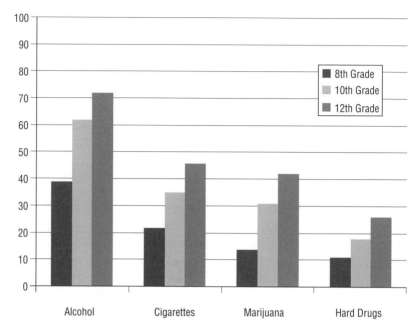

Figure 8.1   Lifetime CAD use by grade.
Source: Data are adapted from NIDA (2007).

Although recent research points to broad experimental use of cigarettes, alcohol, marijuana, and "harder" illicit drugs across adolescence (see Figure 8.1; National Institute on Drug Abuse [NIDA], 2007), a significant number of youth begin CAD use prior to the onset of puberty. For instance, by fourth grade approximately 10% of children have puffed a cigarette and 10% have had more than a sip of alcohol (Donovan, 2007; Maggi, 2008). Of course, because adolescence is a time of trying new things, substance use will continue to grow across development. By the time adolescents are ready to graduate from high school, 72% of students report one or more instances of alcohol use, 46% state that they have smoked cigarettes at least once in their lifetime, 42% claim at least one experimental encounter with marijuana, and 26% report occasional use of "harder" illicit drugs (e.g., amphetamines, inhalants, and cocaine). Additionally, nearly 18% of eighth graders, 42% of 10th graders, and 55% of 12th graders state that they have gotten drunk at least once in their life. Generally speaking, these data suggest that most youth are more likely to just say yes to drugs (and alcohol) than to "just say no."

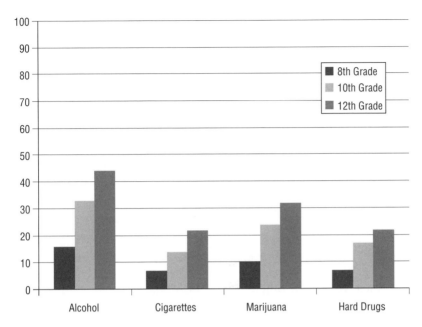

Figure 8.2   Current CAD use by grade.
Source: Data adapted from NIDA (2007).

Although most adolescents experiment with CAD use at least once in their lifetime, fewer report current (i.e., use within the last 30 days) substance use. Nevertheless, the number of youth currently consuming alcohol, drugs, and cigarettes clearly indicates that the War on Drugs is not yet complete. Nearly one fifth of 12th graders are current smokers, 1 in 10 is a current illicit drug user, and more than two fifths are current drinkers. When adolescents consume alcohol, they frequently engage in binge drinking (i.e., consuming five or more drinks in a row). In fact, 10% of 8th graders, 22% of 10th graders, and 26% of 12th graders report recent binge-drinking activity. (See Figure 8.2.) Similar to the data on substance use experimentation, adolescents are more likely to report current use of marijuana than of any other illicit drug (NIDA, 2007).

A couple of cautionary notes are needed when interpreting the aforementioned data. First, the findings are all based on adolescent self-report and not observed behavior. As such, reported drug and alcohol use may not reflect actual CAD use (by either over- or underestimation). Second, although the surveys mentioned above assessed nearly

50,000 youth, data were only collected from students currently *enrolled* in school; high school dropouts were not assessed. However, this subgroup seems to be at greater risk for substance abuse, and they are 1.2 times to 6 times more likely to currently drink and use illicit drugs than youth who stay in school (Swaim, Beauvais, Chavez, & Oetting, 1997). Because nearly 10% of adolescents drop out of high school, the survey data collected by NIDA (2007) may significantly underestimate CAD use across adolescence. Nevertheless, with an estimated 21 million youth in the United States between the ages of 10 and 14 and another 21 million adolescents between the ages of 15 and 19 (U.S. Census Bureau, 2008), even conservative estimates illustrate the grand scale of CAD use across development. Tens of millions of adolescents are engaging in the use of mind-altering substances, and such use is not without consequence.

Outcomes Associated With Adolescent CAD Use

Health Risks

Alcohol
The use and after-effects of alcohol range from relatively benign hangovers to death due to alcohol poisoning. Irrespective of age, alcohol use is thought to cause close to 85,000 deaths annually. The more adolescents consume alcohol, the greater the likelihood that they will develop long-term health risks, such as cirrhosis of the liver, pancreatitis, and hemorrhagic stroke. Alcohol intoxication also negatively impacts decision-making processes and coordination, and as such, individuals who get drunk are prone to accidents. Among individuals under age 21, drinking alcoholic beverages results in 5,000 injury-related deaths each year. For instance, 20% of adolescents killed in car accidents were driving under the influence, and nearly 50% of all adolescent drowning victims were drinking at the time of their death. Additionally, adolescent alcohol use is associated with risky sexual practices, such as engaging in unprotected intercourse, and increased vulnerability to coercive sexual activity by others. Excessive alcohol use can lead to both memory problems in the short term and a reduced ability to learn in the long term. In part, these later effects occur due to alcohol causing physical alterations in a still developing brain (Mokdad, Marks, Stroup, & Gerberding, 2004; U.S. Department of Health, 2007).

Tobacco

Over the course of their lifetime, smokers will increase their risk of death from coronary artery disease, pulmonary disease, and cancer. In fact, each year approximately 440,000 Americans die from smoking-related illnesses. Viewed another way, 1 in 6 deaths in the United States are attributable to smoking. That is more than the combined number of deaths caused by alcohol, illicit drugs, homicide, suicide, car accidents, and AIDS. Of the estimated 1,070 teens who become addicted to tobacco every day, 535 will die prematurely. Unlike the negative consequences associated with alcohol and illicit drug use, most smoking-related outcomes tend to take years to develop (Glantz, 2003).

Illicit drugs   Illicit drug use results in around 17,000 deaths each year. Accidental and intentional overdoses, as well as a reduction in the internal prohibitions against engaging in unsafe behaviors (e.g., driving under the influence), account for this finding (Mokdad et al., 2004). Early drug use is associated with higher levels of aggression, poor academic achievement, deviant and/or criminal behavior during adolescence, and continued drug use throughout adulthood. Physical and mental health risks abound with illicit drug use, most of which vary by the type of drug used. Consider the following as just a limited sampling of the panoply of negative health outcomes associated with illicit drug use: Marijuana use can cause memory impairment, respiratory complications, and cancer; inhalants can result in liver, kidney, bone marrow, and brain damage; and cocaine use can lead to seizures, strokes, disturbances in heart rhythm, and paranoia. Adolescents using illicit drugs are also more likely than other youth to suffer from mental illness, such as anxiety disorders and depression. However, it is important to remember that the mentally ill may seek out illicit drugs in an effort to cope with their psychological problems (NIDA, 2007).

Gateway Hypothesis of Drug Use

Research on adolescents has consistently shown that the use of tobacco and alcohol precedes marijuana use, which in turn occurs prior to the use of illicit drugs, such as hallucinogens, heroin, and cocaine. Some have suggested that tobacco, alcohol, and marijuana are "gateway drugs," thus implying that experimentation with CAD occurs sequentially across development. Evidence for the gateway hypothesis includes correlational studies with adolescents that link alcohol and tobacco use with subsequent marijuana use. Also, the association between marijuana and illicit drug use is stronger than the connection between alcohol or tobacco and illicit drug use. Biologically, tobacco, alcohol, marijuana, as well as the illicit drugs mentioned above primarily operate on the neurotransmitter dopamine, thus providing a potential physiological mechanism for the gateway hypothesis. Nevertheless, rather than early CAD use *leading* to subsequent and harder drug use, it may simply be that users of alcohol, tobacco, marijuana, and illicit drugs share many of the same characteristics (e.g., personality, emotionality, and prevalence of psychopathology) that predispose them to use a *variety* of drugs. Moreover, during adolescence, those who smoke marijuana start hanging out with other drug-using peers. Consequently, these relationships, and the culture of drug use that they engender, lead to greater opportunities to use harder drugs (Golub & Johnson, 2002; Hall & Lynskey, 2005).

Addiction

Without question, both legal and illegal substance use can be problematic for adolescents and adults alike. In addition to the medical and psychological issues mentioned above, CAD use can result in addiction, which is characterized by compulsive and uncontrollable substance use that leads to negative health and social consequences. For instance, problem drinking during adolescence is associated with poor school performance and dropping out of school. Of note, addiction is composed of two related constructs: substance abuse and dependence. Whereas *substance abuse* refers to the behavioral and social consequences of CAD use (e.g., loss of friends, and drug-seeking behavior), *dependence* refers to the accompanying long-term physiological effects, such as tolerance and withdrawal. Unfortunately, animal models have demonstrated that adolescents are particularly vulnerable to addiction. Adolescents are three times more likely than adults to become addicted to marijuana, and teens who start drinking before the age of 15 are four times more likely to become addicted to alcohol than those who wait until they turn 21. Developmental vulnerability to addiction is apparent as well, with the probability of addiction during the life span being the highest for teens beginning CAD use during early adolescence (NIDA, 2007).

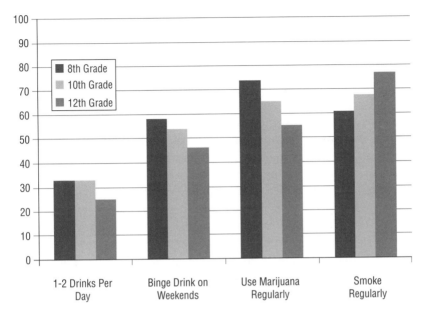

Figure 8.3   Perceived risk of "great harm" from regular CAD use by grade.
Source: Data adapted from NIDA (2007).

Perceptions of CAD Use

Despite the potential for adverse effects, most adolescents fail to perceive great risk associated with regular substance use. From eighth to 12th grade, fewer and fewer teens see significant problems associated with daily alcohol consumption, binge drinking on weekends, and regular marijuana use (see Figure 8.3). Harm associated with cigarette smoking, on the other hand, increases across adolescence. Interestingly, even though marijuana smoke contains higher levels of several toxic compounds than tobacco smoke (e.g., hydrogen cyanide), by the 12th grade, marijuana use is viewed by teens as far less of a health threat than is smoking cigarettes. Adolescents' perception of CAD harm across development may partially explain why high school seniors report the greatest current use of alcohol, followed by marijuana and then cigarette smoking. Two main conclusions can be drawn from the previous review: (a) Substance use is quite common during adolescence, and (b) many adolescents possess a cavalier attitude toward the use of substances deemed inappropriate and illegal for their age.

Prevalence of Substance Use in the Media

Advertisements

Each year, billions of dollars are spent to promote alcohol and tobacco products to consumers. The goal of such advertising is to reach as many potential consumers as possible, as often as possible, even those consumers that cannot legally use the advertised commodity. With the exception of a few magazines targeting cannabis users, such as *High Times*, there are few, if any, nationwide publications available to youth that promote or advertise illicit drugs. Currently, there are no data on youth readership of such brazen magazines. There are, however, plenty of data on alcohol and tobacco advertising in magazines that youth read. Pro-tobacco advertisements in magazines portray smoking to be a positive, normative activity for attractive, independent, and fun-loving young men and women. In a recent assessment of cigarette advertising expenditures, Krugman and colleagues (Krugman, Morrison, & Sung, 2006) found that, over a 10-year period (1993–2002), the three most popular cigarette brands smoked by teens (Marlboro, Camel, and Newport) spent close to $800 million to advertise in magazines that adolescents frequently read. Included in this assessment were magazines considered to be either adult oriented or a youth publication. The term youth publication is reserved for magazines that have at least 2 million adolescent readers or for which 15% or more of the total readership is between the ages of 12 and 17. Magazines meeting this criterion focus on a variety of topics, including fashion (e.g., *Elle* and *Vogue*), sport and fishing (e.g., *ESPN* and *Sports Illustrated*), cars (*Motor Trend* and *Car & Driver*), and entertainment (*People* and *TV Guide*). Data from Krugman and colleagues' (2006) study indicate a dramatic reduction between 1993 and 2002 in the estimated number of cigarette advertisements viewed by adolescents. In 1993, 62% of cigarette ads were placed in youth publications and approximately 93% of adolescent readers had the opportunity for 3+ exposures per year (which is the number needed to be considered an effective campaign). By comparison, in 2002, only 9% of youth had 3+ exposures.

With their loyal (i.e., addicted) customers dying off by the thousands, the profitability of tobacco companies relies on the recruitment of new smokers. But as a result of litigation brought forth by the attorneys general of 46 states against the major U.S. tobacco companies, and the ensuing master settlement agreement (MSA) of 1998, it is now illegal for tobacco companies to advertise directly to youth and/or in a manner that is attractive to youth. Moreover, because of the MSA, no longer can tobacco companies legally advertise in youth publications. Nor can they use cartoon characters, such as Joe Camel, to promote tobacco products. Failure to comply with the MSA can result, and has resulted, in multimillion dollar fines. At this point in time, with the MSA in place, and the threat of fines cogent in the mind of the tobacco industry, the typical child or adolescent will be exposed to few, if any, cigarette advertisements in youth publications. However, 44% of adolescents who read adult-oriented magazines, like *Time*, *Maxim*, *Redbook*, and *Popular Mechanics*, tend to see cigarette advertisements 3+ times annually, for a total of about 9 exposures per year (Krugman et al., 2006).

Each year, the alcohol industry spends approximately $330 million on advertisements in magazines. Typically, these ads show attractive young adults having a great time and enjoying life. Alcohol is almost universally portrayed in the context of partying; only 3% of the time is alcohol promoted in the context of responsible drinking. Between 2000 and 2003 the various trade associations for the beer, wine, and liquor industries restricted alcohol ads to adult magazines, thus prohibiting ads in youth publications. However, these self-imposed standards defined a youth publication as one having greater than 30% readership between the ages of 12 and 20. Thus, publications with 15–30% youth readership are considered to be adult publications with regard to alcohol but youth publications with regard to tobacco (Center on Alcohol Marketing and Youth [CAMY], 2007a; NIDA, 2007). Consequently, when designating a magazine as a "youth publication," tobacco companies are forced to use more stringent criteria than the alcohol industry. In 2001 and 2002, around 10% of alcohol ads appeared in youth publications. That number decreased to less than 4% by 2006. In fact, youth were exposed to 50% fewer alcohol ads in 2006, in comparison to 2001. It appears, then, that the alcohol industry is abiding by its own standards. However, the advertising strategy for alcohol is less altruistic than it appears to be. Approximately 80% of all youth exposure to alcohol advertisements occurs in magazines in which tobacco companies cannot legally place ads (i.e., magazines with 15–30% youth readership). In fact, in 2006 underage youth saw around 90 ads for alcohol-related products in magazines (CAMY, 2007a).

Since 1971, it has been illegal for tobacco advertisements to appear on radio or on television. Although no government restrictions apply to alcohol advertising, the trade associations for the beer, wine, and liquor industries have voluntarily limited radio and television ads to broadcast programs where at least 70% of the audience is of legal drinking age. Each year, advertisers spend close to $90 million to advertise alcohol-related products or sponsored events on the radio. A recent assessment of the 28 largest radio markets in the United States found that, industry wide, nearly 28,000 (8%) alcohol ads occurred in programs with greater than 30% youth listenership. However, 36% of radio advertisements for alcohol occurred during programming with disproportionately large number of youthful listeners, such that individuals under the legal drinking age were more likely to hear advertisements for alcohol than adults 21 and over (CAMY, 2007b).

In 2006, nearly $1 billion was spent to advertise alcohol on television (an increase of 27% from 2001). Even though commercials for alcohol supposedly target consumers at or above the legal drinking age, they also appear to be designed to attract an underage audience. After all, cute dogs and horses that play football easily garner the attention of youth. From 2003 to 2006, the percentage of advertisements occurring on television programs with greater than 30% youth audience was halved from 12% to 6%. However, in 2006 alcohol advertising was placed in 14 of the 15 prime-time television programs with the largest numbers of adolescent viewers (e.g., *Lost*, *Deal or No Deal*, and *CSI*), half of which aired between 8:00 and 9:00 p.m. Thus, although alcohol advertisements were not shown on the Disney Channel or Nickelodeon, such ads were aired during television shows popular with underage youth. As a result, each year, children and adolescents view around 285 television commercials for products containing alcohol (CAMY, 2007b).

Media-Based Story Lines in the Movies and on TV

In addition to the advertising techniques mentioned above, CAD are also being marketed to youth whenever they are embedded in a TV show or movie. At times, such marketing involves paid product placement, in which a particular brand of alcohol or cigarette is contracted to appear on-screen. For instance, in the movie *Superman II*, the superhero from the Planet Krypton was shown bursting out of a truck with the word Marlboro emblazoned in large letters on the side. Currently, both the alcohol and tobacco industries no longer purposefully target movies and television shows designated as youth oriented, as they once did. However, main characters are shown happily using alcohol or tobacco products, thus offering youth the opportunity to see the benefits of CAD consumption. In *American Pie*, for instance, numerous scenes depict hard-partying high school seniors frequently drinking beer. In effect, CAD use on-screen is tantamount to a celebrity-endorsed paid advertisement for the substance being used.

In an assessment of 534 contemporary box-office hits from 1998 to 2002, Sargent and colleagues (2007) identified 3,830 depictions of smoking. Of these, 60% appeared in R-rated films, greatly outnumbering the occurrences of smoking in films rated G (< 1%), PG (4%), and PG-13 (36%). However, because youth are less likely to see R-rated movies than any of the above ratings, children and adolescents are most likely to encounter smoking in films rated PG-13. When simply looking at the presence of alcohol and tobacco in film, the prevalence of each substance becomes even more pronounced. Between 1937 and 2000, Disney released 24 animated feature-length films that were rated G. Of these, only three failed to depict a character drinking alcohol and/or using tobacco. If a child were to watch all 24 films, he or she would see a total of 275 incidents of alcohol consumption and an additional 106 occurrences of pipe, cigar, or cigarette smoking (Ryan & Hoerrner, 2004). Beyond the wholesome entertainment of Disney, a recent study found that around 50% of G- and PG-rated films depicted at least one instance of smoking and/or alcohol use (Polansky & Glantz, 2004; Thompson & Yokota, 2004). For films rated PG-13, alcohol and tobacco use occurs even more often, with the overwhelming majority of films (> 80%) showing characters smoking and/or drinking at least once (Roberts, Henriksen, & Christenson, 1999). See Table 8.1 for a description of the Motion Picture Association of America (MPAA) movie ratings.

It is worth noting that a significant amount of substance use in comedic and dramatic movies involves teenage characters. Recently, Stern (2005) found that 35% of major teen characters in PG-13-rated movies, and 61% of major teen characters in R-rated movies, drank alcohol. Regardless of film rating, 17% of teens in major roles smoked and 30% of major teen characters in R-rated movies engaged in illicit drug use. Such high levels of teenage CAD use are particularly troublesome

Table 8.1   MPAA Ratings

- **G (general audiences)**: All ages admitted. Contains nothing offensive.
- **PG (parental guidance suggested)**: Some material may not be suitable for children.
- **PG-13 (parents strongly cautioned)**: Some material may be inappropriate for children under 13. May contain some violence, nudity, sensuality, or crude language.
- **R (restricted)**: Youth under 17 require a parent or adult guardian for admittance. Material is of an adult nature and may contain violence, nudity, crude language, and sexual situations.
- **NC-17 (no one 17 and under admitted)**: The content of the film is considered too intense for children. Films may contain extreme violence, strong sexual content, aberrational behavior, and drug abuse.

---

given that, relative to older characters, children and adolescents are more likely to view similarly aged characters as appealing role models.

As children age, they are exposed to increasing amounts of alcohol and tobacco use on TV. A 1998 assessment of prime-time television shows popular with 2- to 11-year-old children found that 17% of scenes depict some form of alcohol use. In contrast, smoking occurred in only 2% of scenes (Byrd-Bredbenner, Finckenor, & Grasso, 2003). Another study found that alcohol use was shown at least once in 53% of prime-time programs popular with youth between the ages of 12 to 17. In contrast, tobacco use (11%) and illicit drug use (1%) occurred far less often in these programs. In addition, the amount of tobacco and alcohol use during prime time tends to vary by program rating. Shows rated TV14 contain more instances of alcohol (84%) and tobacco use (24%) than programs rated TVPG (77% and 20%, respectively) or TVG (38% and 6%, respectively). Of note, negative statements about and consequences associated with substance use occur infrequently (14% and 26% of episodes, respectively). Rarely are youth under the age of 18 shown engaging in substance use (Christenson, Henriksen, & Roberts, 2000). Illicit drug use seldom appears during mainstream television programming. However, Roberts and colleagues (1999) found that nearly 20% of movies rated PG-13 illustrated illicit drug use. Youth are also exposed to smoking in movie trailers shown on television. One recent study found that 14% of televised movie trailers depicted tobacco use. It has been estimated that movie trailers expose 95% of 12- to 17-year-olds to at least one instance of smoking, and 89% of teens to at

Table 8.2   The Television Rating System

- **TVY (All Children)**: Appropriate for all children, but content usually targets children between 2 and 6 years of age.
- **TVY7 (Children age 7 and over)**: Elements in programs may include mild fantasy violence or comedic violence. Content may frighten children under the age of 7.
- **TVG (general audience)**: Contains little violence, no strong language, and little sexual dialogue or situations.
- **TVPG (parental guidance suggested)**: Contents, which may be unsuitable for younger children, contain moderate violence, some sexual situations, occasional coarse language, and some suggestive dialogue.
- **TV14 (parents strongly cautioned)**: Contents are suitable for adolescents over 13 years of age. Programs may contain intense violence, intense sexual situations and dialogue, and strong coarse language.
- **TVMA (mature audience only)**: Contents are deemed unsuitable for youth under 17. Program contains graphic violence, explicit sexual activity, or indecent language.

---

least three smoking depictions, each year (Healton et al., 2006). See Table 8.2 for a summary of the television rating system.

Music

From Eric Clapton's "Cocaine" to 50 Cent's "In Da Club," identifying songs that mention substance use is quite easy. From 1960 to 1998, nearly 800 songs lyrically discussed illicit drug use alone (Market, 2001). More recently, Primack and colleagues (Primack, Dalton, Carroll, Argawal, & Fine, 2008) established that 42% of the most popular songs of 2005 referenced CAD use. However, the frequency of such mentions varied by genre of music. Leading the way was rap music, in which 90% of songs had at least one reference to substance use. By comparison, country (41%), rhythm and blues (R&B) and hip-hop (27%), rock (23%), and pop (14%) songs had far fewer references of alcohol, tobacco, and illicit drug use. Across genres, alcohol (24%) was mentioned more often than marijuana (14%), illicit drugs (12%), or tobacco (3%). Alcohol, marijuana, and illicit drugs were more frequently mentioned in rap (53%, 53%, and 37% respectively) than in any other genre. Additionally, 68% of the songs contained more positive consequences associated with substance use than negative ones. More often than not, CAD use occurred in the context of partying and/or sexual activity. Not surprisingly,

Table 8.3   Percentage of Music Videos Showing Explicit or Implied Substance Use

	Substance	
Music Genre	**Alcohol**	**Illicit Drugs**
Rap	56%	31%
Rock	27%	9%
R&B	26%	4%
Pop	27%	0%

Source: Gruber, Thau, Hill, Fisher, and Grube (2005).

Figure 8.4   Music advisory label.

music videos of songs with CAD references also tend to depict actual substance use or evidence of substance use, such as paraphernalia. Recently, an assessment of 359 music videos revealed that 43% showed evidence of frequent substance use. Rap videos showed evidence of alcohol and illicit drug use more often than rock, R&B, and pop (Gruber, Thau, Hill, Fisher, & Grube, 2005). See Table 8.3 for the related percentages. Of note, in an effort to protect children and adolescents from drug-related, violent, and sexually explicit lyrics, the Recording Industry Association of American (RIAA) voluntarily labels music with a warning sticker: "Parental Advisory: Explicit Content" (see Figure 8.4).

Video Games

Information on the presence and use of legal or illicit substances can be found as part of content descriptors appearing on the back of video game boxes. For instance, the listed content of *Grand Theft Auto IV* includes "use of drugs and alcohol." In fact, game play does allow players to drink and drive drunk (complete with blurred vision) and ride around with characters who smoke marijuana. Although substance has found its way into the content of video game story lines, rarely if ever

Table 8.4   ESRB Ratings

- Early childhood (EC): Content suitable for ages 3 and older. Contains no inappropriate material.
- Everyone (E): Content suitable for children ages 6 and older. May contain minimal violence, comic mischief, and/or mild language.
- Everyone 10+ (E10+): Content suitable for children ages 10 and older. May contain more cartoon, fantasy or mild violence, mild language, and/or minimal suggestive themes.
- Teen (T): Content suitable for teens ages 13 and older: may contain elements of violence, mild or strong language, and/or sexually suggestive themes.
- Mature (M): Content suitable for persons 17 years of age and older. Content contains mature sexual themes, intense violence, and/or strong language.
- Adults only (AO): Content meant only for adults: contains graphic depictions of sex and/or violence. Not intended for minors.

does it appear in video games rated E (Thomson & Haninger, 2001). According to the Entertainment Software Rating Board (ESRB), 2% of video games rated T in 2001 and 4% of video games rated M in 2004 depicted substance use. However, recent research has shown that ESRB ratings frequently fail to include content descriptors of substance use in video games that actually depict such behavior. Results from two recent studies indicate that CAD appeared in 15% of T-rated video games and 58% of video games rated M (Haninger & Thomson, 2004; Thompson, Tepichin, & Haninger, 2006). Why is there such disconnect between the ESRB content descriptors and the actual depiction of CAD use during game play? The answer is very straightforward: The ESRB assigns ratings based on *videotaped* footage of game play and content descriptors that are both provided by the game's maker. Thus, it appears as if many submissions to the ESRB omit clips of CAD use encountered during game play, and/or appropriate content descriptors. See Table 8.4 for a description of ESRB ratings.

Websites

Websites for beer and liquor are interactive and high-tech. Visitors can download mixed drink recipes, screensavers, wallpapers, widgets, IM accessories, and customized music. Commercial videos are available for view, blogs can be read, chat rooms can be entered, and flash games, like Budweiser's "Perfect Pour Challenge," can be played. In addition to product-related downloads, many websites offer downloadable images that are sexually provocative. However, arcade-like games (e.g., Air Hockey, Digital Football, and Putting Challenge), which appeared in 67% of beer and 37% of distilled spirits websites in 2003 (CAMY, 2004), are no longer available on most official alcohol-related websites. Moreover, cartoons and cartoon-like characters are no longer found on websites for alcohol products. It appears as if the alcohol industries' prohibition against advertising to youth has made its way to the Internet. Although alcohol product websites virtually "card" potential visitors by having them provide their birth date, no attempt is made to verify that the individual is actually of legal drinking age. Data from the CAMY (2004) study indicated that nearly 700,000 visits to alcohol product websites were made by underage children and adolescents.

Official websites for the Big 3 tobacco companies (R.J. Reynolds, Phillip Morris, and British American Tobacco) are relatively benign, containing sections on product lines, financial information, the health risks of tobacco use, and quitting. In addition, websites for specific brands of cigarettes such as Camel and Marlboro require actual age verification (not just simply entering a birth date) and membership to enter. Absent from such sites are games, videos, and entertaining characters. No attempt is made to appeal to children and adolescents. Nevertheless, pro-tobacco websites (e.g., Forestonline.org) are available, without age restriction, on the Internet for those who wish to find them.

Planning your first Ecstasy experience and uncertain about potential side effects? Need to know what drugs mix well with cocaine? Want to find out how much Ketamine will produce a "good" psychedelic experience? The answers to all these questions and thousands more are just a click away. The Internet has numerous websites, blogs, and forums dedicated to illicit drug use. Although providing warnings about the hazards of drugs, many illicit drug websites, such as Erowid.com and Ravesafe.org, also promote "safe" and "responsible" drug use. Such sites typically have Q & A and "past experience" sections that in effect become a "how to" guide for drug users. Traffic at these websites is astonishing. Erowid.com alone gets 55,000 unique visitors per day (Erowid.com, 2008). The number of youth visiting these websites, however, is currently unknown.

Effects of Substance Use in the Media

Research During Early Childhood

Because preschool-aged children have limited language skills, cannot read, and are easily influenced by the way questions are asked (DeHart, Sroufe, & Cooper, 2004), accurately assessing their attitudes, expectations, and perception of substance use has proven difficult. Recently, Dalton and colleagues (2005) used an innovative role-playing scenario to assess the associations between movie exposure and 2- to 6-year-old children's attitudes toward alcohol and tobacco use. Children were told to pretend that they were adults and were going to have a party for their friends. Children then "shopped" at a Barbie store stocked with 133 miniature products, including nine beer and wine items and six packs of cigarettes. After shopping, the child's character (i.e., a doll) was given an opportunity to use the "purchased" objects with their friend (i.e., doll controlled by an experimenter). Overall, 62% of children bought alcohol and 28% purchased cigarettes. Children buying "smokes" correctly identified them as cigarettes 68% of the time. Alcohol was correctly identified 58% of the time. Although watching movies did not predict purchasing cigarettes during pretend play, preschool-aged children with a history of watching PG-13- and R-rated movies were five times more likely to choose alcohol than those who watched only movies rated G. But rather than movies contributing to the view that alcohol use is a normal part of adult socializing, it may simply be that parents who allow their preschool-aged children to watch PG-13- and R-rated movies raise their children in a lifestyle where alcohol use is prominent (e.g., alcohol is referred to as "daddy's juice"). Such aspects of parenting were not assessed in Dalton and colleagues' study.

As you recall, the MSA prohibits tobacco companies from using cartoon characters in their marketing campaigns, and with good reason. Such characters were extremely effective in developing brand awareness in youth at a very young age. For instance, Mizerski (1995) found that 25% of 3-year-olds, 41% of 4-year-olds, 63% of 5-year-olds, and 72% of 6-year-olds could accurately identify Joe Camel, the mascot for Camel cigarettes. Similar rates of recognition were seen for Ronald McDonald. However, such high rates of recognition were not associated with positive attitudes toward smoking in preschool-aged children.

Virtually all young children viewed smoking as "bad for you" (Henke, 1995; Mizerski, 1995). Given their young age, no studies exist on the effects of media on alcohol- and smoking-related behaviors or the intention to use substances later in life.

Research During Middle Childhood

According to many researchers, the intention to use alcohol and/or tobacco during adolescence or adulthood is influenced by both brand awareness and positive attitudes toward substance use during middle childhood. Media influences, such as advertisements, television, and movies, are thought to create both of these across development.

Tobacco-related attitudes and behaviors
Similar to the findings for preschool-aged children, middle childhood youth demonstrated a high degree of cigarette brand recognition prior to the MSA. For example, Henke (1995) demonstrated that 86% of 7- to 8-year-olds recognized Joe Camel and 46% recognized the noncartoonish red-roof logo of Marlboro cigarettes. Moreover, across the elementary school years, brand recognition of cigarettes was not associated with favorable attitudes toward cigarette use. Little is known about brand recognition post MSA. However, during the first part of middle childhood, exposure to tobacco advertising does not appear to engender a favorable attitude toward its use.

But how are attitudes and the intention to smoke affected when children are exposed to cigarette brands while at the same time getting the opportunity to pleasurably mimic smoking behavior? Of course, I am referring to candy cigarettes, which have traditionally been sold in packaging that approximates the real thing. Packs of candy cigarettes have 10 or so sticks, each of which has a red tip, and if you blow on them, powdered sugar puffs out the end. Some even have names similar to that of brand-name cigarettes, such as Lucky Lights (cf. Lucky Strike). Children between the ages of 4 and 8 are the primary consumers of candy cigarettes. One recent study found that the odds of cigarette smoking in adulthood went up as the reported amount of childhood cigarette candy consumption increased. In fact, eating cigarette candy nearly doubled the odds of becoming a smoker (Klein, Thomas, & Sutter, 2007). However, this study involved the assessment of retrospective memory (i.e., participants are asked to recall information about the past), which is notoriously unreliable and easily impacted by the current mood state of the individual. It is possible, for instance, that nonsmokers were less likely to recall cigarette candy use during childhood because of their current negative views toward smoking. Of note, there is no research on the effects of marijuana-flavored candies on youth.

As reported in a Philip Morris document, "[M]ost of the strong, positive images for cigarettes and smoking are created by cinema and television" (Morris, 1989). Recent research suggests that such images, which are tacitly pro-smoking, do in fact influence the initiation of smoking during middle childhood. After removing the influence of a variety of factors associated with smoking initiation (e.g., parent and peer smoking status, self-esteem, and school performance), viewing smoking in movies at age 9 (as indicated by occurrences of smoking in reported movies watched) was associated with an increased risk of smoking within 3 years. Moreover, smoking in movies accounted for 35% of smoking initiation that occurred by age 12 (Titus-Ernstoff, Dalton, Adachi-Mejia, Longacre, & Beach, 2008). These results are consistent with earlier studies, which also demonstrated that viewing smoking in magazines, movies, and advertising contributed to smoking initiation prior to adolescence (e.g., Aloise-Young, Slater, & Cruickshank, 2006; Wills et al., 2007). Additional research has found that 9- to 12-year-old children prohibited from watching R-rated movies by their parents were about 40% less likely to be at risk for smoking, relative to youth without such prohibitions (Dalton et al., 2006).

Alcohol-related attitudes and behaviors

By the time children enter kindergarten, brand recognition of heavily advertised alcoholic beverages is quite accurate, and it only gets better with time. One study found that 8 out of 10 kindergarteners could identify the red Budweiser logo, which, by the way, was more than could identify the Energizer bunny (61%) or the Cat in the Hat (61%). By second grade, virtually all children could correctly identify the logos for Budweiser (100%) and Bud Lite (96%; Henke, 1995). A survey of 9- to 11-year-olds even found that children were more familiar with Budweiser's television frogs (Bud-Weis-Er) than with Kellogg's Tony the Tiger, Smokey the Bear, or the Mighty Morphin' Power Rangers (Lieber, 1996). Despite such high levels of brand awareness, most children report negative attitudes toward alcohol use during the elementary school years. In fact, one study found that most children aged 7 to 12 do not believe that drinking beer makes one "cool" (93%) or can "make life a lot more fun" (90%). Similarly, 91% of children stated that they did not like commercials for alcohol. Nevertheless, nearly half of all children surveyed had tasted alcohol at least once. It may be that the stated negative attitudes toward alcohol simply reflected what children thought the adult interviewers wanted to hear. At the very least, these data suggest that children are aware of the prevention messages directed at them in school (Austin & Nach-Ferguson, 1995).

Though few studies exist, exposure to alcohol use in advertising and movies during middle childhood has been positively associated with both the intention to drink and actual alcohol use (Austin & Nach-Ferguson, 1995). For instance, fifth and sixth grade children knowledgeable about beer brand logos held more positive beliefs about drinking and intended to drink more often when they were adults than other youth (Grube & Wallack, 1994). More recently, Sargent and colleagues (2006) found in a similarly aged group of children that exposure to alcohol in movies was associated with a greater likelihood of engaging in early onset drinking. Additionally, the aforementioned effect was stronger for preteens considered to be at low risk for alcohol experimentation, relative to deviance-prone youth. Similarly, Dalton and colleagues (2006) found that 9- to 12-year-old children prohibited from watching R-rated movies by their parents were about 40% less likely to be at risk for alcohol use (i.e., either drank alcohol or planned on drinking it in the near future), compared to youth able to watch restricted movies. Of note, these findings are nearly identical to the effects of movie exposure on smoking initiation mentioned earlier.

Research During Adolescence

Tobacco-related attitudes and behaviors
Across adolescence, numerous experimental and correlational studies have indicated that advertising and media-based images of tobacco use create positive attitudes toward smoking and increase the intention to smoke. Consider the following experimental study as an example: Pechmann and Shih (1999) created two versions of the film *Reality Bites*. In one version of the film, smoking scenes were included, but in the

second version they were removed. *Nonsmoking* ninth graders who viewed the smoking version of the film indicated a greater intention to smoke and were more likely to convey positive attitudes about smokers than their counterparts who watched the smoke-free version. A summary of more than 50 articles involving adolescents found that media exposure to smoking increased the odds of both holding positive attitudes toward tobacco use and expressing an intention to smoke by 50% (Wellman, Sugarman, DiFranza, & Winickoff, 2006). Recently, Shadel and colleagues (Shadel, Tharp-Taylor, & Fryer, 2008) demonstrated that the impact of cigarette advertising on the intent to smoke was strongest for early adolescents, relative to older adolescents and teens with well-established identities. Thus, early adolescents (who are struggling to establish an identity) may be especially vulnerable to the effects of encountering positive portrayals of smoking in the media.

More important than the effects of media-based smoking on attitudes and intentions to smoke, is the fact that viewing images of smoking in advertising, magazines, movies, and so on appears to double the odds of actual smoking initiation among teenagers and increases the odds of becoming an established smoker (i.e., smoking more than 100 cigarettes) by 42% (Wellman et al., 2006). In fact, one study estimated that 34% of all smoking experimentation could be accounted for by images of smoking in the media (Pierce, Choi, Gilpin, Farkas, & Berry, 1998). Such effects remain, even after removing the influence of other factors known to impact tobacco use, attitudes, and intentions, such as ethnicity, socioeconomic status, parents, peers, and personality (e.g., sensation seeking; Wellman et al.).

Nevertheless, media-based smoking does appear to impact youth differently depending on the nature of the aforementioned characteristics. For instance, Sargent and colleagues (2007) found that the effects of smoking in movies on already established smokers was 12 times greater for youth low in sensation seeking, relative to youth high in this characteristic. High sensation seekers were more likely to have already started smoking than those low in sensation seeking, thereby increasing the impact of viewing smoking in movies on the latter group. Additionally, Pechmann and Knight (2002) found that a combination of peer factors and exposure to advertising influenced adolescents' intentions to smoke. Adolescents were more likely to view peer smokers in a more positive light (e.g., cool) if they had been exposed to cigarette advertising than if they had no such exposure. Moreover, Aloise-Young and colleagues (2006) found that magazine advertisements augmented the effect of passive peer pressure (i.e., number of peers that smoke) on status as a cigarette smoker. It remains to be seen, however, if the impact of media-based smoking varies across adolescence, as most studies have failed to differentially assess early, middle, and late adolescents in their analyses.

It is interesting to consider why exposure to smoking in the media influences teen smoking initiation to a greater extent than it does the progression to becoming an established smoker. The answer may simply be that it is the symptoms of addiction that drive teens from experimentation to heavier use (Wellman et al., 2006). Thus, from the tobacco industry's perspective, anything that can get adolescents to initiate smoking (from advertisements to images of on-screen smoking) is of the upmost importance. After all, once smoking has begun, the hard part is over, as the addictive nature of cigarettes will sell themselves.

Alcohol-related attitudes and behaviors

In general, the qualities of commercials for alcohol that are attractive to adults, such as music, animal characters, and humor, are also attractive to adolescents. Moreover, when adolescents like an ad, they report a greater desire to buy the promoted alcoholic beverage and expect to have a good time when using it (Chen, Grube, Bersamin, Waiters, & Keefe, 2005). Adolescents, in particular, may be attracted to ads for alcoholic beverages because drinking is a behavior associated with immediate gratification, excitement, and elevated social status, all of which are important to teenagers (Pechmann, Levine, Loughlin, & Leslie, 2005).

Several studies have demonstrated that as general media consumption increases, so too does reported alcohol use. For instance Van den Bulck and colleagues (Van den Bulck, Beullens, & Mulder, 2006) found that for every hour of TV watched per day, teens were 17% more likely to drink alcoholic beverages at home. For adolescents watching multiple hours of music videos per week, the odds of drinking alcohol (when going out) increased by 239%. Similarly, Wingood and colleagues (2003) reported that listening to rap music increased the odds of drinking alcohol by 1.5 times in adolescent females. Unfortunately, the utility of these studies is limited because they all failed to assess the amount of on-screen alcohol use and alcohol advertisements seen by adolescents. It is unclear if youth exposed to more media actually see significantly more images of alcohol than youth with less media consumption.

Additional research, however, has assessed actual exposure to alcohol in the media as it relates to drinking behavior, and found that the relationship alluded to above does in fact exist. For instance, higher exposure to alcohol advertisements was associated with greater levels of alcohol consumption among underage drinkers between 15 and 20 years of age. For each additional ad viewed above the monthly average of 23, the typical underage drinker consumed 1% more alcohol (Snyder, Milici, Slater, Sun, & Strizhakova, 2006). Similarly, a study of seventh graders found that the viewing of television programs containing commercials for alcohol was linked with an elevated risk of drinking beer (44% increase) or wine and liquor (34% increase). This study also found that the likelihood of having a three-drink episode the following year increased by 26% for such viewers (Stacy, Zogg, Unger, & Dent, 2004). Parallel findings have been found for magazine advertisements and movies. Viewing alcohol ads in magazines in the seventh grade has been associated with higher levels of drinking behavior in the ninth grade (Ellickson, Collins, Hambarsoomians, & McCaffrey, 2005), and greater levels of exposure to alcohol in movies were linked with an increased likelihood of engaging in early-onset drinking in the seventh and eighth grades. These effects were especially strong for youth not considered to be at great risk for alcohol use.

Illicit drug-related attitudes and behaviors

Currently, only a handful of studies have assessed the effects of observing media-based drug use on the attitudes and behavior of youth. With regard to attitudes, Mayton and colleagues (Mayton, Nagel, & Parker, 1990) found the depiction of illicit drug use, in movies and in music and music videos, was perceived by adolescents as encouraging such behavior less than 10% of the time. In terms of engaging in illicit drug use, Wingood and colleagues (2003) found that watching copious amounts of rap music videos was associated with greater amounts of illicit drug use by African American female adolescents. These findings remained even after taking into consideration additional factors, such as parental monitoring and commitment to one's faith. However, because actual on-screen drug use was not assessed, it is impossible to know if the above association was influenced by the content of the music videos.

Other studies attempting to link music preferences (e.g., rap, country, and pop) with illicit drug use have been met with mixed results. For instance, Dent and colleagues (1992) found music preference to be a weak predictor of illicit drug use. In contrast, two studies linked listening to "rave" music with the use of drugs (e.g., ecstasy) during adolescence (Forsyth & Barnard, 1998; Forsyth, Barnard, & McKeganey, 1997). What these studies failed to do, however, was assess the lyrical content of the songs. Thus, although liking certain music may be a potential indicator of drug use, it by no means can be stated that music is a cause of it.

In all likelihood, the greatest threat for adolescent illicit drug use comes from the Internet. Research on late adolescents and young adults has shown that drug encyclopedias on the Internet can normalize the use of illicit drugs and create more accepting attitudes in nonusers (Brewer, 2003). For adolescents already engaged in drug use, the Internet has become a handy tool for seeking out information related to the modification and/or enhancement of drug use. Moreover, adolescents report that drug searches on the Internet expose youth to drugs that they had previously never heard about. Although one study found that 75% of drug users used the Internet in an attempt to make their drug use safer, there is no empirical evidence to suggest that the advice given was accurate (Boyer, Shannon, & Hibberd, 2005). Clearly more research is needed to assess the influence of the Internet on drug use, and the magnitude of its effect across development, for both novice and established users.

Developmental Points of Interest

As the previous review illustrates, children and adolescents have ample opportunity to encounter CAD use in the media; and as youth become older, they are exposed to even more. However, just as important as the frequency with which CAD appear in the media, is the nature and context of its presentation. Typically, CAD use is portrayed in a very positive light. Substance use on television and in the movies is done by attractive, high-status main characters, thereby increasing the salience of its consumption. Most CAD use appears as a background activity (e.g., while talking or eating), without directly promoting a message (either pro or con) about its use. Moreover, the use of tobacco, alcohol, and illicit drugs in the media, which is frequently depicted as a normal, carefree activity, tends to be greeted with acceptance by on-screen characters, rather than rejection (Ryan & Hoerrner, 2004).

Like most behaviors, substance use initiation and maintenance are impacted by a multitude of environmental risk factors, such as peers, siblings, and parents. Beyond these influences, does media exposure increase the risk of CAD use during childhood and adolescence? Without a doubt, the answer is yes. Media exposure to both legal and illicit substances appears to increase the initiation of both alcohol and tobacco use across the later part of middle childhood and throughout adolescence. Such effects are not limited to those already at risk for drug use. In fact, for both tobacco and alcohol use, youth considered to be at low risk for substance use were affected more by media depictions of CAD than those at high risk. Even more troubling, however, is the research that suggests that media may be a factor in adolescents moving beyond experimentation, and into the realm of established substance use and concomitant dependency.

However, some developmental differences are evident. Whereas the attitudes of children during early and middle childhood toward smoking and alcohol use seem to be unaffected by images of tobacco in the media (i.e., they are generally negative), media exposure during adolescence appears to create a positive view toward substance use. So, how are we to resolve this age-related contradiction? One possibility is developmental in nature, where media content positively influences smoking and alcohol attitudes as children approach adolescence. Teenagers may be at greater risk from media influences as they strive to come to terms with the social, psychological, and physical changes they are currently undergoing (Shadel et al., 2008). The second possibility may simply be that younger children are more likely to give socially desirable responses than older children and adolescents, thereby eliminating media-related effects that are in fact present at a young age. Given that preteens and teens often feel a need to rebel against authority, social desirability appears to play less of a role as children approach and enter into adolescence.

As the previous review revealed, there are several gaps in the literature that need to be filled. Little is known about the impact of viewing substance use in the media during the preschool years on CAD experimentation later in life. Moreover, no prospective studies on the effects of consuming candy cigarettes or marijuana-flavored confectionaries during childhood have been conducted. Nor is there any research on the impact of viewing illicit drug use in the media on youth in early or middle childhood. Additional research is also needed to determine if certain forms of media (e.g., radio, magazines, and television) impact substance use more than others. Finally, the relative risk of media-related CAD on youth across development has yet to be fully explored.

9

Media and the Sexualization and Sexual Socialization of Youth

During the late 1970s, Brooke Shields made headlines when she portrayed a prostitute in the film *Pretty Baby*; she was 12 years of age at the time. At age 15, she provocatively uttered the now famous tag line for Calvin Klein jeans, "You want to know what comes between me and my Calvins? … Nothing." Some 30 years later, a similar hullabaloo surrounded 15-year-old Disney Channel and music megastar Miley Cyrus after racy pictures of her (a bedsheet is draped across her bare torso, exposing her back) appeared in *Vanity Fair* magazine. Sexual portrayals of adolescents are not limited to girls, as boys too are often presented in a sexualized manner. For example, in the movie *American Pie*, male high school seniors spend the entire movie attempting to lose their virginity. Similarly, teen-centric magazines, such as *Seventeen*, portray adolescent boys as sexually obsessed. These are but a few of the many examples in which media presents to the world a sexualized vision of adolescents; and in some cases, the teens have not even finished puberty.

Sexualization and Sexual Socialization

Such sexually charged portrayals of adolescents have caused great public concern because of their potential to influence two distinct, but related, concepts: sexualization and sexual socialization. Sexualization occurs when any of the four following conditions have taken place: (a) Self-worth is determined by one's sexual appearance or behavior; (b) a person is held to a standard in which physical attractiveness is equated with being sexy; (c) rather than being viewed as a sentient being, a person is made into a "thing" for the sexual use of others, that is, he or she is sexually objectified; and (d) sexuality is inappropriately imposed upon someone. Developmental status is especially important for the fourth condition, for sexuality is almost universally imposed upon preadolescent children rather than chosen by them. Finally, sexualization occurs on a continuum, with sexual evaluation (e.g., leering) at one end and sexual exploitation (e.g., sexual abuse) at the other. Whereas self-motivated sexual exploration and age-appropriate exposure to information about sexual practices are both considered aspects of healthy sexuality, sexualization places the physical and mental health of youth in jeopardy. For instance, sexualized female teens are at greater risk for depression, eating disorders, low self-esteem, and sexually transmitted diseases (CDC.gov, 2008).

In contrast to sexualization, which primarily focuses on the inappropriateness of viewing youth as sexual entities, the broader concept of sexual socialization refers to the process by which children and adolescents acquire knowledge, attitudes, and values about sexuality. Included within this concept is the biology of sex and reproduction, the definitions of different types of sexual acts (e.g., masturbation, oral sex, and vaginal sex), and attitudes toward the appropriateness of various sexual activities at different ages and at different stages of a relationship (e.g., just met, in love, or married; Ward, 2003). Agents of sexual socialization include parents, siblings, peers, religious settings, health care professionals, and school (and adolescents know exactly *who* they want to learn about sex from).

When asked which of the above they would prefer as their source of sexual information, parents were the desired choice of adolescents from ninth through 12th grade; peers and schools were the next in line (Somers & Surmann, 2004). However, when asked which of the above sources they actually received the greatest quantity of information from, media accompanies peers at the top of the list and parents move down toward the bottom. Similar findings have been shown for youth in early adolescence (Alexander & Jurgenson, 1983). Moreover, the messages offered to youth from media and peers differ from those provided by parents. Parents tend to relate the message that sex is something that should be delayed, avoided, and risky. In sharp contrast, peers and the media tend to characterize sex as positive, fun, natural, and casual (Epstein & Ward, 2008). Moreover, many forms of media also relay the importance of engaging in safe-sex practices (Brown & Strasburger, 2007).

Recent data suggest that for many teens, the messages provided by peers and the media are having a bigger impact on sexual behavior than those provided by parents. According to a 2005 survey conducted by the Centers for Disease Control (CDC), 34% of ninth graders, 43% of 10th graders, 51% of 11th graders, and 63% of 12th graders reported having sexual intercourse at least once in their lifetime. By the time they graduated from high school, over 50% of adolescents stated that they engaged in oral sex, and 14% claimed to have had sex with four or more partners (CDC, 2006). In 2006, 22 out of every 1,000 adolescent females between the ages of 15 and 17 became pregnant, and 26% of all adolescent girls were diagnosed with a sexually transmitted disease (STD). It is quite apparent that a significant number of adolescents ignore parental admonitions about premarital sex, as well as media-based messages about engaging in safe sex, as the rates for pregnancy, birth, STDs, and abortion among teenagers in the United States are considerably higher than rates in most developed countries (e.g., Canada, England, France, Ireland, the Netherlands, Sweden, and Japan; CDC, 2008).

So, to what extent do media-based sexualization of youth and exposure to sexual content in the media impact the sexual socialization of youth? If you ask teens directly, rarely is media indicated as an influence on their current level of sexual activity. Instead intimacy, pleasure, and social status are the top three reasons given by teenagers for both sexual intercourse and noncoital sexual behaviors. For instance, in an assessment of ninth graders, pleasure (35%), improving relationships (30%) and popularity and reputation (25%) topped the list as justifications for having oral sex. In contrast, media was listed as a justification for this behavior less than 2% of the time (Cornell & Halpern-Felsheret, 2006; Ott, Millstein, Ofnter, & Halpern-Felsher, 2006). Another study found that only 6% of adolescents felt that televised sexual content affected their own sexual behavior "a lot." Interestingly, 32% of teens felt that sexual behaviors on TV strongly influenced their peers' sexual activities (Kaiser Family Foundation, 1998). Nevertheless, just because adolescents perceive sexual media to have very little effect on their own sexual decision making does not actually mean that sexual media has no effect. To fully address this issue, the frequency and nature of sexually related content in the media will first be reported. Subsequently, I will evaluate the impact of encountering sexual material on the sexual attitudes, expectations, and behaviors of youth.

Sexual Media

The media is filled with sexual content: Magazines such as *Playboy* and *Playgirl* show women and men in various stages of undress, whereas others (e.g., *Club Confidential*) depict sexual acts; on television, both soft-core and hard-core pornography are available on pay-per-view or subscription movie channels; music lyrics portray sex acts in subtle or not-so-subtle ways; and on the Internet, thousands of sexual images and porn sites are just a click away. Rather than reviewing the prevalence of all sexual media, in the sections below, I review the amount and type of sexual material that children and adolescents are most likely to encounter.

Sexual Content Observed by Children and Adolescents

Advertisements
Picture a man and woman, both attractive, in a passionate embrace, eyes closed, lips parted and inches away from touching. His long-sleeve shirt is fully buttoned; her shirt is mostly unbuttoned, nearly fully exposing a breast. Is this a magazine advertisement for erectile dysfunction? Not even close! Rather, it was an advertisement for Guess apparel. The successful use of sexual images and overtones (i.e., sex appeal) in advertising for products not directly related to sexual activity has been documented for well over 120 years. For instance, during the early 1910s, Woodbury's facial soap sales increased following an advertising campaign utilizing images of romantic couples. Sexual appeal in advertising can take many forms, including body display (e.g., partial nudity, or well-defined physiques), sexual behavior (i.e., provocative, nonexplicit, behavioral displays), sexual referents (e.g., locations, music, and/or lighting), and sexual embeds or symbolism (e.g., a key inserted into a lock; Reichert, 2003).

According to recent research, sexual content appears infrequently during prime-time television commercials, only occurring in about 1 in every 80 ads (1.2%). Rarely do current ads contain any explicit sexual behavior; instead, sexual content is limited to revealing clothing and innuendo (Hestroni, 2007a). Just a decade earlier, 21% of television commercials contained sexual content (Reichert, 2003). Fear of FCC fines for indecency has been credited with the aforementioned reduction (Hestroni, 2007b). When sexual objectification does occur in commercials, it usually involves female models. For instance, Fullerton and Kendrick (2001) found that 12% of women and 2% of males were provocatively dressed during prime-time television advertisements.

With apparent little concern of government fines, print advertisements are far more salacious than those aired on television, demonstrating higher levels of body exposure and heterosexual behavior. When men and women are depicted *together* in a magazine advertisement, sexually suggestive contact is portrayed more than half the time (Reichert, Lambiase, Morgan, Carstarphen, & Zavoina, 1999). When appearing alone, however, females, more so than males, tend to be the focal point for sexual objectification. Reichert and colleagues (1999) found that revealing clothing was more than twice as likely to be worn by women in magazine advertisements, relative to men. More recently, a study of close to 2,000 advertisements in 58 popular magazines found that 52% of advertisements presented women as sex objects. However, additional analyses indicated that the amount of sexual objectification in advertisements varied by magazine type, with more than 6 out of 10 ads that objectify women appearing in magazines that target a teen audience. Overall, advertisement in men's magazines (e.g., *Maxim* and *ESPN*) sexually objectified women the most, followed by magazines for teenage girls (e.g., *Cosmo Girl* and *Teen People*), women's magazines (e.g., *Self* and *Vogue*), magazines focusing on entertainment (e.g., *National Enquirer* and *Entertainment Weekly*) and news and business magazines (*Time* and *Newsweek*; Stankiewicz & Rosselli, 2008). See Figure 9.1.

Magazines

When the data are averaged together, magazines popular with adolescents (e.g., *Teen People* and *Teen Style*) appear to contain relatively few instances of sexual material. As an example, Pardun and colleagues (2005) found content related to sexuality in only 8% of magazines read by early and middle adolescents. However, just as the sexual content of advertisements varies by magazine type, so too do the amount and type of sexual material found in the magazines directed at youth. Headlines related to sex, such as "Orgasms Dos and Don'ts" and "Your Body: What Turns Him On," are commonplace in fashion and women's magazines. In fact, sex and romance constitute the most frequently written about topic in magazines read by teenage girls and women;

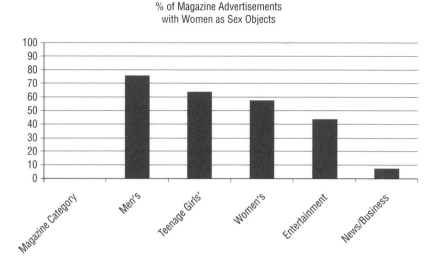

Figure 9.1   Sexual objectification in magazine advertisements.

with one study reporting that 21% of headlines focused on issues of sexuality (Davalos, Davalos, & Layton, 2007).

Typically, the photographs, articles, and cover lines in these magazines convey one simple message: Looking "hot" and being "sexy" comprise the primary way to attract the opposite sex. Yet, conflicting messages are also given, as magazines also tend to portray the sexual nature of men and women in a manner consistent with a sexual double standard, in which sexuality is controlled, restricted, and punished for females but tolerated and encouraged for males. In addition, whereas magazines typically describe males as having a near insatiable sexual appetite, female sexual behavior is characterized as being cautious, discreet, and responsible (Ward, 2003). Of note, explicit discussion of sexual content is not limited to magazines targeting an adult audience, as teen magazines frequently discuss issues of sexuality. One study found that 52% of articles in *Seventeen* focused on sexual behavior and health (Carpenter, 1998).

It almost goes without saying that many teenagers read magazines meant for a much older audience. For instance, I have a "friend" who when visiting his grandparents would always use the master bedroom bathroom, for that was where the stash of porno magazines was kept. My "friend's" experience is not uncommon, as by age 15, virtually all

Table 9.1   Some Recent Hit Songs That Sexualize Women and Reached the #1 Position on Billboard's Hot 100

- Mariah Carey (2008), "Touch My Body"
- Usher (2008), "Love in This Club"
- Lil Wayne (2008), "Lollipop"
- Flo Rida (2009), "Right Round"
- Emimen, Dr. Dre, and 50 Cent (2009), "Crack a Bottle"

adolescent males (92%) and most adolescent females (84%) have been exposed to nudity and sexual content in adult-oriented magazines. Another study found that adolescents' initial exposure to pornographic magazines occurred during early adolescence, 5 years before the magazines could be legally purchased by them (Bryant & Brown, 1989).

Music and music videos
Relative to other traditional media popular with youth, music and music videos contain the greatest proportion of sexual content. As an example, Pardun and colleagues (2005) recently found that 40% of the lyrics listened to by teens contain both direct and indirect references to sexuality. In contrast, movies, TV, and magazines lagged far behind (12%, 11%, and 8%, respectively). The sexual content associated with music becomes even more prevalent in accompanying music videos. Content analyses of music videos conducted across multiple decades indicate that between 44% and 81% of music videos depict revealing clothing, sexual readiness, indications of sexual behavior, and sexual innuendo (Zurbriggen et al., 2007). As before, sexual objectification in music videos (involving revealing clothing, provocative dancing, and the like) is much more likely to involve female characters than male ones. For instance, Seidman (1992) found that women were provocatively dressed in 37% of music videos; only 4% of men could be described similarly. Table 9.1 presents a list of recent hit songs that sexualize women.

Television
During the average prime-time television hour, the typical viewer will encounter about four instances of sexual talk (e.g., jokes, innuendo, and double entendres), but less than one instance of touching, kissing,

or implied sexual intercourse. Put another way, for every 50 hours of television programming watched, viewers will see an implied act of explicit sexual behavior only once. In fact, the frequency of sexual content during prime time has been decreasing ever since its peak during the late 1970s (Hestroni, 2007b). Once again, concerns about FCC fines have led to this reduction. However, when the popularity of shows among teenagers is taken into consideration, the proportion of sexual material encountered increased. Pardun and colleagues (2005) found that 11% of the total televised content typically viewed by teens is sexual in nature. Similarly, Kunkel and colleagues (2005) demonstrated that 70% of the top 20 shows popular with teens display at least one instance of sexual content, averaging nearly seven scenes per hour. Of these, around two involve some form of sexual behavior (e.g., touching or kissing). Sexual content is not limited to prime-time or live-action programming, for that matter. Fisher and colleagues (2004) found in a sampling of 121 children's cartoons that 26% of the episodes had sexual content and 21% had some mild sexual interactions (e.g., flirting, kissing, or touching); however, there were no instances of explicit sexual behavior. Moreover, the animated movies of today (e.g., *Little Mermaid* and *Pocahontas*) depict female leads wearing skimpier clothing and showing more cleavage then the animated movies of yesteryear (e.g., *Snow White* and *Cinderella*; Zurbriggen et al., 2007).

Movies

Despite the fact that adolescents attend movies to a greater extent than any other age group, little is known about the sexual content of the films that they view. The most recent assessment, which assessed sexuality depicted within the 50 top-grossing films of 1996, found that 57% of R-rated movies contained at least one sex scene. Comparatively, one third of PG- rated and one third of PG-13-rated movies depicted sex. Sex scenes were absent from movies rated G (Bufkin & Eschholz, 2000). Other studies have found that females are four times more likely to appear nude in R-rated films, relative to men (Zurbriggen et al., 2007). Although R-rated films are limited to patrons 17 years of age and older, younger adolescents have relatively little difficulty seeing the film. A recent study by the Federal Trade Commission Report (FTC; 2004), found that 25% of 13-year-olds, 29% of 14-year-olds, 35% of 15-year-olds, and 62% of 16-year-olds were able to buy tickets to an R-rated movie without parental consent. Teens were even more successful at buying DVDs from merchants, with 79% of 13-year-olds, 82% of 14-year-olds, 79% of 15-year-olds, and 92% of 16-year-olds purchasing an R-rated DVD without a parent or guardian being present. Where there is a will, there is a way.

Video games

Unlike video games meant for children, video games meant for adolescents and adults (rated T or M) present a significant proportion of female characters in a highly sexualized manner. For instance, in the *Grand Theft Auto* series, women, and in particular minority women, were portrayed as prostitutes (Dill, Gentile, Richter, & Dill, 2005). Such sexualized females tend to wear very revealing clothing, exposing arms, bellies, legs, and cleavage. For instance, nearly 50% of the female characters assessed wore either halter tops, tank tops, or bathing suits (Beasley & Standley, 2002). A separate study found that close to 20% of hypersexualized female characters exposed their midriffs, with an additional 7–8% of females fully exposing their breast and/or buttocks (M-rated games only). Although less sexualized, about 37% of female avatars in E-rated games wore revealing clothing or were partially nude. Male characters tend to wear revealing clothing about half as often as female characters. More often than not, male exposure of skin was meant to highlight overdeveloped muscles (Children Now, 2001). Similarly, sexual themes (i.e., partial nudity, sexual dialogue, and sexual behavior) have been observed in a significant number of T-rated and M-rated video games (27% and 36%, respectively; Haninger & Thompson, 2004; Thompson, Tepichin, & Haninger, 2006).

Internet

By all indications, the musical *Avenue Q* was correct: The Internet was indeed made for porn. There are websites dedicated to adult film stars and their movies, search engines specifically programmed to track down pornographic material, file-sharing programs for downloading porn for free, and blogs and moblogs for uploading homemade pornography, including pictures taken on cell phones. There are websites committed to the display of erotic art, erotic stories, erotic pictures, and erotic videos involving men, women, and/or cartoon characters. Name a fetish, be it animal, vegetable, or mineral, and there is a website promoting it. If so inclined, a person could create an avatar version of him or herself, visit a SIMS-like online bar, "pick up" a date, go to a private chat room, and engage in video-camera-enabled sex. All of the aforementioned websites are legal, as long as the pornographic participants and viewers are 18 years of age. Although access to most pornographic sites require an "age check," free sites simply have the visitor "agree" that they are 18 or over, without any verification of its veracity.

Exposure to pornography on the web by youth occurs both purposefully and by accident. One recent study found that 42% of adolescent Internet users were exposed to online explicit sexual content within the previous year. Of those, 66% report that the viewing of pornographic content was by accident. Unwanted exposure to pornography most often occurred after using a search engine and clicking on resultant links or through pop-up advertisements. Across development, the purposeful viewing of Internet porn increased with age, but varied by gender. For boys, 1% of 10- to 11-year-olds, 11% of 12- to 13-year-olds, 26% of 14- to 15-year-olds, and 38% of 16- to 17-year-olds reported successfully seeking out online sexually explicit content. The percentages for girls were far lower, with only 2% to 5% of girls visiting X-rated websites on purpose, and by age 16 to 17, only 8% of girls reported seeking out online pornography (Wolak, Mitchell, & Finkelhor, 2007). However, these data may underestimate actual exposure to online sexually explicit content, as other studies consistently report that around 70% of late adolescents have been exposed to Internet pornography (Peter & Valkenburg, 2007; Zurbriggen et al., 2007).

Sexualization of Youth in the Media

Children

Although the sexualization of adult men and women is commonplace in the media, the sexualization of children and adolescents occurs far less often. For instance, over a 40-year period, only 38 ads (1.5%) in popular magazines could be viewed as depicting children in a sexual way, with girls being sexualized in 85% of these ads (O'Donohue, Gold, & McKay, 1997). Rarely are prepubescent children sexualized on screen, with the exception of dramas related to sexual abuse. In such instances, the sexual encounters are never pleasurable, and the consequences are always severe.

Adolescents

With regard to teens, Kunkel and colleagues (2005) found that during prime time, only 3% of televised scenes implied sexual intercourse involved teens. However, just a few years earlier, 32% of shows with sexual content depicted adolescents talking about or engaging in sexual intercourse (Kunkel et al., 2003). In a sampling of shows with television characters aged 12 to 22, Aubrey (2004) found that 91% of episodes contained at least one sexual reference, with an average of eight sexual references per hour of programming. Thus, the presence or absence of sexualized adolescents on TV can vary from year to year, and from show to show.

It is important to note that the majority of televised sexual activity appears to occur without consequence, either positive or negative. Aubrey found that following teenage sexual activity, negative physical (e.g., STD or pregnancy; 5.5%) and emotional consequences (e.g., humiliation or guilt; 24%) were uncommon, and positive consequences of sex (e.g., increases in self-esteem and pride) occurred even more rarely (4%). Such data are consistent with other studies findings that "risks and responsibilities" of sexual activity are discussed around 5% of the time (Kunkel et al., 2003). Aubrey's (2004) study also demonstrated the presence of a sexual double standard for adolescent males and females. For instance, negative consequences were more likely to occur during scenes in which teenage girls initiated sexual activities, in comparison to when teenage boys did.

In contrast to televised media, the sexualization of youth is far more common in print media. In order to attract boys, *Seventeen* tells teenage girls that they should present themselves submissively, alluringly, and with an appealing physical appearance. Even self-improvement tips given to readers are geared toward gaining the attention of boys. Recent tag lines on the cover of *Seventeen* read, "Look Hot" and "Get Irresistible Lips." Conversely, adolescent males tend to be portrayed as either inept romantic partners or sexually obsessed. Also, teen-centric magazines tend to focus on sexual pleasure more so than sexual health (Hust, Brown, & L'Engle, 2008). One study examining the content of *Seventeen* found that only 3% of the articles addressed STDs and 2% dealt with the issue of teen pregnancy. It is worth noting that sexuality and health advice columns in *Seventeen* offer up extremely explicit talk about sex. From 1982 to 2001, 25% of the sex advice dealt with the issue of virginity, and in particular discussing which sexual acts (e.g., partial insertion of penis, fingering, and oral sex) actually constitute a loss of virginity (Garner, Sterk, & Adams, 1998; Medley-Rath, 2007). Similar content can be found on the website of *Seventeen* (www.seventeen.com), which has an entire section devoted to "health+sex+fitness." Sexually related questions are asked by girls of all ages, with their age posted next to their question (e.g., "Is it safe and normal to have sex while you have your period? Kathleen, Age15").

When she was just 17, Britney Spears burst onto the music scene with her #1 song "Hit Me Baby One More Time." The music video featured Spears in Lolita fashion, donning pigtails and a school uniform as she danced around in a short skirt with her bare midriff on display. Though the percentage of videos featuring the sexualization of teenage girls is unknown, the video illustrates a phenomenon known as "pedophilic fashion," in which older teens and young women are dressed up as little girls (Kilbourne, 1999; Zurbriggen et al., 2007). For instance, during a televised *Victoria's Secret* fashion show in 2005, one segment involved having sexy models walk down the runway, which was surrounded by toys, wearing baby doll teddies and pulling stuffed animals.

Rather than simply observing the sexualization of youth (as occurs in traditional media), the Internet sadly affords children and adolescents the opportunity to experience sexualization directly. One recent study found that 13% of 10- to 17-year-old Internet users report being sexually solicited (e.g., asked about personal sexual information) in the past year. Additionally, 4% of these youth experienced aggressive sexual solicitation (i.e., an attempt was made to make offline contact). Most solicitations came from online acquaintances who youth did not know in person (86%), with 61% of the solicitors being self-described as teenagers themselves (though their true age is not known; Wolak et al., 2007). Noteworthy is the fact that the rate of sexual solicitation went up for youth who frequently posted personal information online and/or communicated with others through chat, IM, and social-networking sites. For instance, Mitchel and colleagues (2008) found that for adolescents who either blogged and/or personally communicated with others on the Internet within the past year, 85% were subject to some form of sexual solicitation, with nearly a quarter of adolescents being aggressively solicited for sex. Regardless of who started the conversation, 34% of adolescents report talking about sex.

The Effects of Viewing Sexual Media on Adolescents

Research on the effects of a sexual media diet on youth has focused on three main outcomes related to sexuality: attitudes, expectations, and behavior. Sexual attitudes refer to the extent to which adolescents believe sex to be recreational, risk free, and superficial. Thoughts surrounding the social reality of sex (e.g., what is normal and prevalent) constitute sexual expectations and attributions. Finally, sexual behavior refers to the types of sexual activities that youth engage in. Each is addressed in turn. Of note, due to ethical considerations, there are no experimental studies in which aspects of adolescent sexuality are assessed following exposure to explicit sexual content. For similar reasons, there are no studies (of any design type) involving the effects of sexual media on youth in early or middle childhood.

Attitudes Toward Sex

Although the frequency and nature of sexual content in the media have been consistently researched over a period of decades, far fewer studies have assessed the impact of sexual media on adolescents' attitudes related to sexuality. However, the studies that have been conducted suggest that explicit sexual media does, in fact, impact sexual attitudes. For instance, adolescents who have watched X-rated movies report a greater dislike toward condom use, relative to other youth (Wingood et al., 2001). Another study found that, across adolescence, watching sexually oriented television shows was associated with a greater permissiveness toward sex (Ward, 2003). Other research has found that adolescents with high levels of exposure to sexual content on television felt dissatisfied with being a virgin (Courtright & Baran, 1980) and normalized unusual sexual activities (e.g., group sex; Greenberg & Smith, 2002). Recently, Peter and Valkenburg (2007) found that higher levels of sexual media consumption were linked with stronger beliefs that women are sex objects. Importantly, the aforementioned association was hierarchical in nature, with exposure to explicit sexual content (e.g., pornography) creating this attitude more strongly than nonexplicit sexual content (e.g., MTV videos). Taken together, these studies suggest that both the amount of sexual media encountered and the explicitness of the sexual media consumed can influence sexual attitudes.

Sexual Expectations and Attributions

Adolescents' perceptions of peer norms and behaviors are key factors in the decision to become sexually active. It may be hard for adolescents to abstain from sex when they perceive that "everyone is doing it." Indeed, believing that friends are sexually active is judged by adolescents to be a valid reason to initiate a sexual relationship (Rosenthal,

Senserrick, & Feldman, 2001). But do media depictions of sexual acts make them seem more widespread among peers than they really are? Perhaps, as research has shown that youth watching more talk shows or spending more time watching television (all types of shows) make higher estimations for their peers' level of sexual activity (Davis & Mares, 1998; Eggermont, 2005). Yet, these studies failed to assess the total amount of *sexual media* consumed, thereby making it possible to conjecture that nonsexual content (e.g., antisocial attitudes) accounted for the aforementioned findings. Interestingly, one recent study found that sexual media consumption and perceptions of peer norms about sexual issues were only indirectly related, with other sex-related factors mediating the relationship (e.g., perceived peer exposure to sex-related media and perceived influence of media on peers; Chia, 2006).

Sexual Behavior

Attempts to link the total amount of television consumed with adolescent sexual activity have failed to yield evidence of a significant connection between the two. This is not surprising given that total television viewing incorporates both sexual and nonsexual programs. In contrast, heavy viewing of sexual content during adolescence has been positively associated with increases in the onset of intercourse and the amount and type of noncoital sexual activity (e.g., breast and genital touching). Recently, Collins and colleagues (2004) found that, after statistically removing the influence of a wide range of social factors, teens who were heavy viewers of sexual content were twice as likely to engage in intercourse the following year in comparison to light viewers of sexual content. Furthermore, heavy television viewing was associated with more sexually advanced, noncoital sexual activity (e.g., genital touching). This artificial aging of adolescents' sexuality resulted in 12-year-olds engaging in sexual behavior consistent with that of a 14- or 15-year-old. Finally, these findings held for sexual media that was either physically depicted or inferred from dialogue. Thus, exposure to sexual content may influence adolescents' sexual activity regardless of whether it is seen or heard. Beyond television, additional research suggests that encountering sexual material in magazines, music, movies, and the Internet has the potential to impact adolescents' sexual behavior. One recent study of seventh and eighth graders found that greater consumption of sexual content in music, magazines, or movies predicted increased sexual activity (Pardun, L'Engle, & Brown, 2005).

It seems however, that sexual media may impact youth differently, depending upon the race of the consumer. Recently, Somers and Tynan (2006) found that sexual media was linked to adolescent sexual behavior for Whites but not African Americans. Similarly, Brown and colleagues (2006) demonstrated that White early adolescents with a heavy sexual media diet were twice as likely to engage in sexual intercourse during middle adolescence, relative to White youth with a limited exposure to sexual media. Even though African American adolescents had a larger sexual media diet than Whites, sexual media consumption played no role in predicting their sexual activities. Rather, for African American teens, parental and peer influences were the prominent predictors of sexual behavior. Interestingly, in both studies, African American teens were more sexually advanced, on average, than White teens. It may be that the ability of sexual media to impact adolescents' sexual behavior is more limited in youth who are already sexualized.

Additional research suggests that the sexual media influence may have the strongest impact on early adolescents with limited sexual experience. In support of this contention, Kim and colleagues (2006) found that early adolescents watched significantly more sexually oriented TV than older teens. As mentioned above, for early adolescents, heavier TV viewing was linked with a more rapid initiation of sexual intercourse the following year (Collins et al., 2004). Additionally, Tolman and colleagues (Tolman, Kim, Schooler, & Sorsoli, 2007) failed to find a connection between viewing sexual talk and sexual behavior on television with reported sexual behavior among ninth and 10th graders. As you recall, middle adolescents are more sexually advanced than early adolescents. Thus, it may be that by middle adolescence, sexual behaviors are sufficiently entrenched to limit the impact of sexualized media. As of yet, not enough research has been conducted to confirm or disconfirm this contention.

Although the Internet is teeming with sexual content, few studies have assessed its impact of teenage sexual behavior. I could find no studies involving Internet effects on an adolescent sample. In fact, the lone study related to adolescence is a retrospective online study involving adults in their late 20s. Findings from that study indicate that adults who had accessed Internet pornography between ages 12 and 17 reported younger ages for sexual initiation, compared to participants without access to online sexual content (Kraus & Russell, 2008). However, it was unclear as to whether the viewing of Internet pornography occurred before or after the loss of virginity.

Additional research indicates that, beyond sexual media consumption, the nature of the sexual media (e.g., explicit, degrading, or innuendo) encountered may also be an important determinant of future sexual activities during adolescence. For instance, using a sample of 12- to 17-year-olds, Martino and colleagues (2008) found that frequent listening to sexually degrading lyrics, but not sexual lyrics, was associated with a range of sexual behaviors, including noncoital activities and sexual intercourse. Because such distinctions have not been made in other media, it is difficult to know if the above effect was idiosyncratic to music lyrics or characteristic of all media.

Developmental Points of Interest

Currently, there is relatively little explicit sexual content in most media aimed at a youthful audience. That is not to say, however, that sexual content is absent from media that children and adolescents frequently encounter. For instance, sexually suggestive clothing and sexual objectification of females have become commonplace in a variety of different media, including animated films and video games. Moreover, popular music (and accompanying video) and certain teen-centric magazines (including the advertisements within and their online companion websites) offer up plenty of sexual fare. The sexual content of these types of magazines is particularly noteworthy because it involves teenagers; thus providing youth with a sexualized vision of adolescence. Given that the intended audience for the teen magazine is between 13 to 19 years of age, and that younger girls comprise part of their readership, such magazines may be normalizing sexual behavior for all teenagers, even those not yet old enough to understand the physical and psychological consequences of sexual relationships.

Along with peers, the media's portrayal of sex appears to be an important influence in adolescents' decision making regarding sexual activity, as sexual attitudes, expectations, and behaviors are all affected by it. In fact, media is frequently described as an encouraging and sympathetic "super peer" that affirms the appropriateness of adolescents' sexual activities. In support of this contention, L'Engle and colleagues (2006) found that teenagers perceiving the media to be supportive of teenage sexual relationships reported more sexual activity than other youth. However, the vast majority of research in this area

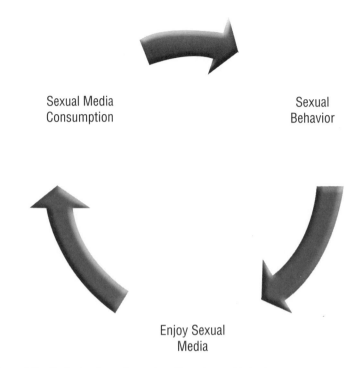

Sexual Media
Consumption

Sexual
Behavior

Enjoy Sexual
Media

Figure 9.2   Cyclical pattern of sexual media and sexual behavior.

has focused on only one medium, television. Currently, few studies have been conducted on the effects of advertising, magazines, music, video games, and the Internet on adolescents' sexual attitudes and behaviors. In fact, only 1% of studies relating adolescent sexuality with sexual media have addressed this issue (Escobar-Chaves et al., 2005).

Numerous studies have clearly linked the consumption of sexual media with both the initiation of sexual activity and the sexual aging of adolescents. It is important to remember that romantic and sexual relationships are both novel and important to the adolescent experience. As such, many teenagers seek out information from the media to help them traverse the new sexual landscape before them. In fact, sexually intrigued teens consume more sexual media than other youth (Kim et al., 2006). Taken together, these studies provide empirical evidence for a reciprocal and reinforcing relationship in which media influences the onset and trajectory of sexual activities. In turn, engaging in sexual activities leads youth to seek out more sexual media (see Figure 9.2).

Finally, to date, no study has assessed the influence of media, in which younger teen characters behave in a sexual manner, on adolescent's sexual attitudes, expectations, and behaviors. Do media depictions of *teen* sexual activity, relative to similar behaviors performed by adults, lead to more permissive attitudes toward sex, increase the perceived frequency of sex among real-life peers, and sexually advance youth? Only more research will tell.

10

Violent Media Part 1

Comic Books, Music, and Video Games

For decades, the impact of violent media on youth has been debated. Some have argued that media violence is harmful to children and adolescents, a bonafide health threat on par with the danger that smoking poses to youth (Anderson & Bushman, 2001). In fact, as early as the 1940s, magazine articles warned that violent comic books and violent television, with their portrayals of rape, murder, and assault, were training grounds for criminals, putting youth on the pathway to juvenile delinquency (Kirsh, 2006). Others have said that such claims are overstated and that media violence may actually be good for youth. For instance, Jones (2002) contended that violent video games help children and adolescents feel strong, powerful, and in control of their lives. Others, like Bettelheim (1967), have suggested that exposure to violent imagery, such as that depicted in *Grimm Brothers' Fairy Tales*, can have a cathartic effect on the child, resulting in the purging of aggressive impulses. As interesting as these latter claims may be, however, there are no data to support them (Kirsh, 2006). In contrast, there is plenty of evidence to suggest that violent media, both directly and indirectly, impacts aggression in youth. Although hundreds of studies have investigated the effects of televised media violence on children and adolescents (Paik & Comstock, 1994), the impact of violence in other media has received significantly less empirical attention. Addressed in the current chapter are three of these underresearched areas, namely, comic books, music, and, surprisingly, video games. Of note, the influence of violent cartoons and live-action programming on youth will be addressed in the next chapter. However, prior to reviewing the literature, a bit of background knowledge on aggression is needed.

A Brief Primer on Aggression

Human aggression refers to any action intended to cause emotional, physical, psychological, or social injury to another. When done purposefully, each of the following is considered to be an act of aggression: hitting, name calling, yelling, spreading rumors, teasing, stabbing, and shooting. As these examples illustrate, aggressive acts can vary in both intensity and severity. As such, the term *violence* is reserved for acts of aggression that lead to serious physical and/or psychological harm. When studying media violence, the devil really is in the details, for just as the intensity of aggressive acts differ from situation to situation, so too do the outcomes associated with media violence exposure. In particular, violent media can impact both aggressive behavior and aggression-related constructs.

There are three main types of aggressive behavior: physical, relational, and verbal. Physical aggression damages flesh and bone; relational aggression injures social relationships and/or level of group inclusion; and verbal aggression, through name calling and teasing, causes psychological harm (Crick, Grotpeter, & Bigbee, 2002). Both verbal and physical forms of aggression involve altercations that take place in person, and are thus direct in nature. In contrast, relational aggression can be either direct or indirect. In this latter form of aggression, direct confrontations do not occur; rather, the victimization takes place in a circuitous manner, through another person or with the aid of media (e.g., spreading a rumor on the Internet).

Aggression-related constructs refer to person-based factors that increase or decrease the likelihood that an individual will act aggressively. In particular, research has focused on four aggression-related constructs: aggressive emotions, aggressive traits, physiological factors associated with aggression, and aggressive thoughts. Feelings associated with the onset of aggressive acts (e.g., anger) as well as feelings that follow aggressive behavior (e.g., shame and guilt) comprise aggressive emotions. *Aggressive traits* refer to personality characteristics, such as impulse control and thrill seeking, which increase the likelihood that an individual will act aggressively. Changes in physiology associated with aggression, such as increased heart rate and blood pressure as well as the release of hormones, constitute physiological factors associated with aggression. Finally, aggressive thoughts are the cognitive processes accompanying the events surrounding aggressive acts, such as beliefs about the appropriateness of using aggression to solve problems and potential responses to an unprovoked act of aggression.

Both aggressive behavior and aggression-related constructs are important outcomes to consider when studying the impact of media violence on children and adolescents. The reason for studying aggressive behavior is clear: Aggression can be harmful to others. But aggression-related constructs cannot directly cause harm to another person. So why do researchers study them? Acts of aggression and violence are the end result of an internal process, a process in which aggressive thoughts, emotions, traits, and physiology reciprocally interact to influence the decision to act or not act aggressively (Anderson & Bushman, 2001). Thus, the degree to which media violence can alter aggression-related constructs (e.g., increasing aggressive thoughts, feelings, and associated hormones) becomes a crucial component in the internal process leading to the enactment of aggressive behavior.

Violent Comic Books

Through artistically rendered drawings and speech balloons, comic books relay a narrative story. There are over 15 different genres of comic books, including crime, horror, humor, science fiction, and pornographic. Depending on the genre and target audience of the comic book, the reader may encounter relational, verbal, and/or physical aggression, as well as depictions of violence. Comic books targeting children under the age of 10, such as *Rugrats* and *Archie*, may portray mild acts of aggression, with little or no violence. In contrast, comic books written for an older audience frequently contain extreme acts of violence (e.g., *Spawn* and *Evil Ernie*). In this latter type of comic book (which would be rated R if it were a movie), copious amounts of blood and gore are depicted, including amputations, decapitations, eviscerations, and bloody holes where tissue and bone used to be. Historically, the prototypical comic book reader was a 10- to 14-year-old boy. However, since the 1990s, nearly 25% of comic book sales have been generated by adults (Antonucci, 1998).

In comic books, unlike other media, story lines are presented in frames that are only partially continuous. For instance, in one frame of a comic book, a gun is shown with a fiery bullet an inch out of its barrel. In the next frame, a bloody, gaping hole is seen in the head of a prone victim. Although the impact of the bullet is not depicted, the reader can easily visualize the bullet tearing through flesh. Thus, when reading a comic book, children and adolescents are required to engage their imaginations and visualize the elements in the story that were not graphically portrayed (McCloud, 1993). Moreover, when reading a comic book, youth can self-regulate the intake of information. As such, children and adolescents can spend as much time as they like reading dialogue and viewing graphic images, thus affording youth a detailed encoding of violent material.

Decades ago, concerned politicians believed that the engrossing nature of comic books, and the violent images depicted within, posed a grave threat to children. As an example, during the 1940s, nearly 50 cities attempted to ban the sale of comic books altogether. Some 10 years later, the first "scientific" research on this topic was conducted. Fredrick Wertham (1954), who published his findings in a book entitled *The Seduction of the Innocent*, concluded that comic book reading led to the following negative outcomes: illiteracy, racial prejudice, deviant sexual beliefs, and the endorsement of, and desire to follow, a lifestyle of delinquency (i.e., engaging in criminal behavior and acts of violence). However, the methods used by Wertham to collect data were extremely flawed (e.g., anecdotal), and have subsequently been discredited (Kirsh, 2006).

Beyond Wertham, the few empirical studies that have investigated the influence of comic book violence on youth have produced contradictory findings. For instance, in a sample of middle school-aged youth, Tan and Scruggs (1980) failed to find a significant relationship between reading violent comic books and indices of physical and verbal aggression. Similarly, Blakely (1958) found that exposure to violence in comic books was unrelated to behavior problems during early adolescence. Moreover, in an assessment of aggression-related constructs, comic book reading was not related to feelings of aggression in 12-year-olds (Brand, 1969). In contrast, Belson (1978) found that during adolescence, boys who frequently read violent comic books engaged in more acts of aggression and violence than other youth. Consistent with these findings, Hoult (1949) found that, in comparison to adolescents who have never been arrested, delinquent teens read more violent and crime-themed comic books. It is worth noting that no studies have been conducted on children in middle childhood or younger. In summary, there is little evidence to support the contention that reading violent comic books influences aggressive behavior or aggression-related constructs. However, with so little research done on the topic, and none from a developmental perspective, additional evidence is needed before any hard-and-fast conclusions can be drawn.

Music Violence

Violent Lyrics

Violent lyrical content can be found in a variety of musical genres, including rap, heavy metal, and country. At times, such lyrics describe or extol violence directed at the self, including suicide. At other times, the focus of violent lyrical content revolves around hurting somebody else. For instance, in the country hit "Goodbye Earl," the Dixie Chicks sing about the poisoning, murder, and disposal of an abusive husband. A more graphic version of murder can be found in a death metal song by Dismember called "Bleed for Me," which graphically describes slicing into a body while the victim's life slowly bleeds away. However, since the mid-1980s, it is the violent, misogynistic, homophobic, and antisocial lyrics of rap, and in particular gangsta rap, that have received considerable public criticism, with most of it being negative (Kurbin, 2005).

Gangsta rap, which started in the streets of South-Central Los Angeles and other urban areas of California, diverged from earlier genres of rap during the 1980s, which were more socially conscious and political. Artists such as NWA, Dr. Dre, Snoop Dogg, and Tupac Shakur quickly found success rapping about the violent aspects of gang and urban life from the perspective of a criminal. Not surprisingly, the impact of such violent lyrics on youth has been a cause of grave concern for over 2 decades. Exemplifying this point is the fact that nearly 50% of mothers with school-aged children believe that violent rap music is an important contributor to the problem of school violence (Kandakai, Price, Telljohann, & Wilson, 1999). Detractors of gangsta rap, and violent music lyrics in general, contend that violence in music exalts the aggressor and condones the excessive use of force, a critique that appears to be accurate. As an example, a recent analysis of rap lyrics found that aggressive and violent acts are frequently used in response to being disrespected or otherwise wronged. Moreover, rap lyrics suggest that it is *OK* to kill women who are disobedient, cheat on their lovers, or are rejecting of sexual advances (Adams & Fuller, 2006). To illustrate this point, consider "Stan" by Eminem, in which a women (described as being tied up) can be heard screaming in the trunk of a car. Thus, it is clear that such lyrics do extol the use of violence and glorify the aggressor. But do they impact aggressive behavior (directed at the self or others) and aggression-related constructs across development? Let us see.

Boulevard of Broken Lyrics?

The results of studies conducted more than 2 decades ago suggest that during adolescence, memory for lyrics is generally poor (there is no research on children). For instance, Desmond (1987) found that 60–70% of adolescents could not recall the lyrics to their favorite song. Unlike in the previous millennium, in which lyrics could only be found on album or tape inserts, today's youth can go online and look up lyrics. However, whether or not this increased accessibility to lyrics translates into better recall is unknown. Nevertheless, even when lyrics are correctly remembered, they are often subjectively experienced (Prinsky & Rosenbaum, 1987). In fact, the inability to correctly *interpret* lyrics is so commonplace that numerous websites (e.g., lyricinterpretations.com) have devoted themselves to deciphering musical prose. But when studying the influence of violent music on youth, is lyrical recall really that important? Not necessarily, as youth can be affected by the lyrics they are currently listening too, even if they cannot recall them hours or days later. All that needs to happen is that the lyrics be understood. Comprehension, in other words, is the key to influence.

Currently, there is little research on lyrical comprehension across development. The few studies that exist suggest that the ability to understand lyrics generally improves with age. However, it is not until early adolescence that the capacity to understand *abstract* lyrics becomes more commonplace (younger youth tend to interpret abstract lyrics in a literal fashion). For instance, Greenfield and colleagues (1987) found that 20% of fourth graders, 60% of eighth graders, and 95% of 12th graders correctly understood that, in the song "Born in the USA," the lyrics referred to being in a predicament. Moreover, the overarching abstract theme of despair and disillusionment that runs throughout the song was lost on most youth (only 40% of 12th graders correctly interpreted it). With regard to violent music, when lyrical comprehension is lacking, the ability to perceive underlying themes of violence becomes more difficult, and the negative effects associated with exposure are reduced. However, not all songs that youth listen to present abstract concepts. As the lyrics to "Bleed for Me" (discussed above) illustrate, the content of many violent songs is pretty straightforward: Shoot, kill, and maim. In fact, the lyrics of rap and heavy metal, with their common themes of violence and defiance of authority, are easily understood by most youth. Finally, adolescents are more likely to attend to, and comprehend, the lyrics of songs that they enjoy (Roberts & Christenson, 2001). Across development, does the liking of a song translate into a greater influence on aggression? Currently, there are no data to answer this very important question.

Violent Music and Aggressive Actions

Research on early childhood and middle childhood youth
To date, not a single study on the impact of violent music on youth has been conducted with children during early or middle childhood. Given that youth begin to listen to music alone several years prior to adolescence, it is astonishing that no research exists during the elementary school years. By contrast, the lack of research during early childhood is not nearly as surprising, as the idea of 4-year-olds willfully listening to death metal or gangsta rap on their own seems unlikely. However, even the youngest of children may be exposed to violent music through their older siblings and parents. For instance, my preschool-aged nephew, Jesse, was introduced to heavy metal (i.e., Slipknot's "Psychosocial") and rap (e.g., Beastie Boys' "Girls") through his older brothers, Jacob and Joshua. Jesse not only learned most of the lyrics to Eminem's "Just Lose it" but also imitated Eminem's rhythmic overhead hand movements as he sang along with the song. On youtube.com, there are many postings of preschool aged children singing and/or rapping along to adult-themed songs, such as "My Humps" and "Smack That." Thus, for many children, their first introduction to violent music is through a family member. Whether or not early exposure to violent lyrics influences aggression-related constructs and aggressive behavior during childhood, or even the future musical preferences of youth, is, however, unknown.

Research on adolescents
During adolescence, less than a handful of studies have assessed the impact of violent music on aggression (and none on aggression-related constructs). The results of several of these studies indicate that preference

for violent heavy metal and rap music is associated with verbal aggression, behavior problems in school, and street gang involvement (Atkin, Smith, Roberto, Fediuk, & Wagner, 2002; Miranda & Claes, 2004; Took & Weiss, 1994). However, because the aforementioned studies involved correlational designs, the possibility exists that both directionality and third variable issues were at play. With regard to directionality, rather than violent music *causing* deviant behavior, it may be that aggressive youth *prefer* to listen to violent music. In fact, there is research to support this contention (Gardstrom, 1999). Third variables, such as personality characteristics, could also explain the association between violent music and aggressive behavior. For instance, rebellious adolescents prefer music with defiant and antiestablishment themes, the lyrics of which are often violent (Carpentier, Knoblauch, & Zillmann, 2003). Even if the preference for violent music is the "effect" of an aggressive lifestyle rather than the "cause" of one, violent music may influence youth nonetheless. The phenomenon known as the downward spiral model provides the explanation. According to the downward spiral model, aggressive youth seek out violent media, which, in turn, reinforces and intensifies their aggressive behavior, aggression-related constructs, and desire for violent media. In the end, a negative feedback loop develops with both violent media and aggression stimulating and reinforcing one another (Slater, Henry, Swaim, & Anderson, 2003).

Violent Music Videos

As previously stated, musical lyrics are often difficult to interpret, especially if they are of an abstract nature and involve symbolic meaning. Such is the case for the lyrics to "Jeremy" by Pearl Jam, which discusses a boy talking in class, but doing so without saying a word. How do I know that the innocuous-sounding lyrics of the song are truly violent? The answer: I have seen the music video, during which an adolescent boy sticks a gun in his mouth and "speaks" to his classmates by pulling the trigger. As this example illustrates, music videos can provide clear and powerful visual images to accompany lyrics that, on their own, can be difficult to comprehend. Moreover, when the lyrical message is clear, the images found in music videos add an additional dimension of violence to the already violent lyrics; a double dose, if you will.

Unfortunately, the concern generated by violence in music videos has failed to engender a significant amount of research on youth. Only two studies have been published with adolescents and there are no published studies involving children. Moreover, the research that has been conducted has focused solely on the cognitive component of aggression-related constructs: namely aggressive attitudes and perceptions. Greeson and Williams (1986) found that 10th graders became less disapproving of violence after watching violent rap videos. However, no such differences were evident for seventh graders. Similarly, Johnson, Jackson, and Gatto (1995) found that adolescents watching violent rap music videos were more accepting of the use of violence to solve problems than youth watching nonviolent videos. Taken together, these two studies suggest that violent music videos have the potential to influence the cognitive component of aggression-related constructs. What remains to be seen, however, is the extent to which music videos impact other aggression-related constructs and/or aggressive behavior across development.

Violent Music and Suicide

According to recent statistics, suicide is the third leading cause of death for adolescents 15 years of age and older (Center for Disease Control and Prevention, 2006). As such, the identification of factors that increase the likelihood that an adolescent will attempt suicide is of great importance. For decades, the lyrical content of music has been suspected to be one of those potential influences (Brown & Hendlee, 1989). Songs about suicide are found in nearly all genres of music, including rap, country, and opera. However, it is heavy metal that has been consistently singled out as a potential *cause* of suicide during adolescence. For instance, the lyrics to Alice in Chains' "Dirt," which describe placing a gun in one's mouth and the aftermath of pulling the trigger, commend the use of suicide as a form of revenge.

The themes of alienation, death, and despair that frequent many heavy metal songs would seem to put adolescents at risk for suicide. However, adolescents with a preference for heavy metal music also tend to have many other risk factors for suicide, including depression, delinquency, and family conflict. When such factors are taken into consideration, the apparent link between heavy metal music and suicide is broken. Thus, there is no direct evidence to support the contention that heavy metal music, or any other genre of music for that matter, causes suicidal behavior among adolescents (e.g., Scheel & Westefeld, 1999).

Nevertheless, there is evidence to suggest that frequent listening to music with suicidal themes indicates the presence of suicidal ideation. Suicidal ideation refers to both nonspecific thoughts of death and specific thoughts involving the intent to die, accompanied by a plan of action. Accordingly, an intense focus on lyrics involving death and suicide would constitute suicidal ideation. Although suicidal ideation is not considered to be a threat of imminent suicide, the American Academy of Child and Adolescent Psychiatry suggested that youth preoccupied with suicidal and mortality focused lyrics themes should be considered for a mental health evaluation (Alessi, Huang, James, Ying, & Chowhan, 1992).

Violent Video Games

In 1962, the first violent video game was released. Spacewar, as it was called, was a mainframe computer game in which two spaceships battled to the death in head-to-head competition. Although the graphics were crude by today's standards (the spaceships looked like a small needle and a triangular wedge), Spacewar quickly became an online success. However, it was not until 1976, with the commercial release of Death Race, that a violent video game became the source of public concern. The object of this electronic arcade game was to run over tiny black and white stick figures, called "gremlins," that, when hit, screamed and turned into crosses. The controversy over *Death Race* was so great that the video game was quickly pulled from store shelves. Since the late 1970s, the furor over video game violence has never really died down.

Fueled by school shootings, in which many of the perpetrators reported a penchant for violent video game play, the controversy surrounding the impact of violent video games has grown worldwide. In the United States, Senate subcommittees have held hearings on the potential impact of violent video games on children and adolescents. In Germany, because it is illegal to take a virtual human life, video game avatars are depicted as humanoid robots that release springs when wounded or killed; and in Australia, violent video games such as Manhunt and Grand Theft Auto III have been banned from public sale. Nevertheless, violent video games have been incredibly popular for over 2 decades and today are consistently among the top-selling video games. For instance, on its first day of release, the violent video game

Halo 3 racked up $170 million in sales. Just as impressive, that same day more than 1 million people played the game online (McDougall, 2007).

Violent Video Games and Increasing Realism

Over the past 30 years, video game technology has dramatically improved. Far from the abstract and sticklike representations of the human form of yesteryear, modern graphics render bodies that are authentic looking when whole and just as lifelike when holes have been ripped into them by bullets, arrows, and machetes. In fact, many of the "violent" video games of the 1970s, such as Missile Command and Asteroids, would be considered minimally violent or even nonviolent today. When comparing violent and nonviolent video games, the relative difference between the two, in terms of the perceived level of violence, has become greater over time (Gentile & Anderson, 2003). Thus, when investigating the influence of violent video game play on children and adolescents, the technology involved during game play becomes an important consideration.

Based on the degree of graphic realism, Gentile and Anderson (2003) have divided the history of video games into three eras: Atari (1977–1985), Nintendo (1985–1995), and Sony (1995–present). During the Atari era, violent video games rarely involved humanoid violence. Instead, games such as Defender and Centipede required simple geometric shapes and/or drawings to destroy other simple geometric shapes and/or drawings. As video game technology improved, the number of violent video games using humanoid forms increased. In fact, it was during the Nintendo era that many violent video game series that continue today, such as Street Fighter and Mortal Kombat, were first introduced. It was also during the Nintendo era that realistic representations of violent actions, like punching and shooting, resulted in realistic outcomes, such as bleeding and dismemberment. For instance, one of the special killing moves in Mortal Kombat II resulted in the opponent's torso being ripped in half, blood spurting into the air, as the word *fatality* appeared on the screen. Such graphic realism involving violence and gore continued to increase during the Sony era. Moreover, improvements in gaming software allowed virtual bodies to move about the virtual environment and respond to the physical world in a more lifelike fashion. For violent video games, this meant characters shot in the head fall to the ground differently then characters shot in the chest.

Over time, such technological improvements have led to the incredibly realistic representations of violent actions and their outcomes, found in modern video games.

Violent Video Games and Youth: Effects of Era, Age, and Research Design

As you recall, different conclusions can be drawn from correlational and experimental studies, with causality only being associated with the latter. Moreover, each type of design has its own unique strengths and weaknesses. For instance, because aggressive behaviors shown in laboratory experiments (e.g., lacing food with hot sauce and blasting white noise) are so distinctly different from most acts of real-life aggression (e.g., hitting), many scientists believe that these types of experiments have low external validity (Ritter & Eslea, 2005). In contrast, Anderson and Bushman (1997) contended that laboratory and real-life aggression are conceptually similar (they both deal with aggression) and are therefore high in external validity. In other words, increases in aggressive behavior observed in the laboratory following violent video game play should also occur following violent video game play in the home or in an arcade. However, aggressive behavior is less likely to be observed in real life because the environmental conditions surrounding aggressive actions are very different in the experimentally controlled environment of a laboratory (which are set up to allow for aggressive actions) and the parentally controlled environments of home and school (which are set up to prevent aggressive actions). Given these differences, the research presented below will be reviewed by research design, in addition to video game era and age.

Atari era

Correlational research   The first purported link between aggressive behavior and video game play was established during the Atari era. Studies by both Dominick (1984) and Kestenbaum and Weinstein (1985) found associations between video game play and delinquency during early adolescence. Unfortunately, not a single study conducted during this era assessed the relationship between *violent* video game play and aggression. Rather, it was the total amount of video game play, in general, that was related to aggressive outcomes. There are two potential interpretations of these data. First, it may be that, regardless of content, video game play influences aggression via activation of aggression-related constructs. However, this contention can be discarded, as most theories of aggression contend that aggressive behavior results from youth encountering *violent* content. Saying general video game play influences aggression is like saying eating leads to heart disease. Although there may be some truth to the statement, it is not nearly specific enough to have any practical utility. Second, video game play may have been predictive of aggression because youth spending the greatest amount of time in arcades happened to be more aggressive than other youth to begin with. As an example, delinquent youth may eschew interacting with their family members in order to "hang out" with friends in entertaining locations, like arcades, for long periods of time. Of note, few homes had video game consoles during the Atari era.

Experimental research In contrast to Atari era correlational research, experimental studies conducted during this time period did evaluate the impact of *violent* video games on youth. However, the results of these studies were far from impressive. Across middle childhood and adolescence, not a single study found any evidence that violent video game play affected either aggressive behavior or aggression-related constructs (Kirsh, 2006). The lone study finding an effect assessed the influence of violent video games on peer-directed aggression during free play (i.e., children interact in an unstructured setting) in early childhood (Silvern & Williamson, 1987). However, one of the major critiques levied against this type of "free-play" assessment is that observations of "aggression" may be in actuality instances of rough-and-tumble play. Rough-and-tumble play is a nonaggressive, high-action activity involving running, chasing, jumping, and wrestling. During rough-and-tumble play, children smile, cooperate, take turns, and engage in role reversals. Moreover, after the roughhousing has ended, children continue to play with one another (Pelligrini, 2002). Unfortunately, Silvern and Williamson (1987) did not differentiate rough-and-tumble play from aggressive behavior in their study. Thus, the possibility exists that preschoolers got excited (physiologically aroused) while playing the "violent" video game, which then carried over into their play in a nonaggressive manner.

Nintendo era
Similar to the Atari era, correlational research conducted during the Nintendo era found significant associations between *general* video game

play and aggression. Unfortunately, just like before, these newer findings are also called into question because the amount of *violent* video game play was not assessed (Fling et al., 1992; Lin & Lepper, 1987). Surprisingly, only two experimental studies were conducted during the Nintendo era, with each assessing the impact of violent video games on the aggressive play of middle childhood youth (e.g., Irwin & Gross, 1995). The results of each study found that children were more physically aggressive after playing a violent video game, relative to a nonviolent one. However, many of the "aggressive actions" observed during play were actually incidences of rough-and-tumble play. Even instances of verbal aggression observed in the Irwin and Gross (1995) study took place while children were engaged in pretend play and, therefore, could have been part of an imaginary story line rather than an interpersonal attack.

Sony era
Research during early childhood   No recent studies have assessed the impact of violent video games on children between the ages of 2 and 5. But even the very young can play video games, and at times, they play violent ones. Take, for instance, Lil Poison, an 8-year-old gaming phenom who currently holds the record for being the world's youngest *professional* video game player. Lil Poison, who started playing his Xbox 360 as a toddler, entered his first video game tournament at age 4 as part of his father's Halo team. By age 5, Lil Poison was ranked as one of the top 64 video game players in the world, and currently he plays video games 6 hours per day (Lilpoison.com, 2008). Although the case of Lil Poison is unique, the degree to which youth in early childhood play, and are subsequently influenced by, violent video games is unknown. Incidentally, most young children experience video game violence through E-rated games (e.g., Super Mario Brothers), and not M-rated ones, like Lil Poison did.

Research during middle childhood   Until the Sony era, no correlational research had assessed the associations between violent video game play and aggressive behavior or aggression-related constructs. A handful of studies now exist for both areas. Of the three studies conducted on aggression-related constructs, two produced significant findings, both of which involved assessments of aggressive cognitions. For instance, in a sample of fourth and fifth grade children, Funk and colleagues (Funk, Bechtoldt-Baldacci, Pasold, & Baumgardner, 2004) found a positive correlation between violent video game play and positive attitudes toward violence. Similarly, Anderson and colleagues (Anderson, Gentile, & Buckley, 2007) found that violent video game play was associated with higher levels of hostile attributional bias in third to fifth graders. A hostile attributional bias is the tendency to over-attribute hostile intent to another individual during ambiguous situations involving harm. With regard to aggressive behavior, Anderson and colleagues (2007) also demonstrated positive associations between violent video game play and both physical and verbal aggression.

Few experimental studies have been conducted with elementary school–aged children during the Sony era. In fact, the majority of experimental research conducted on children and adolescents occurred during the Atari era, the era in which video games were the least realistic and the least violent. Nevertheless, contemporary research does suggest that violent video game play increases aggressive behavior during middle childhood. For instance, Anderson and colleagues (2007) found that after playing a T-rated violent video game (e.g., Street Fighter), 9- to 12-year-olds gave more intense "noise blasts" into the ears of another child during a competitive reaction time task. Of note, the noise blasts were not really delivered to the child's competitor. Nevertheless, Ritter and Eslea (2005) called into question the contention that noise blasts during a competitive game are actually acts of aggression. For instance, rather than sending a noise blast to inflict harm (i.e., the definition of aggression), participants might engage in such behaviors because they are trying to win the game, and believe that the loud noise blasts will disrupt their opponent's ability to win. Moreover, many participants may view the noise blast as just "part of the game" (much like blocking in football, checking in hockey, etc.) and not an aggressive act.

With regard to aggression-related constructs, several studies have addressed the impact of violent video game play on aggressive cognitions. For instance, Kirsh (1998) and Anderson and colleagues (2007) both found that children playing violent video games were more likely to demonstrate a hostile attributional bias than children playing nonviolent video games. Although not all research has found that violent video game play leads to aggressive cognitions (Funk, Buchman, Jenks, & Bechtoldt, 2003), there are more studies indicating the presence of an effect than the absence of one.

Research during adolescence   In the past decade, numerous correlational studies have been conducted across adolescence. However, the findings of these studies have been far from consistent. In fact, there are nearly as many studies that fail to find significant associations between violent video game play and aggressive behavior (e.g., Funk et al., 2002) as there are those that do (e.g., Anderson et al., 2007; Gentile, Lynch, Linder, & Walsh, 2004). Interestingly, correlational studies involving eighth grade boys have consistently produced significant associations between aggression and violent video game play. Developmental vulnerability may be at play here. More so than older adolescents or younger children, eighth grade boys may be particularly susceptible to the effects of violent video games. However, more research is needed to confirm this contention. With regard to aggression-related constructs, several studies have shown positive associations between the violent video game play and aggressive thoughts (e.g., Krahé & Möller, 2004) and aggressive feelings (Gentile et al., 2004).

Although the research is extremely limited, the results of recent *experimental* studies involving adolescents also provide foundational support for the claim that violent video games have the potential to influence aggressive behavior and aggression-related constructs. With regard to the aggression-related constructs, Unsworth and colleagues (Unsworth, Devilly, & Ward, 2007) assessed levels of anger (i.e., an aggressive affect) prior to and following violent video game play (Quake II) in a sample of 12- to 18-year-old adolescents. Youth that were characteristically angry (i.e., high in trait anger) and were feeling angry prior to video game play (i.e., high in state anger) experienced a decrease in state anger after playing Quake. The authors suggested that this is direct evidence of a catharsis effect. However, of the 111 participants in the study, only eight showed the aforementioned decrease. In contrast, adolescents who were high in trait anger and low in state anger prior to game play showed increased levels of state anger following violent video game play. In contrast, characteristically nonaggressive youth were unaffected by game play, regardless of their level of state anger. In fact, 77 of the 111 participants showed no change between their pre- and post-video game play levels of anger. As intriguing as these findings are, there is one serious methodological problem with the study: There was no nonviolent video game condition. As such, it is impossible to know if the findings were due to general factors associated with video game play (e.g., frustration) and/or the violence depicted within.

In one of the few assessments of violent video game-induced aggressive behavior, Konijn and colleagues (Konijn, Nije Bijvank, & Bushman,

2007) assessed the influence of video game violence, immersion in game play, and identification with the aggressor on competition-related aggression. Identification with the aggressor refers to the extent to which youth wish to be like the violent avatars they control and/or believe in and value the similarities between the violent avatars and the self. In this study of 12- to 17-year-old adolescent boys, participants played either a violent or nonviolent video game followed by a competitive reaction time task in which the winner was granted the opportunity to send a loud blast of noise (that ostensibly could cause hearing damage) into the headphones of the loser. What the participants did not know was that the competitive game was rigged and that there really was no opponent. There are several noteworthy findings to this study. First, violent video game play led to louder noise blasts than nonviolent video game play. Second, adolescent boys who *identified* with the violent avatar blasted deafening white noise into their opponent's headphones, more so than nonidentifying violent video game–playing youth. Finally, immersion in game play increased the likelihood that adolescents would identify with violent avatars. Taken together, these findings suggest that immersion during violent video game play may be more harmful to youth than violent video game play alone, because immersion fosters identification with the aggressor. However, given that this was a competitive task, the possibility exists that youth perceived the noise blasts to be "part of the game" and not acts of aggression.

Violent Gaming Online

Tens of millions of children and adolescents from all over the world play together online in a collective environment known as a *massively multiplayer online role-playing game* (MMORPG). Many of these websites offer children nonviolent entertainment, such as that found at Club Penguin. However, there are plenty of other websites, like Runescape, Everquest, and online versions of Call of Duty and Halo, that provide youth with ample opportunity to engage in virtual violence. As my then 10-year-old son said when he was trying to convince me to let him play the MMPROG World of Warcraft, "Online games bring peace throughout the world … even though they're violent." Despite the popularity of MMORPGs, there is no research on the impact of online violent video game play on children or adolescents. Why should MMPORGs be studied in the first place? Should not the research on console and PC violent video game play apply? The answer is both "yes" and "no." Although the impact of violent online play should be similar to that of console and PC violent video game play, MMORPGs have added dimensions that make them especially worthy of study. First, MMORPGs offer opportunities for collective group violence in a way that is not as easily done during offline play. When online, youth can "meet up" at virtual locations and engage in either cooperative or competitive play. Some games, such as Counterstrike, encourage youth to form teams and practice, with the hope of increasing their proficiency at virtual killing, both as individuals and as a team. To date, the impact of cooperative violence versus competitive violence and group versus singular play has yet to be studied in youth. Furthermore, MMORPG are inherently social, with users either engaging in text-based chat during game play or even talking to one another via headsets. In contrast, during most media violence studies conducted to date, youth play violent video games by themselves. Finally, when playing video games online, social interactions between players allow youth to function as a peer group, even engaging in cyber-bullying.

Cyber-bullying
Cyber-bullying involves repeated acts of hostile aggression directed at another individual and can involve verbal (e.g., name calling and teasing) and/or relational (e.g., spreading rumors) aggression. Around 10% of adolescents experience cyber-bullying each year. Given that 97% of adolescents use the Internet, the number of incidences of annual cyber-bullying is in the millions. Developmentally, cyber-bullying appears to peak in middle adolescence, with slight declines occurring thereafter (Kowalski, & Limber, 2007; Williams & Guerra, 2007). However, many of the incidences reported as cyber-bullying were actually brief encounters on the Internet and not repeated incidences of harassment. Often, youth simply delete the annoying comment and/or electronically block the user from further postings. Nevertheless, even brief encounters can lead to psychological pain for the cyber-bullied victim (Stobbe, 2007). Whether playing violent video games online increases the incidence of cyber-bullying is unknown. However, the activation of aggression-related constructs during violent video game play online may increase the likelihood that youth engage in cyber-bullying during play and shortly thereafter. Of course, more research is needed to confirm these contentions. Additionally, content analyses

need to be performed on game-based verbal and written exchanges between players, to ensure that reported instances of cyber-bullying were aggressive in nature, and not simply an expected part of game play (e.g., equivalent to an online version of rough-and-tumble play).

Developmental Points of Interest

Given that many youth begin to play violent video games in early childhood, why have so few experiments been conducted during this age period? The answer is simple: ethics. In fact, prior to conducting research, the most important question a social scientist needs to address is whether or not the procedures involved in the study could result in either physical or psychological harm to the participants. According to *The Publication Manual of the American Psychological Association* (5th ed.; American Psychological Association, 2001), it is unethical for researchers to inflict harm on participants of any age. Although violent video game play will most likely not lead to immediate physical harm, the violence, blood, and gore depicted within have the potential to cause psychological harm. As a result of this concern, many believe that exposure to violent media during early childhood must be eschewed. However, it is considered ethical to conduct surveys about violent video game play and then connect the responses to reported incidences of aggressive behavior and/or indices of aggression-related constructs. Nevertheless, 3 decades worth of research has failed to address the potential influence of violent video games on very young children.

The ethical picture becomes cloudier when conducting research on youth in middle childhood or older. Researchers such as Funk and colleagues (2003) have believed that it is unethical to have children in middle childhood play M-rated video games as part of a research experiment. By law, M-rated video games can only be sold to youth 17 years of age and older. Video games such as Hit Man and Doom 3 receive this restrictive rating because game play contains one or more of the following elements: mature sexual themes, intense violence, and/or strong language. However, research has shown that children over the age of 7 can readily buy M-rated video games in stores without their parents' consent. In addition, nearly 80% of 13-year-olds report recently playing an M-rated game (Walsh, Gentile, Gieske, Walsh, & Chasco, 2003). Thus, future research may want to consider investigating the effects of

Table 10.1   Questions Left Unanswered About Video Games and Youth

- How does violent video game play impact different types of aggression-related constructs across development?
- How does the frequency of game play influence the effects of violent video game play across development?
- What are the long-term effects of violent video game play? Does the age of onset of violent video game play influence the effects?
- Does developmental status influence the short-term and long-term effects of violent video game play differently?
- How does the perception of video game violence, regardless of violent content, influence aggressive responding?

extremely violent video games on older children and adolescents, even if the video games are rated above the child's current age level.

Some media violence critics contend that far beyond increasing aggressive behavior, violent video games instill in youth a desire to kill, while at the same time teaching them how to do it (Grossman & DeGaetano, 1999). Such sensationalistic claims are most likely to occur following incidents of school shootings. Despite such concerns, there has been relatively little research involving violent video games during early and middle adolescence, the two age periods that are most frequently associated with school shootings (Kirsh, 2003). With regard to killing, there are little experimental (or correlational) data to suggest that media violence is a significant *cause* of school violence or homicide.

Despite over 30 years worth of research on video game violence, there are many important issues that have yet to be addressed. Table 10.1 presents a list of the questions most relevant to children and adolescents. Although research on adults has addressed several of these, it is important to remember that children are not adults. Effects present in adults may be absent during childhood and/or adolescence, or the magnitude of the effect may vary across development. If child and adolescent outcomes were reliably predicted by adult data, then there would be no need to conduct research on youth or study development, for that matter. However, the history of developmental psychology has demonstrated that this is not the case.

11

Violent Media Part 2

Traditional Screen Media

Like many kids growing up in the 1970s I watched quite a lot of TV, and as it turns out, most of it was violent. I saw superhero after superhero fight petty criminals and battle supervillains. I witnessed stake after stake being driven into the hearts of vampires and more silver bullets than I can remember being shot into the bodies of werewolves. My steady diet of media violence also included hours of watching professional wrestling, with its colorful language, colorful characters, and nonstop violent altercations. Be it comedy or drama, live-action or animated, horror or science fiction, dubbed or subtitled, if there was violence depicted on-screen I watched it. As I got older, and I was able to attend movies without my parents, the body count went up and the blood flowed more freely. Good times, good times! My youthful enthusiasm for television and movie violence, however, was not shared by all during the 1970s. For instance, the U.S. surgeon general warned that exposure to violent television could lead to aggression in youth (U.S. Surgeon General's Scientific Advisory Committee, 1972). But, to what extent does exposure to violence in traditional on-screen media (i.e., live-action television, cartoons, and movies) impact youth today? The purpose of this chapter is to answer that very question.

Violence in Traditional Screen Media

Violent content abounds in both cartoons and live-action television programs. In fact, it has been estimated that youth will see more than 8,000 murders and 100,000 total acts of on-screen violence by the time they finish elementary school (Huston et al., 1992). In the last decade, television violence has dramatically increased during prime time, with depictions of violence increasing by 45% during the 8:00 p.m. hour, 92% during the 9:00 p.m. hour, and 167% during the 10:00 p.m. hour. On a typical night, the amount of violent acts encountered doubles with each additional hour of TV watched (2.34 violent acts between 8:00 and 9:00 p.m., 4.63 acts of violence between 9:00 and 10:00 p.m., and 9.43 violent acts between 10:00 and 11:00 p.m.; Parents Television Council, 2007).

In addition to the hour of the evening, the amount of violence on television varies by program genre, such as drama, wrestling, comedy, and reality. In terms of both the quantity and intensity of violence, by far, professional wrestling gives the "people's elbow" to the competition. One recent study found that *all* televised wrestling programs contained violent content, at an average of nearly 14 violent scenes per hour. Of those violent scenes, 23% were of an extreme nature (defined as 21 or more consecutive violent actions) with an average of 46 separate violent acts each. In comparison to a typical prime-time TV show, professional wrestling offered up twice the number of violent acts per hour and three times the amount of extreme acts of violence. Children's programs were the second most violent genre on TV, with 80% of the programs containing violence, at an average of 12 scenes per hour. However, only 3% of the violent acts were considered extreme (Tamborini et al., 2005).

Children and adolescents are also exposed to violence during commercials and on the news. For instance, Larson (2003) found that over one third of commercials targeting youth contained aggressive elements. Similarly, Tamburro and colleagues' (Tamburro, Gordon, D'Apolito, & Howard, 2004) research established that 50% of the commercials aired during major sporting events watched by youth (e.g., the Super Bowl and World Series) contained aggressive and/or unsafe behaviors. On the news, reports of death, destruction, and sexual assault are commonplace. One study found that over 50% of televised news stories involved violence, conflict, and suffering (Johnson, 1996). In recent years, war, genocide, and acts of terrorism have frequented the airways, accompanied by graphic scenes of violence and its aftermath. Interestingly, television broadcasts go unrated in the United States, making it impossible for parents to know in advance if they should turn the channel to something less violent and disturbing.

Violence has also proven to be an essential component of both cartoons and animated films. One study found that children and adolescents were more likely to view acts of violence during Saturday morning cartoons than during prime-time television hours (Gerbner, Gross, Morgan, & Signorielli, 1994). Similarly, cartoons have been shown to depict more violent acts than live-action drama or comedic programs (Potter & Warren, 1998). Even in G-rated movies, which are supposed to "contain nothing offensive," violence is routinely observed. For instance, an assessment of 74 G-rated films, released over a 62-year period, revealed that 100% of the films had at least one act of violence. On average, there was 9.5 minutes of violence in each movie (Yokota & Thompson, 2000). Additional research has shown that animated films with a rating of G depict more on-screen violence than live-action, G-rated films (Thompson & Yokota, 2004).

Factors That Influence the Perception of Violence

Just as "beauty is in the eye of the beholder," so too, apparently, is violence, for the manner in which violence is depicted on-screen and the context in which it occurs may affect youthful viewers' perceptions of those violent acts. Such factors include sanitization, consequences, comedy, justification and legitimation, perceived reality, graphicness, and glamorization. Each will be addressed in turn.

Sanitization and Consequences

Sanitization occurs when, contrary to reality, the victims of violence do not die or suffer in realistic pain; that is, the consequences of violence are benign. As an example, during the ultraviolent cartoon *Batman: The Animated Series*, numerous battles take place without any significant harm occurring to the main characters. Despite the fact that bullets are ricocheting everywhere and bombs are exploding all around, the villains almost always live to terrorize another day, with Batman alive to confront them. Whether or not an act of violence is seen as trivial or serious depends on the consequences to the victim and the perpetrator. When victims display little realistic pain or when the perpetrator fails to act remorseful and sorrowful, violent acts are perceived to be trivialized (Gunter, 1985). Although television cartoons frequently sanitize the outcomes of violence, sanitization is less common in animated films and prime-time television shows. For instance, Yokota and Thompson

(2000) found that in G-rated films, death (or presumed death), injury, and pain were quite common (47%, 62%, and 24%, respectively). Similarly, prime-time dramas regularly highlight the pain and suffering of those harmed by violence. One study found that 64% of violent acts resulted in harm and 56% depicted pain (Tamborini et al., 2005).

Comedy

Comedic elements, and in particular slapstick humor, have the potential to camouflage and trivialize depictions of violence. Slapstick humor is a type of comedy in which the humor derives from physical action. Acts of aggression-related slapstick humor include being poked in the eye with a finger, hit on the head with a hammer, or driven into the ground by an anvil. Comedy is thought to trivialize violence for several reasons: (a) Comedic elements signal to the viewer that the seriousness of the events they are watching should be downplayed, resulting in a cognitive transformation that renders serious acts of violence as trivial; (b) schemas for comedies (which contain expectations and rules regarding the type and pacing of jokes, the variety of characters involved, and the typical endings) exclude violence, and as such, violence in comedies becomes camouflaged; and (c) when paired together, violent and comedic elements activate (i.e., prime) constructs (e.g., thoughts, feelings, scripts) related to both humor and aggression. As a result of this dual priming, the perceived level of violence is lessened, relative to when only aggression-related constructs are activated.

Justification and Legitimation

Violence is considered justified when it is presented as a necessary component to the resolution of a conflict. Whenever acts of violence are rewarded or go unpunished, they are considered legitimate; that is morally correct. On television, nearly 70% of "heroes" go unpunished when using violence, and 32% of the time they are rewarded for their violent actions. Even violent acts by villains go unpunished over 80% of the time. Similarly, acts of aggression occurring during programs geared at children are met with positive consequences. For instance, the *Powerpuff Girls* are consistently lauded by the people of Townsville for pummeling the string of villains that terrorize the city on a daily basis. One study found that 27% of children's programs justified acts of violence, with the highest degree of legitimation occurring in cartoons (Wilson et al., 2002). Additional research has demonstrated that violence that is justified or legitimized ultimately becomes trivialized (Potter & Warren, 1998).

Perceived Reality

Perceived reality is composed of two related factors: perceived actuality and perceived similarity. Perceived actuality refers to the degree to which media depicts realistic portrayals of events, settings, and characters, with greater realism resulting in greater perceived actuality. As an example, children's shows containing little perceived actuality, such as *The Mighty Morphin' Power Rangers* and *Ben 10*, depict characters that do not really exist (e.g., superheroes, mutant creatures) engaged in activities that do not occur in the real world (e.g., fighting gigantic alien creatures, transforming one's body into another creature). In contrast, perceived similarity refers to the level of resemblance occurring between the viewer and the events and characters on-screen. For instance, a 15-year-old boy should experience greater perceived similarity with the teenage superhero sidekicks in the movie *Sky High*, in comparison to the 60-something, whip-wielding archeologist Indiana Jones. In comparison to violent images high in perceived reality, media violence with little perceived reality has lower levels of both perceived actuality and perceived similarity. Moreover, depictions of violence low in perceived reality tend to be rated as less violent than depictions of violence deemed to be more realistic (Atkin & Block, 1983).

Graphicness

Often, what differentiates the assigned rating code from one TV program (or movie) to the next is the level of violence depicted within. For instance, whereas programs rated TV-14 (suitable for youth aged 14 and over) contain "intense violence," shows rated TVG (suitable for all) contain "little or no violence." A key determinant of what constitutes "intense violence" is graphicness. The more graphic the depiction of blood and gore, the higher the level of violence attributed to that scene. In addition, acts of violence that cause viewers to feel uneasy or lesson their enjoyment are perceived to be more violent than scenes without these characteristics. According to research, it is easier to trivialize violence that contains little in the way of graphic blood, gore, or otherwise offensive material. Not surprisingly, violence in cartoons and animated films, which has limited blood and gore, is often overlooked by the viewer (Potter & Warren, 1998).

Glamorization

Violence becomes glamorized whenever it is presented in an appealing manner, such that it looks "cool." Think of Neo in *The Matrix*, with his black trench coat, black sunglasses, slick hair style, catchy dialogue, and smooth, gravity-defying martial arts moves. Typically, glamorized violence is perpetrated by physically attractive, charismatic, and charming individuals. Such characteristics are particularly appealing to a youthful audience (Wilson et al, 2002). The glamorization of violence during children's television programs is commonplace. This is particularly troubling because children are more likely to imitate and learn from models who are attractive (Kirsh, 2006).

Research on the Factors That Influence the Perception of Violence in Media

Not only do the characteristics above influence children's and adolescent's perception of on-screen violence, but they also affect their aggressive behavior. For instance, research has established that violence that is punished or depicts the pain and suffering of the victim tends to decrease the likelihood that youth will become aggressive. As an example, adolescents with a history of watching television shows that realistically portray the negative outcomes of violent behavior (e.g., *Cops*) are less likely than other youth to accept the use of justified violence (Krcmar & Valkenburg, 1999). In contrast, the viewing of sanitized, trivialized, and realistic violence encourages aggressive behavior (Wilson et al., 2002). A study by Hartnagel and colleagues (1975) found that youth perceiving television violence to be justified engaged in more violent acts than youth lacking this perception. Among children and early adolescents, the greatest acceptance of justified violence comes from youth with a history of watching fantasy violence on television. During such programs, violence is presented in the context of "aggression for the greater good," with a hero violently and justifiably defeating a villain. One study found that 87% of violence depicted in children's programs occurs in a fantasy context (Wilson et al., 2002).

The Effects of On-Screen Violence on Youth

More research has been conducted on the impact of violent television and movies on youth than on any other type of violent media, including video games. Below are selected studies meant to illustrate four prominent effects that result from viewing televised violence: (a) aggressive disinhibition, (b) changes in aggression-related constructs, (c) desensitization to violence, and (d) becoming fearful.

Aggressive Disinhibition

Aggressive disinhibition occurs when reservations about acting aggressively are lifted. As a result, youth perform aggressive behaviors already in their arsenal or newly learned behaviors resulting from violent media consumption. Aggressive disinhibition is also evident when youth witness one type of realistic aggressive act (e.g., knife fight) but engage in aggressive behaviors that did not occur on screen (e.g., name calling). Aggressive disinhibition is an important concept in media violence research because certain aggressive actions do not occur in reality and, therefore, cannot be imitated or learned by children and adolescents (Hapkiewicz, 1979). Cartoons, animated films, and fantasy programs are replete with impossible acts of aggression. But no matter how many times children try to use the "dark side" of the Force to choke someone (Darth Vader style), they will never be successful. However, children do not necessarily have to be able to perform the aggressive acts viewed on-screen in order to be affected by them. This is because *previously* learned acts of aggression can follow the viewing of on-screen violence, even if the on-screen violence and the child's aggressive behavior look nothing alike. Aggressive disinhibition is different from imitation because when youth imitate what they see on-screen, their behaviors may not necessarily be based on an intent to harm, which is a necessary condition for aggression. For instance, Bandura and colleagues (1961) demonstrated that after observing an adult throw, kick, and yell at a Bobo Doll, preschool-aged children mimicked those actions during free play. However, rather than acting with an intent to harm, the children may simply have been imitating behaviors in the context of rough-and-tumble play.

Correlational/survey research

Through longitudinal studies and cross-sectional surveys, numerous studies have set out to assess the impact of on-screen violence on youth at different stages of development. Research using a preschool sample has found a positive association between the amount of aggressive behavior shown during free play (e.g., hitting, pushing, and seizing toys) and the frequency of violent TV shows watched during prime time (Singer & Singer, 1981). More recently, Ostrov and colleagues (2006) found that 4-year-old boys with higher levels of exposure to on-screen violence (as reported by parents) were associated with greater amounts of observed physical, relational, and verbal aggression. For girls, the aforementioned association was limited to verbal aggression.

Research on middle childhood youth has been a bit more mixed, with the impact of on-screen violence varying by gender and age. For instance, one study found positive associations between watching violent television and aggressive behavior in 10-year-olds, but not 8-year-olds (Viemero & Paajanen, 1992). Another study found that after factoring out a wide range of potential confounds (such as parenting style, SES, IQ, initial levels of aggression), violent television viewing at age 8 significantly predicted aggression at age 19. However, these results were only evident for boys (Eron, Huesmann, Lefkowitz, & Walder, 1972). In contrast, Huesmann and colleagues (Huesmann, Lagerspetz, & Eron, 1984) found that for first and third grade girls, but not boys, violent television exposure significantly predicted levels of aggressive behavior 2 years later. Some 15 years after the original assessment, Huesmann's original sample was contacted once again and participants' adult levels of aggression were assessed. Findings indicated that, for boys, violent television consumption during childhood predicted adult levels of physical aggression. For girls, both physical and indirect forms of aggression were significantly predicted by childhood consumption of violent television (Huesmann, Moise-Titus, Podolski, & Eron, 2003).

During adolescence, higher levels of violent television consumption have time and again been associated with increasing amounts of aggressive behavior. One study of seventh and 10th graders found significant positive correlations between viewing violent television and self-reported acts of aggressive behavior (McLeod, Atkin, & Chaffee, 1972). Another study of sixth and seventh graders demonstrated that violent media consumption predicted current levels of aggressive behavior, as well as the amount of aggressive behavior engaged in 2 years later (Slater et al., 2003). Similarly, a recent assessment of late adolescents found that, in comparison to nonviewers, teens watching wrestling six times per week were 144% more likely to get into a fight, 119% more likely to have threatened someone with a weapon, and 184% more likely to have used a weapon in an attempt to hurt someone (DuRant, Neiberg, Champion, Rhodes, & Wolfson, 2008).

Reverse hypothesis   In addition to media impacting aggressive behavior during childhood and adolescence, aggressive youth may selectively seek out violent media for consumption. Because aggressive behavior predicts violent media use, rather than the other way around, this phenomenon has been referred to as the reverse hypothesis (Huesmann et al., 1984). Thus, youth are not just passive recipients of violent media, as they selectively expose themselves to it. Moreover, the reciprocal interaction of violent media consumption and aggressive behavior has provided supporting evidence for the downward spiral model. For instance, in an assessment of over 1,800 sixth and seventh graders, Slater and colleagues (2003) found that (a) current levels of aggressive behavior predicted violent media use across a 2-year period; and (b) violent media consumption predicted current and future levels of aggression. These findings are consistent with those of Vidal and colleagues (2003), who found that the more youth watch violence, the more they tend to enjoy it. However, additional research has shown that levels of *childhood* aggression do not significantly predict *adult* levels of violent television consumption (Huesmann et al., 2003). These findings suggest that the downward spiral model may only be in place during childhood and adolescence. However, little is known about which period(s) of development the downward spiral model is at its strongest.

Experimental research
During early and middle childhood, both laboratory and field experiments have consistently demonstrated the negative impact of violent television consumption on aggressive behavior. For instance, after watching 20 minutes of *Batman* and *Superman* cartoons, three times a

week for a month in a preschool setting, young children became aggressively disinhibited, acting more disobedient and less tolerant of delay. Moreover, after viewing violent cartoons, children known to be aggressive at the start of the experiment engaged in even more acts of aggression (Friedrich & Stein, 1973). Similarly, in a laboratory setting, Bjorkqvist (1985) found older preschoolers exposed to violent movies engaged in higher levels of aggression and aggressive play than youth viewing nonviolent films.

In a study of *indirect aggression* in elementary school-aged children, exposure to violent television clips increased the likelihood of youth pushing a button that they thought would prevent another child from winning a competitive game (Liebert & Baron, 1971). Using a slightly older sample of 7 to 9-year-old boys, Josephson (1987) established that youth exposed to violent movies were more likely to engage in aggressive disinhibition during a school-based game of floor hockey, in comparison to youth watching a nonviolent film. Acts of aggression identified in this study included, hitting, elbowing, tripping, kneeing, hair pulling, and occasional name calling. More recently, Boyatzis and colleagues (1995) demonstrated that youth exposed to the Mighty Morphin Power Rangers during school hours exhibited seven times as many acts of aggression during recess, in comparison to youth not viewing the program. However, because Boyatzis and colleagues failed to differentiate aggressive behavior from aggressive play (i.e., rough-and-tumble play), it is impossible to tell if youth were truly acting in an aggressive manner.

At the very least, Boyatzis' data suggest that beyond the preschool years, children continue to imitate the aggressive actions that they see on TV, a finding that has also been demonstrated during adolescence. As an example, research has shown that teenage viewers of professional wrestling programs aped the statements (e.g., "Give me a hell yeah") and moves of wrestlers, such as body slams, choke holds, and clotheslines (i.e., a forearm across the neck), during school (Bernthal, 2003). During early and middle childhood, when imitative behaviors occur in the context of rough-and-tumble play, few problems typically arise, except for the occasional bumps and bruises. As children enter adolescence, however, rough-and-tumble play is more likely to be used to establish or maintain dominance hierarchies than in creating positive peer relationships (Pelligrini, 2002). Thus, the adolescent recipients of choke holds, body slams, and the like may not necessarily view the imitative behaviors enacted upon them in a positive light. In such contexts, the imitated behaviors are clear acts of aggression, and not benign playful activities.

Not all studies have found that watching television results in aggressive disinhibition. For instance, several studies exposing children in both early childhood and middle childhood to violent cartoons failed to show increases in physical and verbal aggression towards peers (Kirsh, 2006). However, these "failed" studies typically assessed direct aggression in the laboratory. Given that interpersonal aggression among youth is frowned upon by society, and that acts of physical aggression are often punished, being in a laboratory spotlight may increase youth's awareness of their own behaviors, resulting in aggressive *inhibition*, rather than *disinhibition*. In contrast, when participating in a field experiment, youth are more likely to act as they normally would, as they are less aware of, or do not even know, that they are being observed.

There is little experimental research on aggressive disinhibition during adolescence. However, the research that has been conducted has produced findings consistent with the results demonstrated for much younger participants. As an example, one recent study found that viewing televised acts of either direct or indirect aggression, increased 11- to 14-year-olds' use of indirect aggression (Coyne et al., 2004). Similarly, studies from both sides of the Atlantic Ocean indicate that *delinquent* youth are more likely to act aggressively toward their peers after watching violent films, relative to when they watch nonviolent ones (Leyens et al., 1975; Parke et al.,1977). Research on normative adolescents is needed to determine if these effects generalize to nondelinquent adolescents.

Introduction of television in a community
Today, it is hard to imagine any North American city without television. However, that was indeed the case in isolated areas of Canada during the early 1970s. Of course, television soon arrived, and when it did, the impact of its introduction on the aggressive behavior of youth was assessed. As part of this natural experiment, Williams (1986) compared the amount of physical and verbal aggression in youth from three towns (listed by pseudonyms): Notel, a town that did not receive television; Unitel, which received one television channel; and Multitel, a town that received four television channels. After television reached Notel, Williams discovered that the amount of physical and verbal aggression displayed by Notel youth increased above and beyond the

levels of aggression shown in youth from Unitel or Multitel. Even though some have interpreted this finding as *causal* evidence that violent television increases aggressive behavior, there are serious problems with this study that invalidate such conclusions. Most damaging is the fact that Williams assessed general television viewing and not violent television consumption. It is quite plausible that, as opposed to violent images on-screen, factors related to general patterns of television viewing (e.g., less parental monitoring) and undocumented social changes (e.g., unemployment and divorce rates) accounted for the observed increases in aggressive behavior.

Changes in Aggression-Related Constructs

As you recall from the previous chapter, aggression-related constructs are factors that increase the likelihood that youth will act aggressively. Aggression-related constructs known to influence youth across development, include hostility, attitudes toward the use of aggression, fantasizing about aggression, and identification with the aggressor.

Hostility

Hostility refers to the presence of negative beliefs and attitudes about others, as well as the corresponding negative emotions (e.g., anger, irritation). Youth that are characteristically hostile tend to engage in more acts of aggression than other youth (Moeller, 2001). Violent television has been shown to moderate the hostility levels of young viewers. For instance, Graña and colleagues (2004) found that viewing televised bullfights led to increases in hostility for 8- to 12-year-old boys and girls. Similarly, research has shown that watching violent hockey clips increased the hostility levels of high school seniors. However, the observed effects were limited to teens already characteristically hostile to begin with (Celozzi et al., 1981). By comparison, in pleasant teens, hostility levels were unaffected by violent on-screen images. These findings suggest that the impact of television violence may vary as a function of an individual's characteristic (i.e., trait) hostility level.

Attitudes toward the use of aggression

Aggressive youth not only enjoy acting in a hostile manner but also praise their friends for their successful use of aggression in social situations (Kirsh, 2006). Does consuming violent television engender bully-like attitudes? It seems plausible, as several studies have established a link between violent television consumption and more positive attitudes toward the use of aggression. As an example, one study of fourth to sixth grade boys and girls found that higher levels of violent television consumption were associated with a greater *willingness* to act aggressively in situations that did not require force. Moreover, youth consuming copious amounts of violent television also perceived violence to be a more *effective* solution to life's social problems (Dominick & Greenberg, 1972). Similar results have been demonstrated using slightly older participants, aged 9, 12, and 15 (Greenberg, 1974). Additionally, when asked to provide a solution to hypothetical scenarios involving aggressive provocations (e.g., getting bumped on the playground), 4- to 16-year-old youth responded more aggressively after watching a violent television program, in comparison to when they had previously viewed a nonviolent show (Leifer & Roberts, 1971). Across middle childhood and adolescence, exposure to violent cartoons and movie clips has also produced positive attitudes towards the use of aggression (Nathanson & Cantor, 2000; Wotring & Greenberg, 1973). At times, developmental differences were also evident, with positive attitudes toward the use of force increasing with age. However, this finding has not been consistently demonstrated. The extant body of research has been focused on children's attitudes towards physical aggression. Little is known about the impact of violent television on attitudes toward the use of relational and verbal aggression across development.

Fantasizing about aggression

Have you ever imagined beating up that annoying, loud-talking, cell phone user who refuses to move to a location away from others? Ever been cut off while driving and pictured in your mind crashing the assailant into a tree? If so, then you have engaged in an aggressive fantasy. Across middle childhood, numerous studies have demonstrated that aggressive youth fantasize about aggressive behavior more so than nonaggressive youth (Huesmann et al., 1984; Viemero & Paajanen, 1992). By thinking about aggressive behavior, and by engaging in fantasy play, it has been suggested that youth are practicing aggressive scripts (i.e., internal screenplays in which the beginning, middle, and end of altercations are clearly and explicitly illustrated), thereby increasing the likelihood that they will act aggressively in the future (Anderson & Bushman, 2001). Unfortunately, there is little evidence to support this contention. For instance, Huesmann and colleagues (1984) failed to find a significant connection between violent television exposure and aggressive fantasies during middle childhood. In contrast, Viemero and Paajanen (1992) did find that boys with higher levels of violent television exposure exhibited the greatest number of aggressive fantasies. However, because the authors did not assess current levels of aggression, the possibility exists that preexisting behavioral differences accounted for the findings, and not violent television consumption.

Identification with the aggressor
Identification with the aggressor refers to the situation in which youth desire (either consciously or unconsciously) to pattern themselves after an aggressive individual. Interestingly, the object of identification does not necessarily have to exist in reality. Just as youth can identify with Eminem, so too can they identify with James Bond. Because children and adolescents may imitate the behaviors of those with whom they perceive as role models, identification with aggressive individuals, such as *Spiderman* or *Xena: Warrior Princess*, is of potential concern. In fact, research has shown that youth who identify with aggressive individuals act more aggressively following exposure to media violence, in comparison to nonidentifying youth. Moreover, Huesmann and colleagues (2003) found that, after controlling for the amount of violent television consumed, identification with violent television characters during middle childhood predicted levels of physical and verbal aggression 15 years later. Moreover, Huesmann found that for boys, the combination of high levels of violent television consumption and strong identification with a violent character during middle childhood resulted in the greatest amount of aggression during young adulthood. Thus, violent television exposure and identification with the aggressor appear to influence aggression independently, with the presence of one or more of these factors resulting in ever increasing levels of aggression.

Desensitization

For decades, concern has been raised that exposure to violent on-screen images will result in youth that are both callous and indifferent to real-world violence. As a result of numerous investigations, two media-related processes have been identified: habituation to media violence and desensitization to real-world violence.

Habituation to media violence
When habituation occurs, an individual's responsiveness to violent media decreases with repeated viewings (i.e., becomes less intense). For instance, whereas the first light-saber battle viewed by children might cause feelings of excitement and physiological arousal, repeated viewings of similar battles will produce less pronounced physiological effects (or none at all). Although few media violence-related studies have been conducted, Cline and colleagues (1973) did find evidence of habituation in 7- to 14-year-olds. Specifically, youth with a history of watching lots of television became less physiologically aroused (e.g., possessed higher skin resistance or reduced blood volume) to a violent movie than other youth. Of note, the television programs viewed at home and the movies viewed in the laboratory were different. As such, this finding indicates that habituation occurs for violent media in general, and not just for specific scenes or programs.

Desensitization to media violence
Desensitization refers to the situation in which youth become less affected by, and more indifferent and callous to, genuine violence occurring in the real world. Four distinct types of media-induced desensitization have been identified: behavioral, cognitive, emotional, and physiological. Behavioral desensitization refers to a reduction in prosocial behavior when witnessing acts of aggression. As an example, Drabman and Thomas (1974) measured the amount of time it took third and fourth graders to intervene (i.e., find an adult) in a fight between preschoolers (observed on a "live" video feed). Results indicated that children viewing a violent film took longer to get help than youth watching a nonviolent film. Interestingly, these findings have been replicated using slightly older children (fourth and fifth graders; Molitor and Hirsch, 1994) but not younger children (first and second graders; Horton & Santogrossi, 1978; Thomas and Drabman, 1975). It is quite possible that due to their relative inexperience, younger children have not had enough exposure to violent media to become behaviorally desensitized.

Cognitive desensitization refers to the condition in which youth think about real-world violence in a more positive way (e.g., espouse pro-violence attitudes). By comparison, emotional desensitization refers to a reduction in children's affective responding to real-life acts of violence. Recently, Funk and colleagues (2004) investigated the relationship between television and movie violence consumption on both cognitive and emotional desensitization. Results indicated that fourth and fifth grade children with a history of violent movie exposure reported greater pro-violence attitudes than other youth. However, children's violent television consumption was unrelated to this type of cognitive desensitization. Moreover, Funk and colleagues found that emotional desensitization was not influenced by children's violent movie and television viewing habits. No other studies have been conducted to clarify these mixed findings. Physiological desensitization is evidenced by a reduction in an individual's biological responsiveness to real-life violence. In one of the few studies conducted, Thomas and colleagues (1977) found that children were less physiologically aroused (e.g., skin conductance) by a staged argument between preschoolers after viewing violent movie clips than after seeing nonviolent ones.

Habituation versus desensitization

Although similar, the difference between habituation and desensitization is of the upmost importance. Whereas habituation suggests that youth may be becoming vulnerable to the negative influences of violent media, desensitization implies that a negative impact has already occurred. Additionally, as youth become habituated to violent media, the possibility exists that, like a drug addict chasing their next high, users of "plug-in" drugs seek out increasingly violent imagery in order to experience the same level of arousal that accompanied their initial exposure. In turn, this heightened level of media violence exposure increases the risk that desensitization and aggressive behavior will follow.

Becoming Fearful

Without question, the violent images depicted in television news can instill fear in both children and adolescents. For instance, Buijzen and colleagues (2007) demonstrated that, for 8- to 12-year-old children, familiarity with news reports of a recent assassination in the Netherlands was associated with increased levels of fear and anxiety. Another study found that close to 50% of children report being scared by something seen on the news (Smith & Wilson, 2002). The more often children watch television news, the greater the intensity of fear experienced (Wilson et al., 2005). The fear-inducing effects of television news have also been demonstrated for script-based on-screen programming. Shows like *The Incredible Hulk,* and movies, such as *The Wizard of Oz* (Cantor & Sparks, 1984) have been shown to cause fear in youth days, weeks, and months later. In fact, media-induced fear during childhood is so powerful that the effects have been shown to last into adulthood (Harrison & Cantor, 1999). To this very day, I still get a twinge of anxiety whenever I think about the blue flying monkeys from *The Wizard of Oz.*

Violent media can induce fear via three distinct mechanisms: direct experience, observational learning, and negative information transfer. First, direct experience fear induction occurs when a stimulus activates the fear centers of the brain. Such stimuli can be realistic or fantastical, televised from miles away or occurring right in front of you, or any combination of the two. Thus, whether it is seeing a lion tear through the flesh of a gazelle while on safari or witnessing that same incident on the *Discovery Channel,* such images can induce a state of fear in viewers. Second, observational learning of fear occurs when youth become fearful as a result of seeing others (such as eye witnesses, relatives, and victims) emotional reactions to an event. As an example, watching the distraught relatives of victims killed in a terrorist attack can create an emotional reaction (i.e., empathy) in youth that induces a state of fear or anxiety. Finally, negative information transfer occurs after hearing others relay frightening content about some situation or event. As a result of the encounter, youth create a cognitive schema of that event or situation, including the component of fear. For instance, after hearing a news story about people dying from eating tainted vegetables, a child may become frightened when spinach is put on his plate. As a side note, parental warnings aimed at preventing children from doing something (such as wandering too far away) can also induce fears, especially if a scary or painful consequence is involved (Valkenburg, 2004). As an example, telling children that they should not pet a strange cat because it is really a monster named Bucci can lead to the fear of all cats, even familiar ones.

Not all violent media images are alike: some are real (e.g., news), some are realistic (e.g., *CSI*), and some are fantasy (e.g., *Star Trek*). Across development, the realism of the images viewed appears to differentially impact the onset of fear. Younger children tend to be more scared by fantasy violence than older children and adolescents. In contrast, older youth tend to be frightened by realistic violence the most (Cantor & Sparks, 1984).

In part, these findings occur because older children understand the difference between fantasy and reality. Between 6 and 10 years of age, youth begin to realize that the images they see on-screen are not real and cannot become real. For youth, once the fantasy–reality distinction has been made, fantasy violence becomes much less frightening.

When children and adolescents are scared by realistic violence, they tend to be frightened by different types of images, with older children and adolescents being affected by abstract notions of violence (e.g., terrorism and nuclear war) and younger children being impacted by concrete images (such as injuries and bombs exploding; Cantor et al., 1993). This finding is consistent with Piaget's contention that children are not able to think about abstract concepts until the onset of formal operations, around 11 years of age. Moreover, with increasing age, advances in empathy and cognitive development give children and adolescents a greater ability to understand the causes, consequences, and emotional experiences of violence. As such, for middle childhood-aged youth and older, observational learning effects and the negative transfer of information lead to more generalized concerns about violence. The end result of these developmental advances is the realization for older youth that (a) fantasy violence poses little concern to their health and well-being, and (b) violence can occur at any time and at any place.

Developmental Points of Interest

Children and adolescents witness countless acts of violence on television and in the movies. More often than not, these violent images are deemed to be "age appropriate." Acts of on-screen violence vary in the degree to which they are glamorized, sanitized, justified, comedic, graphic, and realistic. However, relatively little research has systematically investigated the impact of multiple combinations of these factors on children and adolescents. It may be that certain combinations of these variables (e.g., noncomedic, realistic and/or, graphic) influence aggression in youth to a greater extent than others (e.g., sanitized, justified, glamorized). Moreover, different combinations of these variables may impact youth in different ways, depending upon their developmental status.

Additional research is needed to assess these variables as a function of the age of the on-screen characters. Acts of violence performed by child and adolescent characters may affect youth to a greater extent than identical behaviors performed by adults. In support of this contention, Wilson and colleagues (2002) found that children were more likely to duplicate aggressive behaviors performed by same-aged peers than adults. Because children's favorite television characters are likely to be under 18 years of age, identification with on-screen violent youth may occur more readily than with characters who are older (Kirsh, 2006). In comparison with adult characters, acts of violence performed by youth are more likely to be sanitized, less likely to be punished, and more likely to be performed by attractive, "good guy" characters (Wilson et al., 2002). Clearly, these findings point to a larger impact of television violence performed by youthful characters than adults; however, additional research is needed to validate this contention.

Across development, results from numerous correlational studies have demonstrated an empirical link between viewing on-screen violence and aggressive behavior directed at peers and/or objects. Moreover, the findings from several studies indicate that the effects of traditional screen violence consumption can influence youth years later. However, the consistency of these findings varies by age, with the greatest uniformity occurring during adolescence. Once again, adolescence appears to be a time during which youth are particularly vulnerable to the effects of media. More research is needed, however, to isolate the specific ages of adolescence (e.g., early, middle, or late) during which this vulnerability is at its apex.

Surprisingly, few correlational studies have investigated the impact of live-action television and movie violence on preschool-aged children. Rather, the majority of the research conducted during the preschool years has involved cartoon violence. As such, additional research is necessary to determine if cartoon violence and live-action violence differentially influence young children. Moreover, documented associations between cartoon violence and aggressive disinhibition in early childhood could have easily been accounted for by parenting variables, such as levels of warmth and hostility, as well as disciplinary style. Unfortunately, such variables were not typically assessed in the aforementioned studies. During middle childhood, the findings have been mixed, with some studies finding significant effects for girls but not boys, and other studies finding the opposite. It may be that differences between studies in the realism, sanitization, glorification, etc. of on-screen violence accounts for these inconsistencies—an issue worthy of study. The results from experimental studies suggest that throughout early and middle childhood, exposure to on-screen violence results in not only short-term imitative behavior but immediate acts of aggressive disinhibition as well. Less is known, however, about the short-term effects of on-screen violence on adolescents. Nor does the current body of literature provide data on the duration of the aforementioned effects across development. It may be that the impact of on-screen violence lingers longer at certain ages than at others.

In comparison to developmental research on aggressive disinhibition, far fewer studies have investigated the influence of on-screen violence on aggression-related constructs. For instance, from early childhood to late adolescence less than a handful of studies have been conducted on aggression-related emotions. During early childhood, there are few if any studies on aggressive cognitions. In addition, research on desensitization has been primarily limited to middle childhood, and there are no studies with adolescents. Interestingly, desensitization effects have been primarily demonstrated for older elementary school children, suggestive that development may moderate the effect. But given the paucity of research, additional studies are needed to confirm this notion.

Finally, future research needs to more clearly differentiate the impact of violence watched on television from violence viewed in movie theaters. Let me explain. First, previous research has demonstrated that larger television screens (e.g., 56″) produce greater physiological arousal in adults than smaller ones (e.g., 13″; Heo, 2004). Thus, the possibility exists that screen size impacts the physiological arousal of youth as well. Second, the presence of vocal and reactive co-spectators, which is more commonplace in movie theaters than at home, has been shown to increase postviewing aggression in college students (Dunand et al., 1984). Third, televised advertisements may potentially mask the outcomes and consequences of program-related violence. For instance, one study found that commercials aired during a violent television program made it more difficult for third grade children to realize that an aggressive act had been punished (Collins, 1973). As a whole, these findings suggest that violent images and sounds viewed in movie theaters may affect youth to a greater extent than the identical content consumed at home, even if the television screen is 60 inches. However, whether or not screen size and the presence of co-viewers actually moderate the effects of media violence across development has gone largely unexplored.

12

Media Effects: Magnitude, Risk, and Media Literacy

As the previous chapters have revealed, infants, children, and adolescents are clearly influenced by the media that they consume. Whereas some of these effects are beneficial to youth, others have the potential to be harmful. But, to what extent should parents, teachers, and politicians laud the positive outcomes and be concerned about the negative ones? In other words, just how big an influence do the omnipresent media wield in the lives of youth? To help answer this question, social scientists make use of the statistical concept of variance. Variance is the percentage of a dependent variable that is accounted for by an independent variable. In media effects research, attitudes, thoughts, feelings, arousal and behavior serve as the dependent variables and the various forms of media (e.g., violent, sexual, academic, prosocial, etc.) are the independent variables. Thus, media effects research attempts to reveal the percentage of behaviors, thoughts, feelings, and so on, that can be attributed to the consumption of media.

If you think of a pie as the dependent variable under study, then the independent variables are the ingredients that make up that pie. Of course, when you make a pie, some ingredients are more prominent than others. That is, they make up a greater percentage of the total amount of ingredients used; and such is the case in variance, as some independent variables account for more of a dependent variable than others. For instance, when considering delinquent behavior in youth, peers account for 25% of the variance, whereas the quality of family relationships accounts for 3% of the variance. Typically, small effects account for around 1% of the variance, medium effects account for approximately 10%, and large effects account for at least 25%. But even when effect sizes meet the threshold for being considered large, as much as 75% of the variance is left unaccounted for by the factors included in the study. More often than not, in social science research, we cannot fully explain the causes of an effect under study. Although this fact is dissatisfying, it is not surprising, as the complexity of human behavior is immense. Moreover, in developmental research, single variables rarely explain enough of the variance to be considered the primary *cause* of an effect. Nevertheless, an independent variable that accounts for any amount of variance, both large and small, brings science one step closer to explaining the phenomenon under study (Kirsh, 2006).

Meta-Analysis

Rarely are empirical studies replicated in an identical manner. Rather, new research tends to repeat the essence of the original work, with modifications made to the sample, design, and the independent and dependent variables. But with so many studies using different sample sizes, ages, methods, and so on, generating an estimation of variance for any one media effect can be difficult. Fortunately, even with a large number of methodological differences occurring between studies, systematic evaluations of variance can still be made through the statistical procedure known as the meta-analysis. Meta-analysis combines the numerical findings from independent research projects, while taking into consideration differences between studies. By combining separate research projects into a singular study, the weaknesses found in individual studies (e.g., small sample size or poor generalizability) become less troubling. Meta-analysis is especially useful when the findings from multiple studies are contradictory. In essence, meta-analysis creates a large sample out of a number of smaller ones, thereby increasing the ability to detect real differences, if indeed they are present (i.e., power). In doing so, meta-analysis helps to clarify effects that had previously been inconclusive (Comstock & Scharrer, 2003).

In addition to identifying the presence of an effect, meta-analysis also measures the size of the effect. To do so, researchers frequently make use of the effect size correlation (r_+), which refers to the average strength of the relationship between an independent and a dependent variable. Effect size correlation coefficients are considered small when around .10, medium in the region of .30, and large when in the vicinity of .50. Finally, meta-analysis can provide an estimate for the total amount of variance accounted for by any one factor.

There are many important issues to bear in mind when evaluating a meta-analytic study. For instance, the overinclusion of multiple studies with noteworthy methodological problems can render statistically significant effects invalid. Conversely, the inclusion of numerous studies with poor methodology can also make it more difficult to find evidence of an effect. As an example, consider the following: Anderson's (2004) meta-analytic study of violent video games on aggressive thoughts, feelings, and behavior revealed that effect sizes were at their largest when only "best practice" studies were used in the analyses (i.e., those studies with few methodological flaws). Although the statistics involved in meta-analysis are objective, researchers are still required to make subjective decisions about which articles to include and how to categorize different aspects of the study (e.g., emotion or arousal level). For instance, in an assessment of the effects of TV on prosocial behavior, Hearold (1986) included borrowing books from the library as a prosocial act. Given that prosocial behavior is defined as direct acts of helping, sharing, and cooperating with others, Hearold's decision has been subsequently called into question (Mares & Woodard, 2001).

Additionally, many social science journals are hesitant to publish articles in which "nonsignificant" findings occur. As such, the studies included in a meta-analysis are more likely to be skewed toward the presence of an effect than the absence of one. This phenomenon is commonly referred to as *publication bias*. Even though researchers may try to track down studies that ended up in a file drawer unpublished, it is impossible to know if all relevant studies were identified. It is, however, possible to estimate the influence of publication bias on the results of a meta-analysis. One such method, called the *fail-safe N*, calculates the number of *additional* nonsignificant studies needed to make a statistically significant finding become statistically nonsignificant. For meta-analyses with a high-fail-safe N, numerous nonsignificant studies are required to alter the results. In such cases, the influence of publication bias is thought to be minimal. In contrast, when a low-fail-safe N is present, only a few studies are needed to impact the results, thereby greatly increasing the likelihood that publication bias is influencing the findings (Ferguson, 2007).

Findings From Meta-Analyses of Media Effects Research

In terms of magnitude, the results from numerous meta-analyses indicate that media accounts for anywhere between 1% to 14% of the

Variance Accounted for by Media

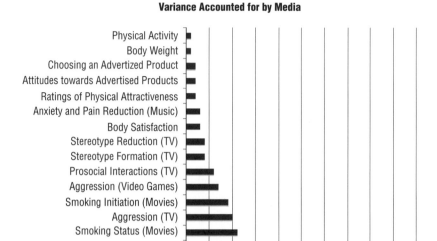

Figure 12.1   Percentage of variance accounted for by media.
*Parentheses indicate the meta-analysis was limited to a specific type of media.

variance, differing by the dependent variable under study. As indicated in Figure 12.1, across development media appears to have the biggest impact on prosocial behavior, aggression, and smoking. In contrast, media appears to have far less of an influence on body weight and physical activity (Desmond & Carveth, 2007; Groesz, Levine, & Murnen, 2001; Klassen, Liang, Tjosvold, Klassen, & Hartling, 2008; Mares & Woodard, 2007; Marshall, Biddle, Gorely, Cameron, & Murdey, 2004; Oppliger, 2007; Wellman, Sugarman, DiFranza, & Winickoff, 2006). However, there are no meta-analytic studies indicating how media effect sizes compare against other powerhouse environmental influences of development (such as parents, peers, and siblings). It may be that, relative to other environmental factors, media consumption has a bigger influence on certain outcomes more so than others. As such, the relative risks and benefits of media, in the context of other environmental factors, require additional investigation.

A few caveats are needed when interpreting these data. First, there are no current meta-analyses on the effects of media on drug use, alcohol use, or sexual activity. However, research indicates that media typically accounts for between 5% and 10% of the variance in these areas (e.g., Sargent et al., 2006). Second, the fail-safe N, for certain areas of

Table 12.1   Age Grouping Typically Used in Developmental Research

Developmental Period	Associated Age Range
Infancy	Birth to 1 year
Toddlerhood	1–3 years of age
Early childhood	3–5 years of age
Middle childhood	6–12 years of age
Adolescence	11–19 years of age

media effects research, such as media violence, is relatively small, suggesting the possibility that publication bias is present in the literature (Ferguson, 2007). Third, cultural influences may moderate the effects of media on youth. For instance, the effect sizes for computer aided instruction are far greater in Taiwan (effect size =.55) than in the United States (effect size = .13; Liao, 2007). Taken together, these findings suggest that media does not impact youth in an all-or-none fashion; rather, its influence occurs in the context of other environmental factors. Additional research is needed to see how the effects of different types of media (e.g., TV, video games, etc.) and genres (e.g., sex, aggression, and drugs) vary by culture as well.

Fourth, across a variety of genres, most meta-analytic studies have not found consistent evidence of developmental differences. For instance, a meta-analysis of violent media failed to support the contention that, across development, the impact of media violence on aggression varied by age (Anderson & Bushman, 2001). Ostensibly, the lack of developmental differences is surprising given that the primary focus of this book has been to assess the differential influence of media on children and adolescents. However, to date, most meta-analytic studies have not adequately assessed media influences using developmentally appropriate age breakdowns. Instead, research tend to combine youth based on the gross age groupings of infancy, toddlerhood, early childhood, middle childhood, and adolescence. (See Table 12.1.) But why is it inappropriate to blindly combine data from children that are part of the same age grouping? The answer is simple, yet often overlooked: Too much development occurs within age groupings. For instance, 6-year-olds and 10-year-olds are both in middle childhood. But, as any sibling pair will tell you, 6- and 10-year-olds are different physically, cognitively, socially, and emotionally. As an example, when my son was 6, he lacked a key component in the understanding of language-based humor, known as *meta-linguistic awareness*, which can be broadly defined as thinking about the formal aspects of language (e.g., syntax and grammar: DeHart, Sroufe, & Cooper, 2004). As such, he told the following joke: "Knock-Knock," (Who's there?), "Banana," (Banana who?), "Banana Orange!" While my son was busy rolling on the floor laughing, his 10-year-old sister, who had a well developed sense of metalinguistic awareness, said, "Um, that doesn't make sense." Of course she was right, and in most instances, creating a singular group of children or adolescents that vary by more than 2–3 years of age doesn't make sense either. There are just too many physical, cognitive, social, and emotional changes that occur within a short period of time. Failure to make these distinctions may result in data that are confounded with developmental status.

Typically, the creation of large age-based grouping in meta-analytic research occurs out of necessity. As it turns out, there is relatively little consistency between studies in the age ranges used or the combined age based grouping created. For instance, whereas one study might assess 6- to 10-year olds, another study might sample 8- and 10-year-olds. Limited by age-based overlapping, the only way to combine these two studies would be to create a large age grouping of 6- to 10-year-olds. As a result, any developmental differences evident between ages 6 and 10 disappear in the data. Unfortunately, because there are no systematic rules that establish which ages are considered developmentally appropriate to combine, this type of overlapping is common. As such, researchers are forced to use larger age-based categories created along broad developmental lines.

Finally, critics of media effects research frequently point out that the amount of variance accounted for by media in any one outcome is relatively small. As mentioned above, even large effects leave 75% of the variance unaccounted for. Nevertheless, in the real world, even small effects can have a big impact on society. For example, the amount of variance accounted for by aspirin in heart attack prevention is only around 1%. Yet prescribing daily aspirin is considered to be a standard health care procedure known to reduce the risk of heart attacks. Similarly, lead is no longer allowed to be used in paint or put in gasoline even though exposure to lead accounts for around 2% of the variance in children's IQ. Despite the fact that it accounts for only 4% of the variance, condom use is lauded as an important factor in the prevention of sexually transmitted HIV. Such examples, which are commonplace in health research, clearly illustrate the importance of "small" effects on public health and public policy. Thus, when thinking about the effects of media on youth, the 1–14% of variance accounted for by media is not only of statistical importance, but also of societal importance (Anderson & Bushman, 2001; Anderson, Gentile, & Buckley, 2007).

Risk, Protective, and Beneficial Factors

Media has the potential to impact youth in three distinct ways: as a risk factor, as a protective factor, and as a beneficial factor. Whereas risk factors increase the likelihood that negative outcomes will occur, protective factors decrease that chance. Rather than protecting against negative outcomes, beneficial factors promote positive outcomes. For instance, in the battle against heart disease, obesity has been identified as an important risk factor, as obese people are more likely to have heart disease than individuals of normal weight. Taking medication to lower cholesterol is a protective factor, because it prevents the naturally occurring build up of plaque along arterial walls. Having bypass surgery is a beneficial factor as it makes a poorly working heart function better (but it does not prevent future blockages). At times, factors can have both beneficial and protective qualities. Exercising and eating healthy are beneficial factors, as they promote heart health (e.g., size and strength) and protective factors as they reduce the risk of heart disease (e.g., arterial blockage; M. M. Kirsh, personal communication, June 2008).

With regard to media effects, it is important to remember that no one risk factor causes a negative outcome. Similarly, no one protective factor can guarantee that a negative outcome will not occur. Nor does a single beneficial factor always produce the desired positive outcome. Consider the following examples: Watching sex on TV will not make a puritanical adolescent suddenly become promiscuous; watching *Sesame Street* or playing the computer game Jump Start First Grade will not guarantee academic success. Even the most violent and gory television program imaginable will not cause children to act aggressively. Rather, it is the accumulation of risk, beneficial, and protective factors over time that result in both positive and negative outcomes. As an example, Anderson and colleagues (2007) found that the ability to predict real-life aggression increased dramatically with each additional risk factor taken into consideration. Moreover, only three risk factors, which included exposure to media violence, were needed to generate a high degree of predictive accuracy.

According to Garbarino (1999), most youth are able to cope with one or two risk factors without negative consequences, but when three or more risk factors are present, negative outcomes are more likely to occur than not. However, because protective factors can mitigate the negative influence of multiple risk factors, it is the combined totality of risk and protective factors that produces the observed outcome. Media, therefore, is most likely to negatively impact youth possessing multiple risk factors and few protective ones. Then again, some risk factors (or protective factors) may be more influential than others. Thus, in addition to the quantity of risk and protective factors present, the relative influence of each factor should be taken into consideration. That is where variance comes in, as the amount of variance accounted for by any one risk or protective factor provides an estimate of that factors influence. For instance, when looking at Figure 12.1, it is clear that watching violent media for hours on end is a far bigger risk factor for aggression than it is for obesity.

Reducing the Negative Effects of Media Through Media Literacy

We live in a media saturated world, and, unfortunately, much of the content that children and adolescents are exposed to places them at risk for negative outcomes. However, as mentioned above, protective factors mitigate the potentially harmful effects of media on youth. One such protective factor is mediation. Mediation refers to a class of intervention strategies that attempt to disrupt the effects of consuming media on children and adolescents. Three distinct types of mediation have been investigated over the past 30 years: co-consuming mediation, active mediation, and restrictive mediation. Co-consuming mediation consists of parents, teachers, and so on participating in the media experience along with children. This is a passive type of mediation, where no comments are made about the content of media before, during, or after its use. Restrictive mediation, which typically takes place in the home, refers to the situation in which limitations are placed on the quantity and/or type of media youth are allowed to view. For instance, parents may prohibit their preteen children from playing M-rated video games and seeing R-rated movies. Active mediation refers to the process of talking to children and adolescents about the content of media. For instance, during active mediation of advertising content, a parent or teacher explains to youth the persuasive intent of the commercial, the mechanisms through which this is achieved (e.g., exaggeration), while at the same time making negative comments and judgments about the advertisements.

Unlike co-viewing and restrictive mediation, active mediation attempts to augment children's and adolescents' cognitive defenses and alter their affective responses to media. Cognitive defenses refer to factors that help youth understand the true nature of the media being consumed; such as its realism, intent, and portrayal of those involved. Violent media, for instance, often fails to show realistic portrayals of the outcomes of violence (e.g., pain and suffering). Buijzen and colleagues (Buijzen, van der Molen, & Sondij, 2007) contended that whereas children have cognitive defenses in place by age 8, they do not use them on their own until age 12. Nevertheless, through adult intervention, cognitive defenses can be activated and used much earlier. But even when cognitive defenses are available for use during early adolescence, not all teens actively employ them. Those that do, however, appear to reap the benefits. For instance, adolescents critical of commercial advertisements were less likely to drink alcohol than teens without this media resistant skill (Epstein & Botvin, 2008). As mentioned above, affective responses refer to the liking of, and attitude toward, the media consumed. As such, active mediation attempts to reduce positive emotions and increase negative attitudes toward media.

Media literacy refers to the ability to analyze and evaluate media. Active mediation is the key component of media literacy campaigns targeting children in formal settings, such as schools and religious venues. Many media literacy programs focus on the factual components of media productions, discussing issues related to special effects, camera angles, plot lines, and so on. One of the basic tenets of media literacy is that if you show youth how media is created, then they will be less likely to be influenced by it. Thus, media literacy interventions involve two independent effects: (a) altering youth's cognitive understanding of media, and (b) reducing the negative impact of media on youth. Numerous studies have clearly demonstrated that from kindergarten onward, a child's cognitive understanding of media can be successfully altered through media literacy programs in school. For instance, media literacy campaigns have effectively taught youth about the reality of, and production methods used to create, their favorite media offerings (Nathanson, 2002). Thus, media literacy can clearly change the experience of media consumption. But can it alter the effects of it as well? The answer varies by the type of mediation employed and the age of the child involved.

Research on Co-Consuming Mediation

It is hard to think of co-consuming mediation as an actual attempt to reduce the effects of media, as no critical (or positive) comments are made during the process. The adult simply plays, watches, reads, or listen to the media that the child is currently consuming. By doing so, the adult is tacitly approving the content being consumed, whatever it may be. Relatively little new research exists on the influence of co-consuming mediation. What does, however, suggests that this type of mediation does not mitigate the effects of media consumption. As an example, Nathanson (1999) found that co-viewing violent television with parents was associated with higher levels of aggressive behavior in children. One thing is clear, parents are more likely to engage in co-consuming mediation if they believe that the effects of the media being used are beneficial to youth, or at the very least, not harmful. In contrast, when media consumption is thought to be detrimental, parents are more likely to use restrictive or active mediation (Nikken & Jansz, 2006).

Research on Restrictive Mediation

At times, restrictive mediation has been associated with a reduction in the negative impact of media on youth. For instance, Schooler and colleagues (Schooler, Kim, & Sorsoli, 2006) found that youth whose parents set more restrictions on general television viewing were less sexually experienced than other youth. However, Schooler et al.'s findings are more the exception than the rule. Experimental and correlational research on mediation techniques (in both home and school settings) has found that high levels of restrictive mediation typically fail to effectively reduce the impact of commercial advertisements or media violence on youth. The inability of restrictive mediation to reduce the influence of media on youth is somewhat surprising, because regardless of developmental status, children and adolescents cannot be influenced by the sights and sound of media that they, ostensibly, cannot see or hear. In support of their restrictive efforts, parents can buy remote controls limiting channels to "kid-friendly stations," activate the V-chip on their TVs to prevent access to violent content, utilize *Net Nanny*–type programs to preclude access to pornography on the Internet, or just simply turn off and/or limit the use of media. When I was growing up, my parents used a key that could be inserted into the cable box to block access to movie channels (and soft-core pornography shown at night). However, "Where there is a will, there is a way." Frequently, youth experiencing a highly media-restrictive home consume the prohibited content without their parents' knowledge (Nathanson, 2002). For instance, I found the key and used it liberally when my parents went out. However, moderate amounts of restrictive mediation can be used to successfully reduce the negative impact of media consumption. As an example, in comparison to youth experiencing either low or high levels of restrictive mediation, youth encountering moderate levels of mediation tend to be less aggressive than other children (Nathanson, 1999).

Another reason to avoid extremely high levels of restrictive mediation is that it often creates ill will between child and parent. Research has shown that children are more likely to espouse negative attitudes toward their parents if they experience a great deal of media restriction; as more than one youth has said, "It's just not fair." Moreover, restrictive mediation can produce a "forbidden fruit" effect. According to the forbidden fruit theory, prohibitions and admonitions (such as warning labels used for music) increase the attractiveness of media for youth. For instance, preadolescent boys prefer to watch television programs labeled as age inappropriate over those labeled age appropriate (Sneegas & Plank, 1998). However, development and gender seem to moderate the forbidden fruit effect. Warning labels and prohibitions increase the desire to consume the outlawed media more so for boys and for children over the age of 8, in comparison to girls and younger children (Bushman & Cantor, 2003). In contrast, for girls and young children, prohibitions and warnings produce a "tainted fruit effect," which results in youth avoiding tabooed media offerings.

It is worth noting that the aforementioned gender differences related to the forbidden and tainted fruit effects may reflect the manner in which boys and girls are socialized. Whereas boys tend to be socialized to exhibit instrumental role characteristics, girls tend to be socialized to adopt expressive roles. As a result, in an effort to be independent, boys are more likely to be noncompliant to the demands of parents, that is, do what they want to do and not necessarily what they were told to do by their parents. The expressive role rearing of girls, in contrast, results in outlawed media being avoided, as "good girls" cooperate and listen to their elders.

Research on Active Mediation

Relative to the outcomes for co-consuming and restrictive mediation, much greater success in reducing the negative effects of media has occurred with active mediation (Buijzen & Valkenburg, 2005; Robinson, Saphir, Kraemer, Varady, & Haydel, 2001). In fact, for certain types of media, active mediation can influence both cognitive defenses and affective responses throughout middle childhood. For instance, advertising mediation can (a) enhance children's understanding of the persuasive intent of advertising, (b) increase children's skepticism about commercials, and (c) create a more negative attitude toward advertised products. Active mediation can even result in children making fewer product requests from parents (Bijmolt et al., 1998; Buijzen et al., 2007; Prasad et al., 1978). Consistent with these studies, Nathanson (2002) found that mediation statements, such as "The show is wrong, lots of girls do things besides paint their nails and put on makeup" and "The show is wrong, lots of girls like camping and don't complain all the time" lead to less positive evaluations of stereotyped television characters. The effects of active mediation were especially strong for younger children (kindergarten through second grade) and for elementary school-aged youth with parents who did not typically monitor their children's television activities. Additional research has demonstrated that when adolescents talk with their parents about television content, they report less sexual activity, relative to when such conversations do not occur (Schooler et al., 2006).

In contrast to advertising and gender stereotyping mediation, altering cognitive defenses during media violence mediation has been relatively ineffective in reducing aggressive outcomes. Thus, telling youth, "They are really not hitting each other" and "That isn't real blood," does not appear to impact postviewing aggression. At times, focusing on the factual aspects of media violence has actually led to an increase in aggressive behavior, rather than a decrease (Doolittle, 1980). Mediation techniques focusing on an emotional response, such as "How awful—hitting is wrong" and "Stabbing someone is horrifying," do appear to reduce post-media violence aggressive behavior (Cantor & Wilson, 2003). Once again, developmental differences are present, with mediation focusing on emotional responses producing stronger effects on behavior during middle childhood than during early childhood. The combination of being aware of societal prohibitions against aggressive behavior and having better impulse control may explain why older children show greater reductions in aggression following mediation, relative to preschool-aged children (Kirsh, 2006).

Interestingly, research focusing on the impact of media violence mediation on *attitudes* toward violence has revealed a developmental pattern in direct opposition to that shown for mediation research on aggressive *behavior*. Whether the mediator is a parent or another adult, active mediation does appear to make aggressive behavior less normal and less acceptable to most youth. However mediation statements appear to influence younger children more so than preteens. It may be that older children find mediation statements, such as "Murder is wrong," as condescending, thus resulting in a "backlash" toward antiviolence attitudes. Or it may simply be that, in order to avoid a lecture, older children "tune out" antiviolence mediation statements (Nathanson & Yang, 2003). In order to circumvent mediation backlash, focusing on the feelings of the victims, rather than the wrongness of a violent act, may prove more beneficial to older children. For instance, Nathanson and Cantor (2000) found that instructing 7- to 11-year-olds to focus on the feelings of the victim prior to watching a violent cartoon resulted in lower ratings for the program's level of humor and likeability, relative to youth not receiving these instructions. Moreover, boys receiving this type of affectively focused mediation (but not girls) perceived the use of aggression to be less acceptable.

Despite its general success, at times, active mediation has produced undesired effects. As mentioned above, Doolittle (1980) found that cognitively focused mediation during violent programming led to an increase in aggressive behavior among children. Similarly, research on the effects of mediation on alcohol use has demonstrated that when parents talk with their young children about alcohol consumption, brand awareness increases (Austin & Nach-Ferguson, 1995). Most troubling is the research on body image and eating disorders, which found that critical viewing of content on television shows (e.g., discussing the thinness of the actress) was associated with greater levels of body image disturbance across adolescence. When parents talked with their children about the physique of actors, regardless if it was positive or negative, adolescents ended up comparing their own bodies to those they saw on screen. Negative emotions resulted and teens became more likely to develop a strong drive for thinness and symptoms of anorexia (Nathanson & Botta, 2003). Thus, simply knowing that media presents the world in an unrealistic manner does not always mean that the effects of its consumption can be mitigated.

Countermedia

In an effort to limit the negative effects of media consumption on children and adolescents, researchers and concerned public health organizations, have made use of countermedia. This type of intervention relays media-based messages that are in direct opposition to ones typically encountered by youth. For instance, the "Just Say No to Drugs" campaign used television commercials and print media to contradict the positive portrayals of alcohol and drug use frequently seen on television and in the movies. To date, research on countermedia interventions have involved prejudice, gender stereotyping, sexual behavior, and CAD use.

Gender stereotyping

The vast majority of countermedia research on gender stereotyping was conducted prior to 1990 and involved showing youth videos, commercials, and books of males and females in nontraditional roles; which at the time included male nurses and female doctors. Across development, the research was mixed, with only a few studies finding evidence that counterstereotyping media successfully reduced gender stereotypes (Durkin, 1985). One of the most ambitious of these interventions was the Freestyle project of the late 1970s, which exposed 9- to 12-year-old youth to series of television programs. Throughout this 13-part series, youth were exposed to a variety of counterstereotyped messages, such as adults engaging in nontraditional gender roles. The results indicated that the programming was most effective at gender stereotype reduction when it took place in the school and involved postviewing discussion. Viewing the programs without discussion, or at home, failed to produce any significant changes in gender stereotyping. This is not surprising given the risk, protection, and beneficial model presented above. The more protective and beneficial factors youth are exposed to, the greater likelihood they will reap the benefits of countermedia.

Racial stereotyping
Much like the research on gender stereotyping, developing effective countermedia for racial stereotyping has proven to be a difficult task. Bigler (1999) pointed out that typical counterstereotyping techniques, such as providing lessons on ethnic and racial diversity, replacing racially stereotyped textbooks with nonstereotyped ones, and exposing youth to antiracist programs, have been ineffective at reducing stereotyped beliefs and racial bias in children and adolescents. Nevertheless, there are success stories, at least during middle childhood. One of the most prominent of these successes was the school-based intervention program *Different and the Same: A Prejudice Reduction Video Series*, which used racially diverse puppets to model behaviors (e.g., problem solving and resisting peer pressure), thought processes (e.g., challenging stereotypes), and attitudes devoid of racial bias. Each video revolved around a race-related theme (e.g., name calling, cultural identity, and standing against prejudice) and was accompanied by a guide to aid classroom teachers effectively administer the series. An assessment of third grade children of various races (African American, Asian, Caucasian, and Hispanic) revealed that, relative to a control group, youth exposed to the video series, and associated classroom discussion showed marked reductions in stereotyped attitudes and beliefs. Additionally, youth in the experimental group were more likely to offer help to a child of a different race, more likely to make cross-race friendships, and more likely to report knowing how to effectively handle interracial conflict (Graves, 1999).

Sexual behavior
In an attempt to stem the tide of teenage pregnancy and STDs, mass media campaigns have been used to promote abstinence and responsible sexual behaviors. Websites, CD-ROMs, television programs, and the like offer youth a way to learn about "safe sex," or how to say "no" to sex, in nonjudgmental, embarrassment-free settings. At the forefront has been the National Campaign to Prevent Teen and Unwanted Pregnancy, which has been generating prevention-related media (TV shows, websites, and magazines) for over 2 decades. Recently, they partnered with NBC on the reality show *The Baby Borrowers*, in which five 18- to

20-year-old couples were tasked with taking care of infants, toddlers, tweens, teens, and elderly folk on camera. The reality of having children (both pros and cons) was clearly demonstrated, and the overarching message of the series was "Don't get pregnant." A guide was made available, via download, to help parents talk with their children about the show's content. Online discussions for youth took place as well.

Around the world, advertising of condoms and birth control pills has been shown to decrease the rates of teen pregnancy and HIV infection (Brown & Strasburger, 2007). Although few large-scale studies of American adolescents exist, the ones that have been conducted suggest that media-based messages on sexual health can alter adolescents' sexual attitudes and behaviors. For instance, a survey assessing the effectiveness of a joint MTV and Kaiser Family Foundation media campaign (involving websites, PSAs, brochures, CD-ROMs, videos, and television specials) found that 66% of 16- to 24-year-olds stated that they were more likely to delay having sex after encountering campaign materials. For those teens already sexually active, more than two thirds stated that the countermedia campaign made them more likely to use condoms, get tested for STDs, and talk to their partner about safe sex (Kaiser Family Foundation, 2003). Another study found that interactive videos reduced self-reported condom failures and incidence of STDs in adolescent girls 6 months after the intervention (Downs et al., 2004). Similarly, the rates of sexual intercourse and pregnancy in middle school students decreased after exposure to the abstinence promoting "Not Me Not Now Campaign" (Doniger et al., 2001). Research has also shown that mass media campaigns can effectively increase the likelihood that parents will talk with their children about sex (DuRant et al., 2006).

Cigarette, alcohol, and drug use
In my late teens, I was treated to an interesting antidrug PSA created by the Partnership for a Drug-Free America. It showed a man holding up an egg and saying, "This is your brain." Next, he picked up a hot frying pan and said, "This is drugs." He then cracked open the egg and dropped the egg whites and yoke onto the hot pan; the contents bubbled and sizzled. The PSA ended with the man looking into the camera and saying, "Any questions?" I remember thinking, "Yes. Do we have any eggs, because that commercial made me hungry". Although millions of dollars have been spent on antidrug advertisements, there is little research to support the contention that encountering antidrug PSAs actually reduce drug use among teens. For instance, a recent

evaluation of the National Youth Anti-Drug Media Campaign, which placed antidrug advertisements on billboards, radio, the Internet, school book covers, basketball backboards, movie theaters, and television (including Channel One in schools), and in newspapers and magazines, failed to find evidence that adolescent drug use was reduced by this comprehensive campaign. In fact, for marijuana, a boomerang effect was found, with frequent exposure to countermedia being associated with the initiation of marijuana use (Orwin et al., 2006). Additional research has shown that when teens are in Internet chat rooms, antimarijuana advertisements are more likely to lead to positive attitudes toward marijuana use, rather than negative ones (David et al., 2006).

Similar to the ineffectiveness of antidrug media campaigns, media-based campaigns to combat underage drinking have not been that successful either. For instance, Flynn and colleagues (2006) found that anti–alcohol use media advertisements did not impact alcohol use among early adolescents. However, campaigns aimed at reducing drinking and driving among teens can produce significant effects. In fact, a review of the literature revealed that such programs reduced alcohol-related accidents by an impressive 13% (Elder et al., 2004). Nevertheless there is no current research to suggest that anti-alcohol ads have any influence on adolescents' alcohol consumption (Spoth et al., 2008).

Despite the inability of media to reduce alcohol and drug use across adolescence, antitobacco campaigns can influence both the intent to smoke and the onset of smoking in teenagers. For instance, over a 2-year period, during which Florida aired antismoking advertisements (designed with the input of teenagers), current cigarette use (within the last 30 days) declined by 54% among middle school students and 24% among high school students. One ad showcased an "awards show in Hell" in which the prize for the greatest number of deaths went to a tobacco executive (Ruiz, 2000). Not all antitobacco advertisements are effective, and typically those that are the least effective focus on the disease consequences of tobacco use. At times, such ads have even resulted in a boomerang effect, with exposed youth espousing a greater intent to smoke, rather than a reduced one. In contrast, the most effective antismoking campaigns tend to focus on the social consequences of smoking, such as being laughed at by peers or being turned down for a date after lighting up a cigarette (Zhao & Pechmann, 2007).

Of course, antitobacco campaigns do not operate inside a vacuum, and just as important as the ad itself is what youth "bring to the table" when exposed to countermedia. One important individual characteristic, known as regulatory focus, not only differentiates youth from one another but also influences the effectiveness of antitobacco advertisements. Regulatory focus refers to the extent to which youth are either promotion focused, and seek out achievements, or prevention focused, and attempt to avoid hazards. In social settings, whereas promotion-focused youth seek out the approval of others, prevention-focused youth try to avoid social disapproval. With regard to antismoking ads, adolescents are influenced the most by advertisements that match their particular style of regulatory focus. Thus, antitobacco ads that suggest that youth are more likely to experience social approval if they do not smoke, relative to when they do, primarily influence adolescents with a promotion focus. In contrast, youth with a prevention focus are greatly influenced by ads suggesting that smoking leads to social disapproval. Interestingly, ads not matching adolescents' regulatory focus were perceived as irrelevant, and had no discernable impact on smoking behavior (Zhao & Pechmann, 2007). The results of this study clearly suggest that it is necessary to create more than one type of antitobacco advertisement to effectively reach the largest number of adolescents.

Developmental Points of Interest

Overall, when looking at its impact on children's and adolescents' behavior, attitudes, and feelings, media accounts for a relatively small percentage of the variance. This fact is neither surprising, nor troubling, as media is simply one of many risk, protective, and beneficial factors that youth encounter. In most cases media is neither the strongest risk, protective, or beneficial factor nor the weakest. Can media use benefit youth? Is its consumption a cause for concern? The answer for both questions is an unequivocal "yes." In and of itself, media is not a strong enough influence to, alone, cause either positive or negative outcomes. However, its reduction or its inclusion can, in concert with other variables, significantly impact the behaviors, attitudes, and feelings of children and adolescents. Future research needs to clarify differences in the relative risks, protections, or benefits of media across development.

It may be that during certain periods of development youth are more vulnerable to media (or certain types of media, such as sexual or violent) than at other times. Of particular concern is early adolescence; a time during which biological, psychological, and social changes result in the presence of a number of risk factors for virtually all youth. Because of the confluence of risk during early adolescence, adding media as another risk factor may be the proverbial "straw that broke the camel's back," resulting in more frequent negative outcomes. Would beneficial factors be especially powerful during this period of development as well? It is hard to say, as few studies have compared early, middle, and late adolescents. However, the findings from Liao (2007) suggest that it is a distinct possibility, as the mathematical benefits associated with computer aided instruction were much larger on a combined group of early and middle adolescents than on younger children or late adolescents, thus suggesting the presence of developmental specificity.

Research on active and restrictive mediation has been primarily limited to children between the ages of 5 and 12. Though there are few studies on preschoolers and adolescents, the findings from several experiments suggest that the effectiveness of mediation becomes limited once children enter adolescence. For instance, evidence from media violence mediation suggests that active and restrictive mediation do not typically work with adolescents (Kirsh, 2006). Restrictions placed on viewing are easily thwarted by going to a friend's house or sneaking the behavior at home. Active mediation fails to work with adolescents because negative comments made by the mediator are frequently viewed as condescending, which may create backlash behavior (Nathanson & Yang, 2003). Additionally, future research needs to more clearly address the issue of social desirability in mediation research as a function of development. As an example, rather than a true attitudinal change, the fact that active mediation influences the aggressive attitudes of younger children more so than older children may simply reflect their desire to please the experimenter. In contrast, the rebellious nature of preteens and teens may preclude social desirable responding with increasing age. Thus, for younger youth, social desirability may make mediation appear to be more effective than it really is.

Moreover, mediation research on youth has been primarily conducted using media containing either violent content or commercial advertisements. Although additional research can be found relating mediation to self-esteem, body-image, and sexuality. Overall, creating an effective mediation campaign can be quite difficult, as its success varies by mediation type, the content being mediated, and the age of those involved. As in many things in life, moderation is the key to successful restrictive mediation. Eventually youth will come into contact with prohibited media, so, in addition to moderate restrictions, parents should use active mediation techniques to help prepare youth for these inevitable encounters. Interestingly, active mediation in advertising appears to be most effective when it impacts children's affective responses to the commercials. For example, as the greatest likelihood of children requesting products from parents occurs for products advertised in commercials that children like, regardless of whether their cognitive defenses are activated or not (Buijzen, 2007). Similarly, media violence mediation focusing on *emotional* responses has been shown to impact the attitudes and behavior of youth to a far greater extent than research focusing on *cognitive* responses. Additional, research is necessary to determine if emotion-focused mediation reduces the negative effects associated with encountering racial and gender stereotypes, as well as sexual and CAD-related content, in the media. Finally, the long-term effectiveness of mediation has yet to be tested across development. It may be that repeated exposure to mediation influences youth for longer periods of time than short-term exposures. However, repeated mediation could also produce a backlash effect, especially at older ages. As such, future mediation research should investigate a broad developmental spectrum, ranging from preschool to late adolescence.

Although *countermedia* campaigns targeting adolescents have successfully reduced tobacco use and sexual activity, they have been unsuccessful at moderating racial and gender stereotypes or drug and alcohol use. It may be that the perceived social consequences of tobacco use and sexual activity are effectively influenced by countermedia because they inherently involve more social ambiguity surrounding their appropriateness. That is, when youth are unsure as to how their peers will respond to their behaviors and attitudes, media becomes a useful tool to help them clarify the issue. In contrast, because peers play a significant role in enforcing stereotypes, countermedia may be less influential, as peers set clear markers as to what attitudes and behaviors are deemed acceptable. Moreover, because alcohol consumption is so universal, and because using certain drugs (e.g., marijuana) is deemed to be an acceptable rite of passage, there is little ambiguity for countermedia to influence. Of course, such contentions require additional validation.

References

Acuff, D. S. (1997). *What kids buy and why: The psychology of marketing to kids*. New York: Free Press.

Adams, T. M., & Fuller, D. B. (2006). The words have changed but the ideology remains the same: Misogynistic lyrics in rap music. *Journal of Black Studies, 36*(6), 938–957.

Alessi, N., Huang, M., James, P., Ying, J., & Chowhan, N. (1992). The influence of music and rock videos. In *Facts for families: The American Academy of Child and Adolescent Psychiatry* (No. 40). Retrieved May 28, 2009, from http://www.aacap.org/cs/root/facts_for_families/the_influence_of_music_and_music_videos

Alexander, A. (1990). Effects of television on family interaction. In J. Bryant (Ed.), *Television and the American Family* (pp. 211–226). Hillsdale, NJ: Erlbaum.

Alexander, S. J., & Jorgensen, S. R. (1983). Sex education for early adolescents: A study of parents and students. *Journal of Early Adolescence, 3*(4), 315–325.

Aloise-Young, P. A., Slater, M. D., & Cruickshank, C. C. (2006). Mediators and moderators of magazine advertisement effects on adolescent cigarette smoking. *Journal of Health Communication, 11*(3), 281–300.

American Psychological Association. (2001). *Publication manual of the American Psychology Association* (5th ed.). Washington, DC: Author.

Anderman, E. M., & Johnston, J. (1998). Television news in the classroom: What are adolescents learning? *Journal of Adolescent Research, 13*(1), 73–100.

Anderson, C. A. (2000). *Violent video games increase aggression and violence*. U. S. Senate Committee on Commerce, Science, and Transportation hearing on "The Impact of Interactive Violence on Children." Retrieved March 1, 2004, from http://psych-server.iastate.edu/faculty/caa/abstracts/2000-2004/00Senate.html

Anderson, C. A. (2004). An update on the effects of violent video games. *Journal of Adolescence, 27*, 113–122.

Anderson, C. A., & Bushman, B. J. (1997). External validity of "trivial" experiments: The case of laboratory aggression. *Review of General Psychology, 1*, 19–41.

Anderson, C. A., & Bushman, B. J. (2001). Effects of violent video games on aggressive behavior, aggressive cognition, aggressive affect, physiological arousal, and prosocial behavior: A metaanalytic review of the scientific literature. *Psychological Science, 12*, 353–359.

Anderson, C. A., & Bushman, B. J. (2002). Human aggression. *Annual Review of Psychology, 53*, 27–51.

Anderson, C. A., Gentile, D. A., & Buckley, K. E. (2007). *Violent video game effects on children and adolescents: Theory, research, and public policy.* New York: Oxford University Press.

Anderson, D. R., Huston, A. C., Schmitt, K. L., Linebarger, D. L., & Wright, J. C. (2001). Early childhood television viewing and adolescent behavior: The recontact study. *Monographs of the Society for Research in Child Development, 66*(1), vii–147.

Anderson, D. R., & Levin, S. R. (1976). Young children's attention to *Sesame Street. Child Development, 47*, 806–811.

Anderson, D. R., & Pempek, T. A. (2005). Television and very young children. *The American Behavioral Scientist, 48*(5), 505–522.

Angrist, J., & Lavy, V. (2002). New evidence on classroom computers and pupil learning. *Economic Journal, 12*, 735–765.

Ansari, D., & Dhital, B. (2006). Age-related changes in the activation of the intraparietal sulcus during nonsymbolic magnitude processing: An event-related functional magnetic resonance imaging study. *Journal of Cognitive Neuroscience, 18*(11), 1820–1828.

Antonucci, M. (1998). Holy sales slump! Comic-book industry hit with a slow-down. *Knight-Ridder Tribune Business News* [Online]. Available from DIALOG File 20: World Reporter.

Aronson, E., Wilson, T. D., & Akert, R. M. (2004). *Social psychology* (4th ed.). Upper Saddle River, NJ: Prentice Hall.

Atkin, C. K. (1975). *Survey of children's and mothers' responses to television commercials. The effects of television advertising on children* (Report No. 8, ERIC Document Reproduction Service No. ED123675). East Lansing: Michigan State University.

Atkin, C. K., & Block, M. (1983). Effectiveness of celebrity endorsers. *Journal of Advertising Research, 23*, 57–61.

Atkin, C. K., Smith, S. W., Roberto, A. J., Fediuk, T., & Wagner, T. (2002). Correlates of verbally aggressive communication in adolescents. *Journal of Applied Communication Research, 30*, 251–266.

Aubrey, J. S. (2004). Sex and punishment: An examination of sexual consequences and the sexual double standard in teen programming. *Sex Roles, 50*, 505–514.

Aubrey, J. S., & Harrison, K. (2004). The gender-role content of children's favorite television programs and its links to their gender-related perception. *Media Psychology, 6*, 111–146.

Ausbrooks, E., Thomas, S. P., & Williams, R. (1995). Relationships among self-efficacy, optimism, trait anger, and anger expression. *Health Values, 19*(4), 46–53.

Austin, E. W., & Nach-Ferguson, B. (1995). Sources and influences of young school-aged children's general and brand-specific knowledge about alcohol. *Health Communication, 7*(1), 1–20.

Baghurst, T., Carlston, D., Wood, J., & Wyatt, F. B. (2007). Preadolescent male perceptions of action figure physiques. *Society for Adolescent Medicine, 41*, 613–615.

Baker, K., & Raney, A. A. (2007). Equally super? Gender-role stereotyping of superheroes in children's animated programs. *Mass Communication & Society, 10*, 25–41.

Ball, S. J., & Bogatz, G. A. (1973). *Reading with Television: An evaluation of* The Electric Company. Princeton, NJ: Educational Testing Services.

Ballard, K. D. (2003, June). *Media habits and academic performance: Elementary and middle school students' perceptions.* Poster session presented at the National Media Education Conference, Baltimore.

Ballentine, L. W., & Ogle, J. P. (2005). The making and unmaking of body problems in *Seventeen* magazine, 1992–2003. *Family and Consumer Sciences Research Journal, 33*, 281–307.

Bandura, A. (1965). Influence of models' reinforcement contingencies on the acquisition of imitative responses. *Journal of Personality and Social Psychology, 1*, 589–595.

Bandura, A. (1973). *Aggression: A social learning analysis.* Englewood Cliffs, NJ: Prentice Hall.

Bandura, A. (1986). *Social foundations of thought and action: A social cognitive theory.* Englewood Cliffs, NJ: Prentice Hall.

Bandura, A., Ross, D., & Ross, S. A. (1961). Transmission of aggression through imitation of aggressive models. *Journal of Abnormal & Social Psychology, 63*(3), 575–582.

Barner, M. R. (1999). Sex-role stereotyping in FCC-mandated children's educational television. *Journal of Broadcasting & Electronic Media, 43*, 551–564.

Bar-Or, O., Foreyt, J., Bouchard, C., Brownell, K. D., Dietz, W. H., Ravussin, E., et al. (1998). Physical activity, genetic and nutritional considerations in childhood weight management. *Medical and Science in Sports and Exercise, 30*, 2–10.

Barr, R., & Hayne, H. (1999). Developmental changes in imitation from television during infancy. *Child Development, 70*, 1067–1081.

Batada, A., & Wootan, M. G. (2007). Nickelodeon markets nutrition-poor foods to children. *American Journal of Preventive Medicine, 33*, 48–50.

Bauserman, K. L., Cassady, J. C., Smith, L. L., & Stroud, J. C. (2005). Kindergarten literacy achievement: The effects of PLATO integrated learning system. *Reading Research and Instruction, 44*(4), 49–60.

BBC.com. (2008). Ban on junk food ads introduced. Retrieved February 12, 2008, from http://news.bbc.co.uk/2/hi/health/7166510.stm

Beasley, B., & Standley, T. C. (2002). Shirts vs. skins: Clothing as an indicator of gender role stereotyping in video games. *Mass Communication & Society, 5,* 279–293.

Bell, B. T., Lawton, R., & Dittmar, H. (2007). The impact of thin models in music videos on adolescent girls' body dissatisfaction. *Body Image, 4,* 137–145.

Bellieni, C. V., Cordello, D. M., Raffaelli, M., Ricci, B., Morgese, G., & Buonocore, G. (2006). Analgesic effect of watching TV during venipuncture. *Archives of Disease in Childhood, 91*(12), 1015–1017.

Belson, W. A. (1978). *Television violence and the adolescent boy.* Farnborough, UK: Saxon House.

Bernthal. M. J. (2003). The effects of professional wrestling viewership on children. *The Sport Journal.* Retrieved June 5, 2004, from http://thesportjournal. org

Bessenoff, G. R., & Del Priore, R. E. (2007). Women, weight, and age: Social comparison to magazine images across the lifespan. *Sex Roles, 56,* 215–222.

Bettelheim, B. (1967). *The uses of enchantment: The meaning and importance of fairy tales.* New York: Random House.

Bigler, R. S. (1999). The use of multicultural curricula and materials to counter racism in children. *Journal of Social Issues, 55,* 687–705.

Bijmolt, T. H. A., Claassen, W., & Brus, B. (1998). Children's understanding of TV advertising: Effects of age, gender, and parental influence. *Journal of Consumer Policy, 21,* 171–194.

Bjorkqvist, K. (1985). *Violent films, anxiety, and aggression.* Helsinki: Finnish Society of Sciences and Letters.

Blakely, W. P. (1958). A study of seventh grade children's reading of comic books as related to certain other variables. *The Journal of Genetic Psychology, 93,* 291–301.

Bo, L. K., & Callaghan, P. (2000). Soothing pain-elicited distress in Chinese neonates. *Pediatrics, 105*(4), E49.

Board on Children, Youth & Families. (2006). *Studying media effects on children and youth: Improving methods and measures, workshop summary.* Washington, DC: National Academies Press.

Bogatz, B. A., & Ball, S. (Eds.). (1971). *The second year of* Sesame Street: *A continuing evaluation.* Princeton, NJ: Educational Testing Service.

Borzekowski, D. L. G., & Robinson, T. N. (2001). The 30-second effect: An experiment revealing the impact of television commercials on food preferences of preschoolers. *Journal of the American Dietetic Association, 101,* 42–46.

Borzekowski, D. L. G., Thomas, D., Robinson, N., & Killen, J. D. (2000). Does the camera add 10 pounds? Media use, perceived importance of appearance, and weight concerns among teenage girls. *Journal of Adolescent Health, 26,* 36–41.

Boyatzis, C. J., Matillo, G. M., & Nesbitt, K. M. (1995). Effects of *"The Mighty Morphin Power Rangers"* on children's aggression with peers. *Child Study Journal, 25,* 45–55.

Boyer, E. W., Shannon, M., & Hibberd, P. L. (2005). The internet and psychoactive substance use among innovative drug users. *Pediatrics, 115,* 302–305.

Brand, J. (1969). The effect of highly aggressive content in comic books on seventh grade children. *Graduate Research in Education and Related Disciplines, 5,* 46–61.

Braun, C. M. J., & Giroux, J. (1989). Arcade video games: Proxemic, cognitive, and content analyses. *Journal of Leisure Research, 21,* 92–105.

Brewer, N. T. (2003). The relation of internet searching to club drug knowledge and attitudes. *Psychology & Health, 18*(3), 387–401.

Bridges, E., & Briesch, R. A. (2006). The 'nag factor' and children's product categories. *International Journal of Advertising: Special Issue: Food Advertising & Promotion, 25*(2), 157–187.

Brooks, G., Miles, J. N. V., Torgerson, C. J., & Torgerson, D. J. (2006). Is an intervention using computer software effective in literacy learning? A randomized controlled trial. *Educational Studies, 32*(2), 133–143.

Brown, E. F., & Hendee, W. R. (1989). Adolescents and their music: Insights into the health of adolescents. *Journal of the American Medical Association, 262,* 1659–1663.

Brown, J. D., L'Engle, K. L., Pardun, C. J., Guo, G., Kenneavy, K., & Jackson, C. (2006). Sexy media matter: Exposure to sexual content in music, movies, television, and magazines predicts Black and White adolescents' sexual behavior. *Pediatrics, 117,* 1018–1027.

Brown, J. D., & Strasburger, V. C. (2007). From Calvin Klein to Paris Hilton and Myspace: Adolescents, sex, and the media. *Adolescent Medicine, 18,* 484–507.

Brownlee, S. (1999). Inside the teen brain. *US News Online.* Retrieved February 20, 2007, from http://www.usnews.com/usnews/issue/990809/nycu/teenbrain.htm

Bryant, J., & Brown, D. (Eds.). (1989). Uses of pornography. In D. Zillmann & B. Jennings (Eds.), *Pornography: Research advances and policy considerations* (pp. 25–55). Hillsdale, NJ: Lawrence Erlbaum.

Bryant, J., & Miron, D. (2004). Theory and research in mass communication. *Journal of Communication: Special Issue: State of the Art in Communication Theory and Research, 54*(4), 662–704.

Bryant, J., & Rockwell, S. C. (1994). Effects of massive exposure to sexually oriented prime-time television programming on adolescents' moral judgment. In D. Zillmann, J. Bryant, & A. C. Huston (Eds.), *Media, children, and the family: Social scientific, psychodynamic, and clinical perspectives* (pp. 183–196). Hillsdale, NJ: Erlbaum.

Bufkin, J., & Eschholz, S. (2000). Images of sex and rape: A content analysis of popular film. *Violence Against Women, 6,* 1317–1344.

Buijzen, M. (2007). Reducing children's susceptibility to commercials: Mechanisms of factual and evaluative advertising interventions. *Media Psychology*, *9*(2), 411–430.

Buijzen, M., & Valkenburg, P. M. (2000). The impact of television advertising on children's Christmas wishes. *Journal of Broadcasting & Electronic Media, 44*, 456–469.

Buijzen, M., & Valkenburg, P. M. (2002). Appeals in television advertising: A content analysis of commercials aimed at children and teenagers. *Communications, 27*, 349–364.

Buijzen, M., & Valkenburg, P. M. (2003). The unintended effects of television advertising: A parent-child survey. *Communication Research, 30*(5), 483–503.

Buijzen, M., & Valkenburg, P. M. (2005). Parental mediation of undesired advertising effects. *Journal of Broadcasting & Electronic Media, 49*(2), 153–165.

Buijzen, M., van der Molen, W., & Sondij, P. (2007). Parental mediation of children's emotional responses to a violent news event. *Communication Research, 34*, 212–230.

Bushman, B. J. (2002). Does venting anger feed or extinguish the flame? Catharsis, rumination, distraction, anger and aggressive responding. *Journal of Personality & Social Psychology, 28*, 724–731.

Bushman, B. J., & Cantor, J. (2003). Media ratings for violence and sex. *American Psychologist, 58*, 130–141.

Byrd-Bredbenner, C., Finckenor, M., & Grasso, D. (2003). Health related content in prime-time television programming. *Journal of Health Communication, 8*(4), 329–341.

Cafri, G., van den Berg, P., & Thompson, J. K. (2006). Pursuit of muscularity in adolescent boys: Relations among biopsychosocial variables and clinical outcomes. *Journal of Clinical Child and Adolescent Psychology, 35*, 283–291.

Calvert, S. L., & Kotler, J. A. (2003). Lessons from children's television: The impact of the Children's Television Act on children's learning. *Applied Developmental Psychology, 24*, 275–335.

Calvert, S. L., Kotler, J. A., Zehnder, S. M., & Shockey, E. M. (2003). Gender stereotyping in children's reports about educational and informational television programs. *Media Psychology, 5*, 139–162.

Campbell, L. A., & Bryant, R. A. (2007). How time flies: A study of novice skydivers. *Behaviour Research and Therapy, 45*(6), 1389–1392.

Cantor, J., Mares, M. L., & Oliver, M. B. (1993). Parents' and children's emotional reactions to TV coverage of the Gulf War. In B. S. Greenberg & W. Gantz (Eds.), *Desert Storm and the mass media* (pp. 325–340). Cresskill, NJ: Hampton Press.

Cantor, J., & Sparks, G. G. (1984). Children's fear responses to mass media: Testing some Piagetian predictions. *Journal of Communication, 34*, 90–103.

Cantor, J., & Wilson, B. J. (2003). Media and violence: Intervention strategies for reducing aggression. *Media Psychology, 5,* 363–403.

Carpenter, L. M. (1998). From girls into women: Scripts for sexuality and romance in Seventeen magazine, 1974–1994. *The Journal of Sex Research, 35,* 158–168.

Carpentier, F. D., Knobloch, S., & Zillmann, D. (2003). Rock, rap, and rebellion: Comparisons of traits predicting selective exposure to defiant music. *Personality and Individual Differences, 35,* 1643–1655.

Carruth, B. R., Goldberg, D. L., & Skinner, J. D. (1991). Do parents and peers mediate the influence of television advertising on food-related purchases? *Journal of Adolescent Research, 6*(2), 253–271.

Celozzi, M. J., Kazelskis, R., & Gutsch, K. U. (1981). The relationship between viewing televised violence in ice hockey and subsequent levels of personal aggression. *Journal of Sport Behavior, 4*(4), 157–162.

Center on Alcohol Marketing and Youth. (2004). Clicking with kids: Alcohol marketing and youth on the internet. Retrieved January 7, 2008, from http://www.camy.org/research/internet0304/

Center on Alcohol Marketing and Youth. (2007a). Youth exposure to alcohol advertising on television and in national magazines, 2001 to 2006. Retrieved July 31, 2008, from http://camy.org/research/tvmag1207/

Center on Alcohol Marketing and Youth. (2007b). Alcohol advertising and youth. Retrieved July 15, 2008, from http://camy.org/factsheets/index.php?FactsheetID=1

Centers for Disease Control and Prevention. (2006). *Youth risk behavior surveillance.* Retrieved September 12, 2002, from http://www.cdc.gov

Centers for Disease Control and Prevention. (2008a). *Reproductive health.* Retrieved September 12, 2002, from http://www.cdc.gov/reproductive-health/Data_Stats/index.htm

Centers for Disease Control and Prevention. (2008b). Sexual risk behaviors. *Healthy Youth!* Retrieved May 28, 2009, from http://www.cdc.gov/HealthyYouth/sexualbehaviors/

Çepni, S., Taş, E., & Köse, S. (2006). The effects of computer-assisted material on students' cognitive levels, misconceptions and attitudes towards science. *Computers & Education, 46,* 192–205.

Chambers, J. H., & Ascione, F. R. (1987). The effects of prosocial and aggressive videogames on children's donating and helping. *Journal of Genetic Psychology 148,* 499–505.

Chan, P. A., & Rabinowitz, T. (2006). A cross-sectional analysis of video games and attention deficit hyperactivity disorder symptoms in adolescents. *Annals of General Psychiatry, 5*(16). Retrieved May 28, 2009, from http://www.annals-general-psychiatry.com/content/5/1/16

Chang, I. (2007, April). Tweens now occupy a top spot in mind of product marketers. *P.R. Week,* 9.

Chang, K., Sung, Y., & Lin, S. (2006). Computer-assisted learning for mathematical problem solving. *Computers & Education, 46*, 140–151.

Chao, Y. M., Pisetsky, E. M., Dierket, L. C., Dohm, F., Rosselli, F., May, A. M., et al. (2008). Ethnic differences in weight control practices among U.S. adolescents from 1995 to 2005. *International Journal of Eating Disorders, 41*, 124–133.

Chaplin, L. N., & John, D. R. (2007). Growing up in a material world: Age differences in materialism in children and adolescents. *Journal of Consumer Research, 34*(4), 480–493.

Chavez, D. (1985). Perpetuation of gender inequality: A content analysis of comic strips. *Sex Roles, 13*, 93–102.

Chen, M., Grube, J. W., Bersamin, M., Waiters, E., & Keefe, D. B. (2005). Alcohol advertising: What makes it attractive to youth? *Journal of Health Communication, 10*(6), 553–565.

Chia, S. C. (2006). How peers mediate media influence on adolescents' sexual attitudes and sexual behavior. *Journal of Communication, 56*, 585–606.

Children Now. (1999). *Boys to men: Sports media messages about masculinity.* Retrieved February 21, 2008, from http://www.childrennow.org//publications/media/boystomen_1999_sportsb.cfm

Children Now. (2001). *Fair play? Violence, gender and race in video games.* Retrieved January 27, 2008 from http://www.childrennow.org/publications/media/fairplay_2001b.cfm

Children Now. (2004). *Fall colors 2003–2004: Prime time diversity report.* Retrieved November 5, 2007, from http://publications.childrennow.org/publications/media/fallcolors_2000b.cfm

Children's Television Act of 1990. (1990). Publ. L. No. 101-437, 104 Stat. 996-1000.

Christakis, D. A., Zimmerman, F. J., DiGiuseppe, D. L., & McCarty, C. (2004). Early television exposure and subsequent attentional problems. *Pediatrics, 113*, 708–713.

Christenson, P., & Roberts, D. (1998). *It's not only rock and roll: Popular music in the lives of adolescents.* Cresskill: Hampton Press, Inc.

Christenson, P. G., Henriksen, L., & Roberts, D. F. (2000). *Substance use in popular prime-time television.* Washington, D.C.: Office of National Drug Control Policy.

Christmann, E., Badgett, J., & Lucking, R. (1997). Progressive comparison of the effects of computer assisted instruction on the academic achievement of secondary students. *Journal of Research on Computing in Education, 29*, 325–336.

Cignacco, E., Hamers, J. P. H., Stoffel, L., van Lingen, R. A., Gessler, P., McDougall, J., et al. (2007). The efficacy of non-pharmacological interventions in the management of procedural pain in preterm and term neonates. A systematic literature review. *European Journal of Pain, 11*(2), 139–152.

Clark, L., & Tiggermann, M. (2006). Appearance culture in nine- to 12-year-old girls: Media and peer influences on body dissatisfaction. *Social Development, 15*, 628–643.

Clay, D., Vignoles, V. L., & Dittmar, H. (2005). Body image and self-esteem among adolescent girls: Testing the influence of sociocultural factors. *Journal of Research on Adolescence, 15*, 451–477.

Cline, V. B., Croft, R. G., & Courrier, S. (1973). Desensitization of children to television violence. *Journal of Personality and Social Psychology, 27*, 360–365.

Cohen, L. L., Blount, R. L., & Panopoulos, G. (1997). Nurse coaching and cartoon distraction: An effective and practical intervention to reduce child, parent, and nurse distress during immunization. *Journal of Pediatric Psychology, 22*, 355–370.

Collins, M. E. (1991). Body figure perceptions and preferences among preadolescent children. *International Journal of Eating Disorders, 10*(2), 199–208.

Collins, R. L., Ellickson, P. L., McCaffrey, D., & Hambarsoomians, K. (2005). Saturated in beer: Awareness of beer advertising in late childhood and adolescence. *Journal of Adolescent Health, 37*, 29–36.

Collins, R. L., Elliott, M. N., Berry, S. H., Kanouse, D. E., Kunkel, D., Hunter, S. B., et al. (2004). Watching sex on television predicts adolescent initiation of sexual behavior. *Pediatrics, 114*, 280–289.

Collins, W. A. (1973). Effect of temporal separation between motivation, aggression, and consequences: A developmental study. *Developmental Psychology, 8*, 215–221.

Collins, W. A., & Getz, S. K. (1976). Children's social responses following modeled reactions to provocation: Prosocial effects of a television drama. *Journal of Personality, 44*(3), 488–500.

Collins, W. A., Wellman, H., Keniston, A., & Westby, S. (1978). Age-related aspects of comprehension and inference from a televised dramatic narrative. *Child Development, 49*, 389–399.

Commercialfreechildhood.org. (2007). *Facts.* Retrieved December 27, 2007, from http://commercialfreechildhood.org

Comstock, G., & Scharrer, E. (2003). Meta-analyzing the controversy over television violence and aggression. In D. Gentile (Ed.), *Media violence and children* (pp. 205–226). Westport, CT: Praeger.

Coon, K. A., Goldberg, J., Rogers, B. L., & Tucker, K. L. (2001). Relationships between use of television during meals and children's food consumption patterns. *Pediatrics, 107*, 167–176.

Coon, K. A., & Tucker, K. L. (2002). Television and children's consumption patterns. *Minerva Pediatrica, 54*, 423–436.

Cooper, J., & Mackie, D. (1986). Video games and aggression in children. *Journal of Applied Social Psychology, 16*, 726–744.

Copyrights Group. (2008). *The world of Beatrix Potter*. Retrieved February 3, 2008 from http://www.copyrights.co.uk/portfolio/classic_nostalgia/beatrix-potter.aspx

Cornell, J. L., & Halpern-Felsher, B. L. (2006). Adolescents tell us why teens have oral sex. *Journal of Adolescent Health, 38,* 299–301.

Courtright, J., & Baran, S. (1980). The acquisition of sexual information by young people. *Journalism Quarterly, 57*(1), 107–114.

Coyne, S. M., Archer, J., & Eslea, M. (2004). Cruel intentions on television and in real life: Can viewing indirect aggression increase viewers' subsequent indirection aggression? *Journal of Experimental Child Psychology, 88,* 234–253.

Crick, N. R., Grotpeter, J. K., & Bigbee, M. A. (2002). Relationally and physically aggressive children's intent attributions and feelings of distress for relational and instrumental peer provocations. *Child Development, 73,* 1134–1142.

Črnčec, R., Wilson, S. J., & Prior, M. (2006). The cognitive and academic benefits of music to children: Facts and fiction. *Educational Psychology, 26*(4), 579–594.

Dalton, M. A., Adachi-Mejia, A. M., Longacre, M. R., Titus-Ernstoff, L. T., Gibson, J. J., Martin, S. K., et al. (2006). Parental rules and monitoring of children's movie viewing associated with children's risk for smoking and drinking. *Pediatrics, 118,* 1932–1942.

Dalton, M. A., Bernhardt, A. M., Gibson, J. J., Sargent, J. D., Beach, M. L., Adachi-Mejia, A. M., et al. (2005). Use of cigarettes and alcohol by preschoolers while role-playing as adults. *Archives of Pediatrics and Adolescent Medicine, 159,* 854–859.

Davalos, D. B., Davalos, R. A., & Layton, H. S. (2007). Content analysis of magazine headlines: Changes over three decades? *Feminism & Psychology, 17,* 250–258.

David, C., Cappella, J. N., & Fishbein, M. (2006). The social diffusion of influence among adolescents: Group interaction in a chat room environment about antidrug advertisements. *Communication Theory, 16,* 118–140.

Davis, S. (2003). Sex stereotypes in commercials targeted toward children: A content analysis. *Sociological Spectrum, 23,* 407–424.

Davis, S., & Mares, M. (1998). Effects of talk show viewing on adolescents'. *Journal of Communication, 48*(3), 69–86.

Davison, K. K., & Birch, L. L. (2004). Lean and weight stable: Behavioral predictors and psychological correlates. *Obesity Research, 12,* 1085–1093.

De Bens, E., & Vandenbruane, P. (1992). *TV advertising and children: Part 4. Effects of TV advertising on children*. Ghent, Belgium: University of Ghent, Centre for Media Opinion and Advertising Research.

Deci, E. L., & Ryan, R. M. (1985). The general causality orientations scale: Self-determination in personality. *Journal of Research in Personality, 19*(2), 109–134.

DeHart, G. B., Sroufe, L. A., & Cooper, R. G. (2004). *Child development: Its nature and course* (5th ed.). New York: McGraw-Hill.

Dent, C. W., Galaif, J., Sussman, S., Stacy, A. W., Burton, D., & Flay, B. R. (1992). Music preference as a diagnostic indicator of adolescent drug use. *American Journal of Public Health, 82,* 124.

Derenne, J. L., & Beresin, E. V. (2006). Body image, media, and eating disorders. *Academic Psychiatry, 30,* 257–261.

Desmond, R. J. (1987). Adolescents and music lyrics: Implications of a cognitive perspective. *Communication Quarterly, 35,* 276–284.

Desmond, R. J., & Carveth, R. (2007). The effects of advertising on children and adolescents: A meta-analysis. In R. Preiss, B. Gayle, N. Burrell, M. Allen, & J. Bryant (Eds.), *Mass media effects research: Advances through meta-analysis* (pp. 169–179). Mahwah, NJ: Lawrence Erlbaum.

Desrochers, D. M., & Holt, D. J. (2007). Children's exposure to television advertising: Implications for childhood obesity. *American Marketing Association, 26*(2), 182–201.

Diekman, A. B., & Murnen, S. K. (2004). Learning to be little women and little men: The inequitable gender equality of nonsexist children's literature. *Sex Roles, 50,* 373–385.

Diener, E. (1984). Subjective well-being. *Psychological Bulletin, 95*(3), 542–575.

Dill, K. E., Gentile, D. A., Richter, W. A., & Dill, J. C. (2005). Violence, sex, race and age in popular video games: A content analysis. In E. Cole & J. Henderson Daniel (Eds.), *Featuring females: Feminist analyses of the media.* Washington, DC: American Psychological Association.

Din, F. S., & Calao, J. (2001). The effects of playing educational video games on kindergarten achievement. *Child Study Journal, 31*(2), 95–102.

Dittmar, H., & Halliwell, E. (2006). Does Barbie make girls want to be thin? The effect of experimental exposure to images of dolls on the body image of 5- to 8-year-old girls. *Developmental Psychology, 42,* 283–292.

Dodge, K. A. (1986). A social information processing model of social competence in children. In M. Perlmutter (Ed.), *Minnesota symposium on child psychology* (Vol. 18). Hillside, NJ: Erlbaum.

Dohnt, H. K., & Tiggemann, M. (2006). Body image concerns in young girls: The role of peers and media prior to adolescence. *Journal of Youth and Adolescence, 35,* 141–151.

Dolson, L. (2003). *How the diet industry has misled us.* Retrieved September 26, 2008, from http://www.skyhighway.com/~turtleway/Articles/expecta tions.html

Dominick, J. R. (1984). Video games, television violence and aggression in teenagers. *Journal of Communication, 34,* 136–147.

Dominick, J. R., & Greenberg, B. S. (1972). Attitudes toward violence: The interaction of television, family attitudes and social class. In G. A. Comstock &

E. A. Rubinstein (Eds.), *Television and social behavior: Vol. 3. Television and adolescent aggressiveness*. Washington, DC: Government Printing Office.

Doniger, A. S., Adams, E., Utter, C. A, & Riley, J. S. (2001). Input evaluation of the "not me, not now" abstinence-oriented, adolescent pregnancy prevention communications program, Monroe County, New York. *Journal of Health Communication, 6*, 45– 60.

Donovan, J. E. (2007). Really underage drinkers: The epidemiology of children's alcohol use in the United States. *Prevention Science, 8*, 192–205.

Doolittle, J. C. (1980). Immunizing children against possible antisocial effects of viewing television violence. *Perceptual and Motor Skills, 51*, 498.

Downs, J. S., Murray, P. J., de Bruin, W. B., Penrose, J., Palmgren, C., & Fischhoff, B. (2004). Interactive video behavior interventions to reduce adolescent females' STD risk: A randomized controlled trial. *Social Science & Medicine, 59*, 1659–1572.

Drabman, R. S., & Thomas, M. H. (1974). Does media violence increase children's tolerance for real-life aggression? *Developmental Psychology, 10*(3), 418–421.

Dubow, J. S. (1995). Advertising recognition and recall by age-including teens. *Journal of Advertising Research, 35*(5), 55–60.

Dunand, M., Berkowitz, L., & Leyens, J. (1984). Audience effects when viewing aggressive movies. *British Journal of Social Psychology, 23*(1), 69–76.

DuRant, R. H., Neiberg, R., Champion, H., Rhodes, S. D., & Wolfson, M. (2008). Viewing professional wrestling on television and engaging in violent and other health risk behaviors. *Southern Medical Journal, 101*, 129–137.

DuRant, R. H., Wolfson, M., LaFrance, B., Balkrishnan, R., & Altman, D. (2006). An evaluation of a mass media campaign to encourage parents of adolescents to talk to their children about sex. *Journal of Adolescent Health, 38*, 1–9.

Durkin, K. (1985). Television and sex-role acquisition: 3: Counter-stereotyping. *British Journal of Social Psychology, 24*, 211–222.

Eagly, A. H., & Diekman, A. B. (2003). The malleability of sex differences in response to changing social roles. In L. G. Aspinwall, & U. M. Staudinger (Eds.), *A psychology of human strengths* (pp. 103–115). Washington, DC: American Psychological Association.

Edmonds, L. (1986, Fall). The treatment of race in pictures books for young children. *Book Research Quarterly*, 31–41.

Eggermont, S. (2005). Young adolescents' perceptions of peer sexual behaviours: The role of television viewing. *Child: Care, Health & Development, 31*, 459–468.

Eggermont, S., & Van den Bulck, J. (2006). Nodding off or switching off? The use of popular media as a sleep aid in secondary-school children. *Journal of Paediatrics and Child Health, 42*(7–8), 428–433.

Eisenberg, N., Fabes, R. A., & Spinrad, T. L. (2006). Prosocial development. In N. Eisenberg (Ed.), *Handbook of child psychology: Vol. 3. Social, emotional, and personality development* (pp. 646–718). New York: John Wiley.

Elder, R. W., Shults, R. A., Sleet, D. A., Nichols, J. L., Thompson, R. S., & Rajab, W. (2004). Effectiveness of mass media campaigns for reducing drinking and driving and alcohol-involved crashes: A systematic review. *American Journal of Preventive Medicine, 27,* 57–65.

Ellickson, P. L., Collins, R. L., Hambarsoomians, K., & McCaffrey, D. F. (2005). Does alcohol advertising promote adolescent drinking? Results from a longitudinal assessment. *Addiction, 100,* 235–246.

Elliot, A., & Hall, N. (1997). The impact of self-regulatory teaching strategies on "at-risk" preschoolers' mathematical learning in a computer mediated environment. *Journal of Computing in Childhood Education, 8,* 187–198.

Ennemoser, M., & Schneider, W. (2007). Relations of television viewing and reading: Findings from a 4 year longitudinal study. *Journal of Educational Psychology, 99*(2), 349–368.

Epstein, J. A., & Botvin, G. J. (2008). Media resistance skills and drug skill refusal techniques: What is their relationship with alcohol use among inner-city adolescents? *Addictive Behaviors, 33,* 528–537.

Epstein, M., & Ward, L. M. (2008). "Always Use Protection": Communication boys receive about sex from parents, peers, and the media. *Journal of Youth & Adolescence, 37,* 113–126.

Eron, L. D., Huesmann, L. R., Lefkowitz, M. M., & Walder, L. O. (1972). Does television violence cause aggression? *American Psychologist, 27,* 253–263.

Erowid.com. (2008). *Erowid: Documenting the complex relationship between humans and psychoactives.* Retrieved May 28, 2009, from http://www.erowid.com

Escobar-Chaves, S. L., Tortolero, S. R., Markham, C. M., Low, B. J., Eitel, P., & Thickstun, P. (2005). Impact of the media on adolescent sexual attitudes and behaviors. *Pediatrics, 116,* 303–323.

Evans, L., & Davies, K. (2000). No sissy boys here: A content analysis of the representation of masculinity in elementary school reading textbooks. *Sex Roles, 42,* 255–270.

Eyal, K., & Cohen, J. (2006). When good friends say goodbye: A parasocial breakup study. *Journal of Broadcasting & Electronic Media, 50*(3), 502–523.

Farquhar, J. C., & Wasylkiw, L. (2007). Media Images of men: Trends and consequences of body conceptualization. *Psychology of Men & Masculinity, 8,* 145–160.

Federal Communications Commission. (1996). *Policies and rules concerning children's television programming: Revision of programming policies for television broadcast stations.* Washington, DC: Author.

Federal Trade Commission. (2004). *Marketing violent entertainment to children: A fourth follow-up review of industry practices in the motion picture, music recording & electronic game industries.* Washington, DC: Author.

Federal Trade Commission. (2008). *Marketing food to children and adolescents: A review of industry expenditures, activities, and self-regulation.* Washington, D.C.

Ferguson, C. J. (2007). The good, the bad and the ugly: A meta-analytic review of positive and negative effects of violent video games. *Psychiatric Quarterly, 78*(4), 309–316.

Feshbach, S. (1956). The catharsis hypothesis and some consequences of interaction with aggressive and neutral play objects. *Journal of Personality, 24*, 449–462.

Field, A. E., Austin, S. B., Camarge, C. A., Taylor, C. B., Striegel-Moore, R. H., Loud, K. J., et al. (2005). Exposure to the mass media, body shape concerns, and use of supplements to improve weight and shape among male and female adolescents. *Pediatrics, 116*, 214–220.

Field, A. E., Austin, S. B., Gillman, M. W., Rosner, B., Rockett, H. R., & Colditz, G. A. (2004). Snack food intake does not predict weight change among children and adolescents. *International Journal of Obesity, 28*, 1210–1216.

Field, A. E., Camargo, C. A., Taylor, C. B., Berkey, C. S., Roberts, S. B., & Colditz, G. A. (2001). Peer, parent, and media influences on the development of weight concerns and frequent dieting among preadolescent and adolescent girls and boys. *Pediatrics, 107*, 54–60.

Fisch, S. M. (2002). Vast wastelands or vast opportunity? Effects of educational television on children's academic knowledge, skills, and attitudes. In J. Bryant, & D. Zillmann (Eds.), *Media effects: Advances in theory and research* (pp. 397–426). Mahwah, NJ: Lawrence Erlbaum.

Fischer, P. M., Schwart, M. P., Richards, J. W., Goldstein, A. O., & Rojas, J. T. (1991). Brand logo recognition by children aged 3 to 6 years: Mickey Mouse and Old Joe the Camel. *Journal of the American Medical Association, 266*, 3145–3153.

Fisher, D. A., Hill, D. L., Grube, J. W., & Gruber, E. L. (2004). Sex on American television: An analysis across program genres and network types. *Journal of Broadcasting & Electronic Media, 48*, 529–553.

Fletcher-Flinn, C. M., & Gravatt, B. (1995). The efficacy of computer assisted instruction (CAI): A meta-analysis. *Journal of Educational and Computing Research, 12*, 219–242.

Fling, S., Smith, L., Rodriguez, T., Thornton, D., Atkins, E., & Nixon, K. (1992). Video games, aggression, and self-esteem: A survey. *Social Behavior and Personality, 20*, 39–46.

Flynn, B. S., Worden, J. K., Bunn, J. Y., Dorwaldt, A. L.., Dana, G. S., & Callas, P. W. (2006). Mass media and community interventions to reduce alcohol use by early adolescents. *Journal of Studies on Alcohol, 67*, 66–74.

Foehr, U. (2006). *The teen media juggling act: The implications of media multitasking among American youth.* Menlo Park, CA: Kaiser Family Foundation.

Forsyth, A., & Barnard, M. (1998). Relationships between popular music and drug use among Scottish schoolchildren. *International Journal of Drug Policy, 9*, 125–132.

Forsyth, A., Barnard, M., & McKeganey, N. P. (1997). Musical preference as an indicator of adolescent drug use. *Addiction, 92*(10), 1317–1325.

Fouts, G., & Burggraf, K. (1999). Television situation comedies: Female body images and verbal reinforcements. *Sex Roles, 40,* 473–481.

Fouts, G., & Vaughan, K. (2002). Locus of control, television viewing, and eating disorder symptomatology in young females. *Journal of Adolescence, 25,* 307–311.

Francis, L. A., & Birch, L. L. (2006). Does eating during television viewing affect preschool children's intake? *Journal of the American Dietetic Association, 106*(4), 598–600.

Friedrich, K. L., & Stein, A. H. (1973). Aggressive and prosocial television programs and the natural behavior of preschool children. *Monographs of the Society for Research in Child Development, 38,* 1–110.

Frueh, T., & McGhee, P. E. (1975). Traditional sex role development and amount of time spent watching television. *Developmental Psychology, 11,* 109.

Fuchs, L. S., Fuchs, D., Hamlet, C. L., Powell, S. R., Capizzi, A. M., & Seethaler, P. M. (2006). The effects of computer-assisted instruction on number combination skill in at-risk first graders. *Journal of Learning Disabilities, 39*(5), 467–475.

Fullerton, J. A., & Kendrick, A. (2001). Portrayals of men and women in U. S. Spanish-language television commercials. *Journalism & Mass Communication Quarterly, 77,* 128–139.

Funk, J. B., Bechtoldt-Baldacci, H., Pasold, T., & Baumgardner, J. (2004). Violence exposure in real-life, video games, television, movies, and the internet: Is there desensitization? *Journal of Adolescence, 27,* 23–39.

Funk, J. B., & Buchman, D. D. (1996). Playing violent video and computer games and adolescent self-concept. *Journal of Communication, 46*(2), 19–32.

Funk, J. B., Buchman, D. D., Jenks., J., & Bechtoldt, H. (2003). Playing violent video games, desensitization, and moral evaluations in children. *Applied Developmental Psychology, 24,* 413–426.

Funk, J. B., Chan, M., Brouwer, J., & Curtiss, K. (2006). A biopsychosocial analysis of the video game playing experience of children and adults in the United States. *Studies in Media Literacy and Information Education (SIMILE).* Retrieved October 2, 2006, from http://www.utpjournals.com/simile/issue23/Issue23_TOC.html

Funk, J. B., Hagan, J., Schimming, J., Bullock., W.A., Buchman, D. D., & Myers, M. (2002). Aggression and psychopathology in adolescents with a preference for violent electronic for electronic games. *Aggressive Behavior, 28,* 134–144.

Gantz, W., Schwartz, N., Angelini, J. R., & Rideout, V. (2007), *Food for thought: Television food advertising to children in the United States.* Washington, DC: Henry J. Kaiser Family Foundation.

Garbarino, J. (1999). *Lost boys: Why our sons turn violent and how we can save them.* New York: Free Press.

Gardner, J. E. (1991). Can the Mario Bros. help? Nintendo games as an adjunct in psychotherapy with children. *Psychotherapy: Theory, Research, Practice, Training, 28*(4), 667–670.

Gardstrom, S. C. (1999). Music exposure and criminal behavior: Perceptions of juvenile behavior. *Journal of Music Therapy, 36*, 207–221.

Garner, A., Sterk, H. M., & Adams, S. (1998). Narrative analysis of sexual etiquette in teenage magazines. *Journal of Communication, 48*, 59–78.

Garrison, M., & Christakis, D. A. (2005). *A teacher in the living room? Educational media for babies, toddlers, and preschoolers.* Menlo Park, CA: Kaiser Family Foundation.

Gary, D. (1984). *A study of Black characters in Caldecott and Newbery award and honor books for children* (ERIC No. ED354527).

Geis, F. L., Brown, V., Walstedt, J. J., & Porter, N. (1984). TV commercials as achievement scripts for women. *Sex Roles, 10*(7–8), 513–525.

Gentile, D. A., & Anderson, C. A. (2003). Violent video games: The newest media violence hazard. In D. Gentile (Ed.), *Media violence and children* (pp. 131–152), Westport, CT: Praeger.

Gentile, D. A., Lynch, P. J., Linder, J. R., & Walsh, D. A. (2004). The effects of violent video game habits on adolescent hostility, aggressive behaviors, and school performance. *Journal of Adolescence, 27*, 5–22.

Gerbner, G. (1990). Stories that hurt: Tobacco, alcohol, and other drugs in the mass media. In H. Resnik (Ed.), *Youth and drugs: Society's mixed messages* (OSAP Prevention Monograph, 6, pp. 53–129). Rockville, MD: Office for Substance Abuse Prevention.

Gerbner, G., Gross, M., Morgan, L., & Signorielli, N. (1994). Growing up with television: The cultivation perspective. In J. Bryant & D. Zillmann (Eds.), *Media effects* (pp. 17–41). Hillsdale, NY: Erlbaum.

Giles, D. C., & Maltby, J. (2004). The role of media figures in adolescent development: Relations between autonomy, attachment, and interest in celebrities. *Personality and Individual Differences, 36*(4), 813–822.

Glantz, S. A. (2003). Smoking in movies: A major problem and a real solution. *Lancet, 362*(9380), 258–259.

Glascock, J., & Preston-Schreck, C. (2004). Gender and racial stereotypes in daily newspaper comics: A time-honored tradition? *Sex Roles, 51*, 423–431.

Gold, J. I., Kim, S. H., Kant, A. J., Joseph, M. H., & Rizzo, A. (2006). Effectiveness of virtual reality for pediatric pain distraction during IV placement. *CyberPsychology, 9*(2), 207–212.

Goldberg, M. E., & Gorn, G. J. (1978). Some unintended consequences of TV advertising to children. *Journal of Consumer Research, 5*(1), 22–29.

Golub, A., & Johnson, B. D. (2002). The misuse of the "gateway theory" in US policy on drug abuse control: A secondary analysis of the muddled deduction. *International Journal of Drug Policy, 13*(1), 5–19.

Gooden, A. M., & Gooden, M. A. (2001). Gender representation in notable children's picture books: 1995–1999. *Sex Roles, 45,* 89–101.

Gorn, G. J., & Goldberg, M. E. (1978). The impact of television advertising on children from low income families. *Journal of Consumer Research, 4,* 86–88.

Gorn, G. J., & Goldberg, M. E. (1980). Children's responses to repetitive television commercials. *Journal of Consumer Research, 6,* 421–424.

Gorn, G. J., & Goldberg, M. E. (1982). Behavioral evidence of the effects of televised food messages on children. *Journal of Consumer Research, 9,* 200–205.

Gortmaker, S. L., Dietz, W. H., & Cheung, L. W. Y. (1990). Inactivity, diet, and the fattening of America. *Journal of the American Dietetic Association, 90,* 1247–1252.

Graña, J. L., Cruzado, J.A., Andreu, J. M., Muñoz-Rivas, M. J., Peña, M. E., & Brain, P. F. (2004). Effects of viewing videos of bullfights on Spanish children. *Aggressive Behavior, 30,* 16–28.

Graves, S. B. (1999). Television and prejudice reduction: When does television as a vicarious experience make a difference? *Journal of Social Issues, 55,* 707–727.

Graybill, D., Strawniak, M., Hunter, T., & O'Leary, M. (1987). Effects of playing versus observing violent versus non-violent video games on children's aggression. *Psychology: A Quarterly Journal of Human Behavior, 24,* 1–7.

Greenberg, B. S. (1974). British children and televised violence. *Public Opinion Quarterly, 38,* 531–547.

Greenberg, B. S., & Brand, J. E. (1993). Television news and advertising in schools: The "channel one" controversy. *Journal of Communication, 43*(1), 143–151.

Greenberg, B. S., Eastin, M., Hofschire, L., Lachlan, K., & Brownell, K. D. (2003). Portrayals of overweight and obese individuals on commercial television. *American Journal of Public Health, 93,* 1342–1348.

Greenberg, B. S., & Smith, S. W. (2002). Daytime talk shows: Up close and in your face. In J. D. Brown, J. R. Steele, & K. Walsh-Childers (Eds.), *Sexual teens, sexual media* (pp. 79–93). Hillsdale, NJ: Erlbaum.

Greenfield, P. M., Bruzzone, L., Koyamatsu, K., Satuloff, W., Nixon, K., Brodie, M., & Kingsdale, D. (1987). What is rock music doing to the minds of our youth? A first experimental look at the effects of rock music lyrics and music videos. *Journal of Early Adolescence, 7,* 315–329.

Grier, S. A., Mensinger, J., Huang, S. H., Kumanyika, S. K., & Stettler, N. (2007). Fast-food marketing and children's fast-food consumption: Exploring parents' influences in an ethnically diverse sample. *American Marketing Association, 26,* 221–235.

Griffiths, M. (2003). The therapeutic use of videogames in childhood and adolescence. *Clinical Child Psychology and Psychiatry, 8,* 547–554.

Groesz, L. M., Levine, M. P., & Murnen, S. K. (2001). The effect of experimental presentation of thin media images on body satisfaction: A meta-analytic review. *International Journal of Eating Disorders*, 1–16.

Gross, E. F. (2004). Adolescent internet use: What we expect, what teens report. *Journal of Applied Developmental Psychology. Special Issue: Developing Children, Developing Media: Research From Television to the Internet From the Children's Digital Media Center: A Special Issue Dedicated to the Memory of Rodney R. Cocking*, 25(6), 633–649.

Grossman, D., & DeGaetano, G. (1999). *Stop teaching our kids to kill*. New York: Crown.

Grube, J. W., & Wallack, L. (1994). Television beer advertising and drinking knowledge, beliefs, and intentions among schoolchildren. *American Journal of Public Health*, 84(2), 254–259.

Gruber, E. L., Thau, H. M., Hill, D. L., Fisher, D. A., & Grube, J. W. (2005). Alcohol, tobacco and illicit substances in music videos. *Journal of Adolescent Health*, 37(1), 81–83.

Gunter, B. (1985). *Dimensions of television violence*. Aldershot, UK: Gower.

Gunter, B., Oates, C., & Blades, M. (2005). *Advertising to children on TV: Content, impact, and regulation*. Mahwah, NJ: Lawrence Erlbaum.

Haines, J., & Neumark-Sztainer, D. (2006). Prevention of obesity and eating disorders: A consideration of shared risk factors. *Health Education Research*, 21(6), 770–782.

Hale, S. (1990). A global developmental trend in cognitive processing speed. *Child Development*, 61(3), 653–663.

Halford, J. C. G., Boyland, E. J., Hughes, G., Oliveira, L. P., & Dovey, T. M. (2007). Beyond-brand effect of television (TV) food advertisements/commercials on caloric intake and food choice of 5–7-year-old children. *Appetite*, 49, 263–267.

Halford, J. C. G., Gillespie, J., Brown, V., Pontin, E. E., & Dovey, T. M. (2004). The effect of television (TV) food advertisements/commercials on food consumption in children. *Appetite*, 42(2), 221–225.

Hall, T. E., Hughes, C. A., & Filbert, M. (2000). Computer assisted instruction in reading for students with learning disabilities: A research synthesis. *Education and Treatment of Children*, 23(2), 173–193.

Hall, W. D., & Lynskey, M. (2005). Is cannabis a gateway drug? Testing hypotheses about the relationship between cannabis use and the use of other illicit drugs. *Drug and Alcohol Review*, 24(1), 39–48.

Halloran, E. C., Doumas, D. M., John, R. S., & Margolin, G. (1999). The relationship between aggression in children and locus of control beliefs. *Journal of Genetic Psychology*, 160, 5–21.

Hamilton, M. C., Anderson, D., Broaddus, M., & Young, K. (2006). Gender stereotyping and under-representation of female characters in 200 popular children's picture books: A twenty-first century update. *Sex Roles, 55,* 757–765.

Hancox, R. J., Milne, B. J., & Poulton, R. (2005). Association of television viewing during childhood with poor educational achievement. *Archives of Pediatrics and Adolescent Medicine, 159,* 614–618.

Haninger, K., & Thompson, K. M. (2004). Content and ratings of teen-rated video games. *Journal of the American Medical Association, 291*(7), 856–865.

Hansen, J. E. (1933). The effect of education motion pictures upon the retention of informational learning. *Journal of Experimental Education, 2,* 1–4.

Hapkiewicz, W. G. (1979). Children's reactions to cartoon violence. *Journal of Clinical Child Psychology, 8,* 30–34.

Hargreaves, D., A., & Tiggemann, M. (2004). Idealized media images and adolescent body image: "Comparing" boys and girls. *Body Image, 1,* 351–361.

Harman, J. P., Hansen, C. E., Cochran, M. E., & Lindsey, C. R. (2005). Liar, liar: Internet faking but not frequency if use affects social skills, self-esteem, social anxiety, and aggression. *CyberPsychology & Behavior, 8*(1), 1–6.

Harper, K., Sperry, S., & Thompson, J. K. (2008). Viewership of pro-eating disorder websites: Association with body image and eating disturbances. *International Journal of Eating Disorders, 41,* 92–95.

Harrison, K. (2000). Television viewing, fat stereotyping, body shape standards, and eating disorder symptomatology in grade school children. *Communication Research, 27,* 617–640.

Harrison, K. (2001). Ourselves, our bodies: Thin-ideal media, self-discrepancies, and eating disorder symptomatology in adolescents. *Journal of Social and Clinical Psychology, 20,* 289–323.

Harrison, K., & Bond, B. J. (2007). Gaming magazines and the drive for muscularity in preadolescent boys: A longitudinal examination. *Body Image, 4,* 269–277.

Harrison, K., & Cantor, J. (1999). Tales from the screen: Enduring fright reactions to scary media. *Media Psychology, 1,* 97–116.

Harrison, K., & Hefner, V. (2006). Media exposure, current and future body ideals, and disordered eating among preadolescent girls: A longitudinal panel study. *Journal of Youth and Adolescence, 35,* 153–163.

Harskamp, E. G., & Suhre, C. J. M. (2006). Improving mathematical problem solving: A computerized approach. *Computers in Human Behavior, 22*(5), 801–815.

Harter, S. (1987). Developmental and dynamic changes in the nature of self-concept: Implications for child psychotherapy. In S. R. Shirk (Ed.), *Cognitive development and child psychotherapy,* pp. 119-160. New York, Plenum.

Hartmann, T. (1996). *Beyond ADD: Hunting for reasons in the past & present.* Grass Valley, CA: Underwood.

Hartnagel, T., Teevan, J. J., & McIntyre, J. (1975). Television violence and violent behavior. *Social Forces, 54,* 341–351.

Hasselbring, T. S., Goin, L., & Bransford, J. D. (1988). Developing math automaticity in learning handicapped children: The role of computerized drill and practice. *Focus on Exceptional Children, 20*(6), 1–7.

Healton, C. G., Watson-Stryker, E. S., Allen, J. A., Vallone, D. M., Messeri, P. A., Graham, P. R., et al. (2006). Televised movie trailers: Undermining restrictions on advertising tobacco to youth. *Archives of Pediatrics and Adolescent Medicine, 160*, 885–888.

Hearold, S. (1986). A synthesis of 1043 effects of television on social behavior. In G. Comstock (Ed.), *Public communication and behavior* (Vol. 1, pp. 65–133). New York: Academic Press.

Henke, L. L. (1995). Young children's perceptions of cigarette brand advertising symbols: Awareness, affect, and target market identification. *Journal of Advertising, 24*(4), 13–28.

Heo, N. (2004). The effects of screen size and content type of viewers' attention, arousal, memory and content evaluations. *Dissertation Abstracts International, 64*, 9-A. (UMI No. AAI3106253).

Herbozo, S., Tantleff-Dunn, S., Gokee-Larose, J., & Thompson, J. K. (2004). Beauty and thinness messages in children's media: A content analysis. *Eating Disorders, 12*, 21–34.

Hestroni, A. (2007a). Sexual content on mainstream TV advertising: A cross-cultural comparison. *Sex Roles, 57*, 201–210.

Hestroni, A. (2007b). Three decades of sexual content on prime-time network programming: A longitudinal meta-analytic review. *Journal of Communication, 57*, 318–348.

Hetland, L. (2000). Learning to make music enhances spatial reasoning. *Journal of Aesthetic Education, 34*, 179–238.

Hoffner, C., & Cantor, J. (1991). Factors influencing children's enjoyment of suspense. *Communication Monographs, 58*, 41–62.

Holdren, G. W. (2003). Avoiding conflict: Mothers as tacticians in the supermarket. *Child Development, 54*, 233–240.

Horgen, K. B., Choate, M., & Brownell, K. D. (2001). Television food advertising: Targeting children in a toxic environment. In D. G. Singer & J. L. Singer (Eds.), *Handbook of children and the media* (pp. 447–462). Thousand Oaks, Ca: Sage.

Horton, R. W., & Santogrossi, D.A. (1978). The effect of adult commentary on reducing the influence of televised violence. *Personality and Social Psychology Bulletin, 4*, 37–40.

Hoult, T. F. (1949). Comic books and juvenile delinquency. *Sociology and Social Research, 33*, 279–284.

Huesmann, L. R. (1986). Psychological processes promoting the relation between exposure to media violence and aggressive behavior by the view. *Journal of Social Issues, 42*, 125–139.

Huesmann, L. R., Lagerspetz, K., & Eron, L. D. (1984). Intervening variables in the TV violence-aggression relation: Evidence from two countries. *Developmental Psychology, 20*(5), 746–777.

Huesmann, L. R., Moise-Titus, J., Podolski, C. L., & Eron, L. D. (2003). Longitudinal relations between children's exposure to TV violence and their aggressive and violent behavior in young adulthood: 1977–1992. *Developmental Psychology Special Issue: Violent children, 39*, 201–221.

Huntemann, N., & Morgan, M. (2001). Mass media and identity formation. In D. G. Singer & J. L. Singer (Eds.), *Handbook of children and the media* (pp. 309–322). Thousand Oaks, CA: Sage.

Hunter, M. W., & Chick, K. A. (2005). Treatment of gender in basal readers. *Reading Research and Instruction, 44*, 65–76.

Hust, S. J. T., Brown, J. D., & L'Engle, K. L. (2008). Boys will be boys and girls better be prepared: An analysis of the rare sexual health messages in young adolescents' media. *Mass Communication & Society, 11*, 3–23.

Huston, A. C., Donnerstein, E., Fairchild, H., Feshbach, N. D., Katz, P. A., Murray, J. P., et al. (1992). *Big world, small screen: The role of television in American society.* Lincoln: University of Nebraska Press.

Huston, A. C., & Wright, J. C. (1998). Mass media and children's development. In I. E. Sigel and K. A. Renninger (Eds.), *Handbook of child psychology* (Vol. 4, pp. 999–1058). New York: John Wiley.

Irwin, A. R., & Gross, A. M. (1995). Cognitive tempo, violent video games, and aggressive behavior in young boys. *Journal of Family Violence, 10*, 337–350.

Iusedtobelieve.com. (2007). *School.* Retrieved September 29, 2007 at http://www.iusedtobelieve.com

Jackson, L. A., von Eye, A., Biocca, F. A., Barbatsis, G., Zhao, Y., & Fitzgerald, H. E. (2006). Does home Internet use influence the academic performance of low-income children? *Developmental Psychology, 42*(3), 429–435.

Jansz, J., & Martis, R. G. (2007). The Lara phenomenon: Powerful female characters in video games. *Sex Roles, 56*, 141–148.

Janz, K. F., Levy, S. M., Burns, T. L., Torner, J. C., Willing, M. C., & Warren, J. J. (2002). Fatness, physical activity, and television viewing in children during the adiposity rebound period: The Iowa Bone Development Study. *Preventive Medicine, 35*, 563–571.

Jeffrey, D., McLellarn, R., & Fox, D. (1982). The development of children's eating habits: The role of television commercials. *Health Education Quarterly, 9*, 174–189.

Jennings, N. A., & Wartella, E. A. (2007). *Advertising and consumer development.* Mahwah, NJ, US: Lawrence Erlbaum.

Jenvey, V. B. (2007). The relationship between television viewing and obesity in young children: A review of existing explanations. *Early Child Development and Care, 177*, 809–820.

John, D. R. (1999). Consumer socialization of children: A retrospective look at twenty-five years of research. *Journal of Consumer Research, 26*(3), 183–213.

Johnson, C. M., & Memmott, J. E. (2006). Examination of relationships between participation in school music programs of differing quality and standardized test results. *Journal of Research in Music Education, 54*(4), 293–307.

Johnson, J. D., Jackson, L. A., & Gatto, L. (1995). Violent attitudes and deferred academic aspirations: Deleterious effects of exposure to rap music. *Basic and Applied Social Psychology, 16*, 27–41.

Johnson, M. D., & Young, B. M. (2003). *Advertising history of televisual media.* Mahwah, NJ: Lawrence Erlbaum.

Johnson, R. N. (1996). Bad news revisited: The portrayal of violence, conflict, and suffering on television news. *Peace and Conflict: Journal of Peace Psychology, 2*, 201–216.

Johnston, D. D. (1995). Adolescents' motivations for viewing graphic horror. *Human Communication Research, 21*, 522–552.

Jones, G. (2002). *Killing monsters: Why children need fantasy, super heroes, and make-believe violence.* New York: Basic Books.

Jones, L. R., Fries, E., & Danish, S. J. (2007). Gender and ethnic differences in body image and opposite sex figure preferences of rural adolescents. *Body Image, 4*, 103–108.

Jordan, A. B. (2000). *Is the Three-Hour Rule Living Up to Its Potential?* The Annenberg Public Policy Center, University of Pennsylvania.

Jordan, A. B. (2007). Heavy television viewing and childhood obesity. *Journal of Children and Media, 1*, 1478–2798.

Josephson, W. L. (1987). Television violence and children's aggression: Testing the priming, social script, and disinhibition predictions. *Journal of Personality & Social Psychology, 53*, 882–890.

Jowett, G. S., Jarvie, I. C., & Fuller, K. H. (1996). *Children and the movies: Media influences and the Payne Fund controversy.* New York: Cambridge University Press.

Jung, J., & Peterson, M. (2007). Body dissatisfaction and patterns of media use among preadolescent children. *Family and Consumer Sciences Research Journal, 36*, 40–54.

Kaiser Family Foundation (1998). *Kaiser Family Foundation and YM Magazine national survey of teens: Teens talk about dating, intimacy, and their sexual experiences.* Menlo Park, CA: Author.

Kaiser Family Foundation (2003). *Reaching the MTV generation: Recent research on the Impact of the Kaiser Family Foundation/MTV public education campaign on sexual health.* Menlo Park, CA: Author.

Kandakai, T. L., Price, J. H., Telljohann, S. K., & Wilson, C. A. (1999). Mothers' perceptions of factors influencing violence in school. *Journal of School Health, 69*(5), 189–195.

Kassarjian, H. H. (1977). Content analysis in consumer research. *Journal of Consumer Research, 4*, 8–18.

Kestenbaum, G. I., & Weinstein, L. (1985). Personality, psychopathology, and developmental issues in male adolescent video game use. *Journal of the American Academy of Child Psychiatry, 24*, 325–337.

Kilbourne, J. (1999). *Deadly persuasion: Why women and girls must fight the addictive power of advertising.* New York: Free Press

Kim, J. L., Collins, R. L., Kanouse, D. E., Elliott, M. N., Berry, S. H., Hunter, S., et al. (2006). Sexual readiness, household policies, and other predictors of adolescents' exposure to sexual content in mainstream entertainment television. *Media Psychology, 8*, 449–471.

King, B., & Kallis, J. (2006). *The big book of girl stuff.* Utah: Gibbs Smith.

King, C., III, Siegel, M., Celebucki, C., & Connolly, G. N. (1998). Adolescent exposure to cigarette advertising in magazines. *Journal of the American Medical Association, 279*, 516–520.

Kirsh, S. J. (1998). Seeing the world through Mortal Kombat-colored glasses: Violent video games and the development of a short-term hostile attribution bias. *Childhood: A Global Journal of Child Research, 5*, 177–184.

Kirsh, S. J. (2003). The effects of violent video game play on adolescents: The overlooked influence of development. *Aggression and Violent Behavior: A Review Journal, 8*(4), 377–389.

Kirsh, S. J. (2006). *Children, adolescents, and media violence: A critical look at the research.* Thousand Oaks, CA: Sage.

Klassen, J. A., Liang, Y., Tjosvold, L., Klassen, T. P., & Hartling, L. (2008). Music for pain and anxiety in children undergoing medical procedures: A systematic review of randomized controlled trials. *Ambulatory Pediatrics, 8*, 117–128.

Klein, H., & Shiffman, K. S. (2005). Thin is "in" and stout is "out": What animated cartoons tell viewers about body weight. *Kensington Research Institute, 10*, 107–116.

Klein, H., & Shiffman, K. S. (2006). Race-related content of animated cartoons. *The Howard Journal of Communication, 17*, 163–182.

Klein, J. D., Thomas, R. K., & Sutter, E. J. (2007). History of childhood candy cigarette use is associated with tobacco smoking by adults. *Preventive Medicine: An International Journal Devoted to Practice and Theory, 45*(1), 26–30.

Klein, M. E. (1998). A comparison of multicultural characters in the annotations of two recommended high school reading lists published thirty-one years apart. ERIC No. ED423989.

Konijn, E. A., Nije Bijvank, M., & Bushman, B. J. (2007). I wish I were a warrior: The role of wishful identification in the effects of violent video games on aggression in adolescent boys. *Developmental Psychology, 43*(4), 1038–1044.

Kortenhaus, C. M., & Demarest, J. (1993). Gender role stereotyping in children's literature: An update. *Sex Roles, 28,* 219–232.

Kowalski, R. M., & Limber, S. P. (2007). Electronic bullying among middle school students. *Journal of Adolescent Health, 41*(6, Suppl.), S22–S30.

Krahé, B., & Möller, I. (2004). Playing violent electronic games, hostile attributional style, and aggression-related norms in German adolescents. *Journal of Adolescence, 27,* 53–59.

Kraus, S. W., & Russell, B. (2008). Early sexual experiences: The role of internet access and sexually explicit material. *CyberPsychology & Behavior, 11,* 162–168.

Krcmar, M., Grela, B., & Lin, K. (2007). Can toddlers learn vocabulary from television? an experimental approach. *Media Psychology, 10*(1), 41–63.

Krcmar, M., & Valkenburg, P. (1999). A scale to assess children's interpretations of justified and unjustified television violence and its relationship to television viewing. *Communication Research, 26*(5), 608–634.

Krugman, D. M., Morrison, M. A., & Sung, Y. (2006). Cigarette advertising in popular youth and adult magazines: A ten-year perspective. *Journal of Public Policy & Marketing, 25*(2), 197–211.

Ku, H., Harter, C. A., Liu, P., Thompson, L., & Cheng, Y. (2007). The effects of individually personalized computer-based instructional program on solving mathematics problems. *Computers in Human Behavior, 23,* 1995–1210.

Kunkel, D. (2001). Children and television advertising. In D. G. Singer and J. L. Singer (Eds.), *Handbook of children and the media* (pp. 375–394). Thousand Oaks, CA: Sage.

Kunkel, D., Eyal, K., Biely, E., Cope-Farrar, K., Donnerstein, E., & Fandrich, R. (2003). *Sex on TV 3: A biennial report to the Kaiser Family Foundation.* Menlo Park, CA: Kaiser Family Foundation.

Kunkel, D., Eyal, K., Finnerty, K., Biely, E. & Donnerstein, E (2005). *Sex on TV 4.* Menlo Park, CA: Kaiser Family Foundation.

Kurbin, C. E. (2005). Gangstas, thugs, and hustlas: Identity and the code of the street in rap Smith, S. L., & Boyson, A. R. (2002). Violence in music videos: Examining the prevalence and context of physical aggression. *Journal of Communication, 52*(1), 61–83.

L'Engle, K. L., Brown, J. D., & Kenneavy, K. (2006). The mass media are an important context for adolescents' sexual behavior. *Journal of Adolescent Health, 38,* 186–192.

Labre, M. P. (2005). Burn fat, build muscle: A content analysis of men's health and men's fitness. *International Journal of Men's Health, 4*(2), 187–200.

Labre, M. P., & Walsh-Childers, K. (2003). Friendly advice? Beauty messages in web sites of teen magazines. *Mass Communication & Society, 6,* 379–396.

Landold, M. A., Marti, D., Widmer, J., & Meuli, M. (2002). Does cartoon movie distraction decrease burned children's pain behavior? *Journal of Burn Care & Rehabilitation, 23*(1), 61–65.

Lapinski, M. K. (2006). StarvingforPerfect.com: A theoretically based content analysis of pro-eating disorder web sites. *Health Communication, 20*, 243–253.

Larson, M. S. (2003). Gender, race, and aggression in television commercials that feature children. *Sex Roles, 48*, 67–75.

Latner, J. D., Rosewall, J. K., & Simmonds, M. B. (2007). Childhood obesity stigma: Association with television, videogame, and magazine exposure. *Body Image, 4*, 147–155.

Leaper, C., Breed, L., Hoffman, L., & Perlman, C. A. (2002). Variations in the gender-stereotyped content of children's television cartoons across genres. *Journal of Applied Social Psychology, 32*, 1653–1662.

Leaper, C., & Friedman, C. K. (2007). The socialization of gender. In J. Grusec & P. Hastings (Eds.), *Handbook of socialization: Theory and research* (pp. 561–587). New York: Guilford.

Leifer, A. D., & Roberts, D. F. (1971). Children's response to television violence. In J. P. Murray, E. A. Rubinstein, and G. Comstock, (Eds.), *Television and social behavior: Vol. 2. Television and social learning*. Washington, DC: Government Printing Office.

Lenhart, A., Kahne, J., Middaugh, E., Macgill, A. R., Evans, C., & Vitak, J. (2008). Teens video games and civics. *Pew Internet and American Life Project*. Retrieved September 15, 2008 from http://www.pewinternet.org

Lenhart, A., Madden, M., & Hitlin, P. (2005). *Teens and technology: Youth are leading the transition to a fully wired and mobile nation*. Washington, DC: Pew Internet & American Life Project.

Levine, M. P., & Smolak, L. (Eds.). (1996). *Media as a context for the development of disordered eating*. Smolak, Linda; Levine, Michael P.; Striegel-Moore, Ruth . The developmental psychopathology of eating disorders: Implications for research, prevention, and treatment. (pp. 235–257). Hillsdale, NJ, England: Lawrence Erlbaum Associates.

Leyens, J. P., Camino, L., Parke, R. D., & Berkowitz, L. (1975). Effects of movie violence on aggression in a field setting as a function of group dominance and cohesion. *Journal of Personality and Social Psychology, 32*, 346–360.

Liao, Y. C. (2007). Effects of computer-assisted instruction on students' achievement in taiwan: A meta-analysis. *Computers & Education, 48*(2), 216–233.

Lieber, L. (1996). *Commercial and character slogan recall by children aged 9 to 11 years: Budweiser frogs versus Bugs Bunny*. Berkeley, CA: Center on Alcohol Advertising.

Liebert, R. M., & Baron, R. A. (1971). Short-term effects of televised aggression on children's aggressive behavior. In J. P. Murray, E. A. Rubinstein, and G. A. Comstock (Eds.), *Television and social behavior: Vol. 2. Television and social learning*. Washington, DC: Government Printing Office.

Liebert, D., Sprafkin, J., Liebert, R., & Rubinstein, E. (1977). Effects of television commercial disclaimers on the product expectations of children. *Journal of Communication, 27,* 118–124.

Lilpoison.com. (2008). Retrieved January 3, 2008, from http://www.lilpoison. com

Lin, S., & Lepper, M. R. (1987). Correlates of children's usage of video games and computers. *Journal of Applied Social Psychology, 17,* 72–93.

Lindstrom, M. (2003). *BRANDchild.* London: Kogan Page.

Linebarger, D. L., Kosanic, A. Z., Greenwood, C. R., & Doku, N. S. (2004). Effects of viewing the television program Between the Lions on the emergent literacy skills of young children. *Journal of Educational Psychology, 96,* 297–308.

Liss, M. B., Reinhardt, L. C., & Fredriksen, S. (1983). TV heroes: The impact of rhetoric and deeds. *Journal of Applied Developmental Psychology, 4,* 175–187.

Li-Vollmer, M. (2002). Race representation in child-targeted television commercials. *Mass Communications & Society, 5,* 207–228.

Lonigan, C. J., Driscoll, K., Phillips, B. M., Cantor, B. G., Anthony, J. L., & Goldstein, H. (2003). A computer-assisted instruction phonological sensitivity program for preschool children at-risk for reading problems. *Journal of Early Intervention, 25*(4), 248–262.

Lowes, J., & Tiggemann, M. (2003). Body dissatisfaction, dieting awareness and the impact of parental influence in young children. *British Journal of Health Psychology, 8,* 135–147.

Luik, P. (2006). Characteristics of drills related to the development of skills. *Journal of Computer Assisted Learning, 23,* 56–68.

Macaruso, P. (2006). The efficacy of computer-based supplementary phonics programs for advancing reading skills in at-risk elementary students. *Journal of Research in Reading, 29*(2), 162–172.

MacLaren, J. E., & Cohen, L. L. (2005). A comparison of distraction strategies for venipuncture distress in children. *Journal of Pediatric Psychology, 30*(5), 381–396.

Maggi, S. (2008). Changes in smoking behaviors from late childhood to adolescence: 4 years later. *Drug and Alcohol Dependence, 94,* 251–253.

Mallinckrodt, V., & Mizerski, D. (2007). The effects of playing an advergame on young children's perceptions, preferences, and requests. *Journal of Advertising, 36*(2), 87–100.

Maloney, R. S. (2005). Exploring virtual fetal pig dissection as a learning tool for female high school biology students. *Educational Research and Evaluation, 11*(6), 591–603.

Maltby, J., Giles, D. C., Barber, L., & McCutcheon, L. E. (2005). Intense-personal celebrity worship and body image: Evidence of a link among female adolescents. *British Journal of Health Psychology, 10,* 17–32.

Mares, M. L., & Woodard, E. H. (2001). Prosocial effects on children's social interactions. In D. G. Singer & J. L. Singer (Eds.), *Handbook of children and the media* (pp. 183–206). Thousand Oaks, CA: Sage.

Mares, M. L., & Woodard, E. H. (2007). Positive effects of television on children's social interaction: A meta-analysis. In R. W. Preiss, B. M. Gayle, N. Burrell, M. Allen, & J. Bryant (Eds.), *Mass media effects research: Advances through meta-analysis* (pp. 281–300). Mahwah, NJ: Lawrence Erlbaum.

Market, J. (2001). Sing a song of drug use-abuse: Four decades of drug lyrics in popular music-from the sixties through the nineties. *Sociological Inquiry, 71,* 194–220.

Marshall, S. J., Biddle, S. J. H., Gorely, T., Cameron, N., & Murdey, I. (2004). Relationships between media use, body fatness and physical activity in children and youth: A meta-analysis. *International Journal of Obesity, 28,* 1238–1246.

Martino, S. C., Collins, R. L., Elliott, M. N., Strachman, A., Kanouse, D. E., & Berry, S. H. (2006). Exposure to degrading versus nondegrading music lyrics and sexual behavior among youth. *Pediatrics, 118,* 430–441.

Matheson, D. M., Killen, J. D., Wang, Y., Varady, A., & Robinson, T. N. (2004). Children's food consumption during television viewing. *American Journal of Clinical Nutrition, 79,* 1088–1094.

Mayer, C. E. (2003). Nurturing brandy loyalty. *Washington Post,* p. F01.

Mayton, D. M., Nagel, E. A., & Parker, R. (1990). The perceived effects of drug messages on use patterns in adolescents. *Journal of Drug Education, 20*(4), 305–318.

McCabe, M. P., & Ricciardelli, L. A. (2003). Sociocultural influences on body image and body changes among adolescent boys and girls. *The Journal of Social Psychology, 143,* 5–26.

McCabe, M. P., Ricciardelli, L. A., Standord, J., Holt, K., Keegan, S., & Miller, L. (2007). Where is all the pressure coming from? Messages from mothers and teachers about preschool children's appearance, diet and exercise. *European Eating Disorders Review, 15,* 221–230.

McCloud, S. (1993). *Understanding comics.* Northampton, MA: Kitchen Sink Press.

McDermott, P. (1997, March). *The illusion of racial diversity in contemporary basal readers: An analysis of the teacher manuals.* Paper presented at the Annual Meeting of the American Educational Research Association, Chicago.

McDougall, P. (2007). Halo 3 sales smash game industry records. *Information Week.* Retrieved November 2, 2007, from http://www.informationweek.com

McGough, J. J., & McCracken, J. T. (2000). Assessment of attention deficit hyperactivity disorder: A review of recent literature. *Current Opinions in Pediatrics, 12*(4), 319–324.

McIlwraith, R., Jacobvitz, R. S., Kubey, R., & Alexander, A. (1991). Television addiction: Theories and data behind the ubiquitous metaphor. *American Behavioral Scientist, 35*(2), 104–121.

McLeod, J. M., Atkin, C. K., & Chaffee, S. H. (1972). Adolescents, parents, and television use: Adolescent self-report measures from Maryland and Wisconsin samples. In G. A. Comstock & E. A. Rubinstein (Eds.), *Television and social behavior: A technical report to the Surgeon General's Scientific Advisory committee on television and social behavior: Vol. 3. Television and adolescent aggressiveness* (pp. 173–238). Washington, DC: Government Printing Office.

Medley-Rath, S. R. (2007). "Am I still a virgin?" What counts as sex in 20 years of *Seventeen. Sex Cult, 11,* 24–38.

Michel, E., Roebers, C. M., & Schneider, W. (2007). Educational films in the classroom: Increasing the benefit. *Learning and Instruction, 17*(2), 172–183.

Miller, C. J., Marks, D. J., Miller, S. R., Berwid, O. G., Kera, E. C., Santra, A., et al. (2007). Brief report: Television viewing and risk for attention problems in preschool children. *Journal of Pediatric Psychology, 32*(4), 448–452.

Miranda, D., & Claes, M. (2004). Rap music genres and deviant behaviors in French-Canadian adolescents. *Journal of Youth and Adolescence, 33,* 113–122.

Mitchell, K. J., Wolak, J., & Finkelhor, D. (2008). Are blogs putting youth at risk for online sexual solicitation or harassment? *Child Abuse & Neglect, 32,* 277–294.

Mizerski, R. (1995). The relationship between cartoon trade character recognition and attitude toward product category in young children. *Journal of Marketing, 59*(4), 58–70.

Moeller, T. G. (2001). Youth aggression and violence: A psychological approach. New Jersey: Erlbaum.

Mokdad, A. H., Marks, J. S., Stroup, D. F., & Gerberding, J. L. (2004). Actual causes of death in the United States. *Journal of the American Medical Association, 291,* 1238–1245.

Molitor, F., & Hirsch, K. (1994). Children's toleration of real-life aggression after exposure to media violence: A replication of the Drabman and Thomas studies. *Child Study Journal, 24,* 191–202.

Moore, E. S. (2006). *It's child play: Advergaming and the online marketing of food to children.* Mendo Park, CA: Kaiser Family Foundation.

Morgan, M. (1987). Television, sex-role attitudes, and sex-role behavior. *Journal of Early Adolescence, 7*(3), 269–282.

Morris, P. (1989). *Cigarette marketing: A new perspective.* London, England: Kelly Weedon Shute Advertising.

Moschis, G. P., & Moore, R. L. (1982). A longitudinal study of television advertising effects. *Journal of Consumer Research, 9*(3), 279–286.

Mosely, J. J. (1997). *Multicultural diversity of children's picture books: Robert Fulton elementary school library.* ERIC No. ED413926.

Murnen, S. K., Wright, C., & Kaluzny, G. (2002). If "boys will be boys," then girls will be victims? A meta-analytic review of the research that relates masculine ideology to sexual aggression. *Sex Roles, 46*, 359–375.

Naigles, L., & Kako, E. T. (1993). First contact in verb acquisition: Defining a role for syntax. *Child Development, 64*(6), 1665–1687.

Naigles, L., & Mayeux, L. (2001). Television as an incidental language teacher. In D. G. Singer & J. L. Singer (Eds.), *Handbook of children and the media* (pp. 135–152). Thousand Oaks, CA: Sage Publications.

Nathanson, A. I. (1999). Identifying and explaining the relationship between parental mediation and children's aggression. *Communication Research, 26*, 124–143.

Nathanson, A. I. (2002). The unintended effects of parental mediation of television on adolescents. *Media Psychology, 4*, 207–230.

Nathanson, A. I., & Botta, R. A. (2003). Shaping the effects of television on adolescents' body image disturbance: The role of parental mediation. *Communication Reasearch, 30*, 304–331.

Nathanson, A. I., & Cantor, J. (2000). Reducing the aggression-promoting effects of violent cartoons by increasing the fictional involvement with the victim: A study of active mediation. *Journal of Broadcasting and Electronic Media, 44*, 125–142.

Nathanson, A. I., Wilson, B. J., McGee, J., & Sebastian, M. (2002). Counteracting the effects of female stereotypes on television via active mediation. *Journal of Communication, 52*(4), 922–937.

Nathanson, A. I., & Yang, M. (2003). The effects of mediation content and form on children's responses to violent television. *Human Communication Research, 29*, 111–124.

National Institute on Drug Abuse (NIDA). (2007). *Monitoring the future: National results on adolescent drug use, overview of key findings* (NIH Pub. No. 01-4923). Washington, DC: Author.

National Network for Child Care. (2007). *Good times at bedtime.* Retrieved March 1, 2008, from http://www.nncc.org/Series/good.time.bed.html

Nederkoorn, C., Braet, C., Van Eijs, Y., Tanghe, A., & Jansen, A. (2006). Why obese children cannot resist food: The role of impulsivity. *Eating Behaviors, 7*, 315–322.

Neighbors, L. A., & Sobal, J. (2007). Prevalence and magnitude of body weight and shape dissatisfaction among university students. *Eating Behaviors, 8*, 429–439.

Neumark-Sztainer, D. R., Wall, M. M., Haines, J. I., Story, M. T., Sherwood, N. E., & van den Berg, P. A. (2007). Shared risk and protective factors for overweight and disordered eating in adolescents. *American Journal of Preventive Medicine, 33*, 359–369.

Nikken, P., & Jansz, J. (2006). Parental mediation of children's videogame playing: A comparison of the reports by parents and children. *Learning, Media & Technology, 31*(2), 181–202.

Nilsson, N. L. (2005). How does Hispanic portrayal in children's books measure up after 40 years? The answer is "it depends." *The Reading Teacher, 58,* 534–548.

Noguchi, L. K. (2006). The effect of music versus non-music on behavioral signs of distress and self-report of pain in pediatric injection patients. *Journal of Music Therapy, 42*(1), 16–38.

O'Bryant, S. L., & Corder-Bolz, C. R. (1978). The effects of television on children's stereotyping of women's work roles. *Journal of Vocational Behavior, 12,* 233–244.

O'Donohue, W., Gold, S. R., & McKay, J. S. (1997). Children as Sexual Objects: Historical and gender trends in magazines. *Sexual Abuse: A Journal of Research and Treatment, 9,* 291–301.

Ogden, C. L., Carroll, M. D., Curtin, L. R., McDowell, M. A., Tabak, C. J., & Flegal, K. M. (2006). Prevalence of overweight and obesity in the United States, 1999–2004. *Journal of the American Medical Association, 295*(13), 1549–1555.

Oppliger, P. A. (2007). *Effects of gender stereotyping on socialization.* Mahwah, NJ: Lawrence Erlbaum Associates Publishers.

Orwin, R., Cadell, D., Chu, A., et al. (2006). *Evaluation of the national youth anti-drug media campaign: 2004 report of findings executive summary.* Delivered to National Institute on Drug Abuse, National Institutes of Health, Department of Health and Human Services By Westat & the Annenberg School for Communication, Contract No.:N01DA-8-5063.

Oskamp, S., Kaufman, K., & Wolterbeek, L. A. (1996). Gender role portrayals in preschool picture books. *Journal of Social Behavior and Personality, 11,* 27–39.

Ostrov, J. M., Gentile, D. A., & Crick, N. R. (2006). Media exposure, aggression and prosocial behavior during early childhood: A longitudinal study. *Social Development, 15*(4), 612–627.

Ott, M. A., Millstein, S. G., Ofnter, S., & Halpern-Felsher, B. L. (2006). Greater expectations: Adolescents' positive motivations for sex. *Perspectives on Sexual and Reproductive Health, 38*(2), 85–89.

Ozmen, H. (2007). The influence of computer-assisted instruction on students' conceptual understanding of chemical bonding and attitude toward chemistry: A case for Turkey. *Computer & Education,* 1–16.

Paavonen, E. J., Pennonen, M., Roine, M., Valkonen, S., & Lahikainen, A. R. (2006). TV exposure associated with sleep disturbances in 5- to 6-year-old children. *Journal of Sleep Research, 15*(2), 154–161.

Paik, H., & Comstock, G. (1994). The effects of television violence on anti-social behavior: A meta-analysis. *Communication Research, 21,* 516–546.

Palmer, E. L., & Carpenter, C. F. (2006). Food and beverage marketing to children and youth: Trends and issues. *Media Psychology, 8,* 165–190.

Palmgreen, P., Wenner, L. A., & Rayburn, J. D. (1980). Relations between gratifications sought and obtained: A study of television news. *Communication Research, 7*, 161–192.

Pardun, C. J., L'Engle, K. L., & Brown, J. D. (2005). Linking exposure to outcomes: Early adolescents' consumption of sexual content in six media. *Mass Communication & Society, 8*, 75–91.

Parents Television Council (2007). *Dying to entertain: Violence on prime time broadcast TV*. Los Angeles, CA: Parents Television Council.

Parke, R. D., Berkowitz, L., Leyens, J. P., West, S. G., & Sebastian, R. J. (1977). Some effects of violent and nonviolent movies on the behavior of juvenile delinquents. In L. Berkowitz (Ed.), *Advances in experimental social psychology* (Vol. 10, pp. 135–172). New York: Academic Press.

Parsons, S., Leonard, A., & Mitchell, P. (2006). Virtual environments for social skills training: Comments from two adolescents with autistic spectrum disorder. *Computers & Education, 47*, 186–206.

Parsons, T. (1955). Family structure and the socialization of the child. In T. Parsons & R. G. Bales (Eds.), *Family socialization and interaction processes*. New York: Free Press.

Paulsen, G. (2007). *Hatchet*. New York: Aladdin.

Pechmann, C., & Knight, S. J. (2002). An experimental investigation of the joint effects of advertising and peers on adolescents' beliefs and intentions about cigarette consumption. *Journal of Consumer Research, 29*(1), 5–19.

Pechmann, C., Levine, L., Loughlin, S., & Leslie, F. (2005). Impulsive and self-conscious: Adolescents vulnerability to advertising. *Journal of Public Policy and Marketing, 24*, 202–221.

Pechmann, C., & Shih, C. F. (1999). Smoking scenes in movies and antismoking advertisements before movies: Effects on youth. *Journal of Marketing, 63*, 1–13.

Peel, T., Rockwell, A., Esty, E., & Gonzer, K. (1987). *Square One Television: The comprehension and problema solving study*. New Work: Children's Television Worshop.

Pelligrini, A. D. (2002). Rough and tumble play from childhood through adolescence: Development and possible function. *Handbook of childhood social development* (pp. 428–453). Oxford, UK: Blackwell Publishing.

Pescosolido, B. A., Grauerholz, E., & Milkie, M. A. (1997). Culture and conflict: The portrayal of black in U.S. children's picture books through the mid- and late twentieth century. *American Sociological Review, 62*, 443–464.

Peter, J., & Valkenburg, P. M. (2007). Adolescents' exposure to a sexualized media environment and their notions of women as sex objects. *Sex Roles, 56*, 381–395.

Peter, J., & Valkenburg, P. M. (2006). Adolescents' exposure to sexually explicit material on the internet. *Communication Research, 33*, 178–204.

Peterson, K. A., Paulson, S. E., & Williams, K. K. (2007). Relations of eating disorder symptomology with perceptions of pressures from mother, peers, and media in adolescent girls and boys. *Sex Roles, 57,* 629–639.

Pierce, J. P., Choi, W. S., Gilpin, E. A., Farkas, A. J., & Berry, C. C. (1998). Tobacco industry promotion of cigarettes and adolescent smoking. *Journal of the American Medical Association, 279*(7), 511–515.

Pike, J. J., & Jennings, N. A. (2005). The effects of commercials on children's perceptions of gender appropriate toy use. *Sex Roles, 52,* 83–91.

Pine, K. J., & Nash, A. (2002). Dear Santa: The effects of television advertising on young children. *International Journal of Behavioral Development, 26*(6), 529–539.

Polansky, J. R., & Glantz, S. A. (2004). *First-run smoking presentations in U.S. movies 1999–2003.* San Francisco: University of California San Francisco Center for Tobacco Control Research and Education. Retrieved May 15, 2008, from http://www.medscape.com

Potter, W. J., & Warren, R. (1998). Humor as a camouflage of televised violence. *Journal of Communication, 48,* 40–57.

Prasad, V. K., Rao, T. R., & Sheikh, A. A. (1978). Mother vs. commercial. *Journal of Communication, 28,* 91–96.

Primack, B. A., Dalton, M. A., Carroll, M. V., Argawal, A. A., & Fine, M. J. (2008). Content analysis of tobacco, alcohol, and other drugs in popular music. *Archives of Pediatrics and Adolescent Medicine, 162*(2), 169.175.

Primack, B. A., Land, S. R., & Fine, M. J. (2008). Adolescent smoking and volume of exposure to various forms of media. *Journal of Public Health, 122,* 379–389.

Prinsky, L. E., & Rosenbaum, J. L. (1987). "Leer-ics" or lyrics: Teenage impression of rock 'n roll. *Youth and Society, 18,* 384–397.

Puhl, R. M., & Latner, J. D. (2007). Stigma, obesity, and the health of the nation's children. *Psychological Bulletin, 133,* 557–580.

Rau, P. P., Peng, S., & Yang, C. (2006). Time distortion for expert and novice online game players. *CyberPsychology & Behavior, 9*(4), 396–403.

Rauscher, F. H., Shaw, G. L. & Ky, K. N. (1993). Music and spatial task performance. *Nature, 365,* 611.

Redd, W. H., Jacobsen, P. B., Die-Trill, M., Dermatis, H., McEvoy, M., & Holland, J. C. (1987). Cognitive/attentional distraction in the control of conditioned nausea in pediatric cancer patients receiving chemotherapy. *Journal of consulting and clinical psychology, 55*(3), 391–395.

Reep, D. C., & Dambrot, F. H. (1989). Effects of frequent television viewing on stereotypes: "Drip, drip" or "drench"? *Journalism Quarterly, 66,* 542–550, 556.

Reichert, T. (2003).The prevalence of sexual imagery in ads targeted to young adults. *Journal of Consumer Affairs, 37,* 403–412.

Reichert, T., Lambiase, J., Morgan, S., Carstarphen, M., & Zavoina, S. (1999). Cheesecake and beefcake: No matter how you slice it, sexual explicitness in advertising continues to increase. *Journalism and Mass Communication Quarterly, 76*, 7–20.

Reimer, K. M. (1992). Multiethnic literature: Holding past to dreams. *Language Arts, 69*, 14–21.

Reitsma, P., & Wesseling, R. (1998). Effects of computer-assisted training of blending skills in kindergarlners. *Scientific Studies of Reading, 2*(4), 301–320.

Rideout, V. J. (2007). *Parents, children, and media: A Kaiser Family Foundation survey.* Mendo Park, CA: Kaiser Family Foundation.

Rideout, V. J., & Hamel, E. (2006). *The media family: Electronic media in the lives of infants, toddlers, preschoolers, and their parents.* Menlo Park, CA: Kaiser Family Foundation.

Ritter, D., & Eslea, M. (2005). Hot sauce, toy guns, and graffiti: A critical account of current laboratory aggression paradigms. *Aggressive Behavior, 31*(5), 407–419.

Rivadeneyra, R., & Ward, L. M. (2005). From Ally McBeal to Sábado Gigante: Contributions of television viewing to the gender role attitudes of Latino adolescents. *Journal of Adolescent Research, 20*, 453–475.

Roberts, D. F., & Christenson, P. G. (2001). Popular music in childhood and adolescence. In D. G. Singer, & J. L. Singer (Eds.), *Handbook of children and the media* (pp. 395–414). Thousand Oaks, CA: Sage Publications.

Roberts, D. F., Christenson, P.G., & Gentile, D. A. (2003). The effects of violent music on children and adolescents. In D. A. Gentile (Ed.), *Media violence and children: A complete guide for parents and professionals* (pp. 153–170). Westport, CT: Praeger.

Roberts, D. F., Foehr, U. G., & Rideout, V. G. (2005). *Generation M: Media in the lives of 8–18 year-olds.* Menlo Park, CA: Kaiser Family Foundation.

Roberts, D. F., Henriksen, L., & Christenson, P. G. (1999). *Substance use in popular movies and music.* Washington, D. C.: Office of National Drug Control Policy.

Robins, R. W., & Trzesniewski, K. H. (2005). Self-esteem development. *Current Directions in Psychological Science, 14*, 158–162.

Robinson, T. H., Saphir, M. N., Kraemer, H. C., Varady, A., & Haydel, K. F. (2001). Effects of reducing television viewing on children's requests for toys: A randomized controlled trial. *Developmental and Behavioral Pediatrics, 22*, 179–184.

Robinson, T. N., Borzekowski, D. L. G., Matheson, D. M., & Kraemer, H. C. (2007). Effects of fast food branding on young children's taste preferences. *Archives of Pediatrics & Adolescent Medicine, 161*(8), 792–797.

Rosenkoetter, L. I. (1999). The television situation comedy and children's prosocial behavior. *Journal of Applied Social Psychology, 29*(5), 979–993.

Rosenthal, D., Senserrick, T., & Feldman, S. (2001). A typology approach to describing parents as communicators about sexuality. *Archives of Sexual Behavior*, *30*(5), 463–482.

Ross, R. P., Campbell, T. A., Wright, J. C., Huston, A. C., Rice, M. K., & Turk, P. (1984). When celebrities talk, children listen: An experimental analysis of children's responses to TV ads with celebrity endorsement. *Journal of Applied Developmental Psychology*, *5*, 185–202.

Rossiter, J. R., & Robertson, T. S. (1974). Children's TV commercials: Testing the defenses. *Journal of Communication*, *24*(4), 137–145.

Rowley, S. J., Kurtz-Costes, B., Mistry, R., & Feagans, L. (2007). Social status as a predictor of race and gender stereotypes in late childhood and early adolescence. *Social Development*, *16*, 150–168.

Rubin, R. B., & McHugh, M. P. (1987). Development of parasocial interaction relationships. *Journal of Broadcasting and Electronic Media*, *13*(3), 279–292.

Ruiz, M. (2000). Truth campaign drives smoking attitude change in Florida youth. Sarasota Florida: Florida Public Relations Department.

Ryan, E. L., & Hoerrner, K. L. (2004). Let your conscience be your guide: Smoking and drinking in Disney's animated classics. *Mass Communication & Society*, *7*, 261–278.

Ryan, R. M., Rigby, C. S., & Przybylski, A. (2006). The motivational pull of video games: A self determination theory approach. *Motivation and Emotion*, *30*, 347–365.

Sands, E. R., & Wardle, J. (2002). Internalization of ideal body shapes in 9–12-year-old girls. *Internation Journal of Eating Disorders*, *33*, 193–204.

Sargent, J. D., Stoolmiller, M., Worth, K. A., Cin, S., Wills, T. A., & Gibbons, F. X. (2007). Exposure to smoking depictions in movies: Association with established smoking. *Archives of Pediatric and Adolescent Medicine*, *161*, 849–856.

Sargent, J. D., Wills, T. A., Stoolmiller, M., Gibson, J., & Gibbons, F. X. (2006). Alcohol use in motion pictures and its relation with early-onset teen drinking. *Journal of Studies on Alcohol*, *67*(1), 54–65.

Scheel, K. R., & Westefeld, J. S. (1999). Heavy metal music and adolescent suicidality: An empirical investigation. *Adolescence*, *34*, 253–259.

Schellenberg, E. G. (2005). Music and cognitive abilities. *Current Directions in Psychological Science*, *14*(6), 317–320.

Schlaggar, B. L., Brown, T. T., Lugar, H. M., Visscher, K. M., Miezin, F. M. & Petersen, S. E. (2002). Functional neuroanatomical differences between adults and school-age children in the processing of single words. *Science*, *296*, 1476–1479.

Schmidt, M. E., & Anderson, D. R. (2006). The impact of television on cognitive development and educational achievement. In Murray, J.P., Pecora, N., &

Wartella, E. (Eds.). *Children and Television: 50 Years of Research*, (65–84). Mahweh, NJ: Erlbaum Publishers.

Schooler, D. (2008). Real women have curves: A longitudinal investigation of TV and the body image development of Latina adolescents. *Journal of Adolescent Research, 23*, 132–153.

Schooler, D., Kim, J. L., & Sorsoli, L. (2006). Setting rules or sitting down: Parental mediation of television consumption and adolescent self-esteem, body image, and sexuality. *Sexuality Research & Social Policy: A Journal of the NSRC.Special Issue: Through a Lens of Embodiment: New Research from the Center for Research on Gender and Sexuality, 3*(4), 49–62.

Schooler, D., Ward, L. M., Merriwether, A., & Caruthers, A. (2004). Who's that girl: Television's role in the body image development of young white and black women. *Psychology of Women Quarterly, 28*, 38–47.

ScienceDaily.com. (2007). American Psychiatric Association considers "video game addiction." Retrieved June 26, 2008, from http://www.sciencedaily.com/releases/2007/06/070625133354.htm

Seidman, S. A. (1992). An investigation of sex-role stereotyping in music videos. *Journal of Broadcasting and Electronic Media, 36*, 209–216.

Shadel, W.G., Tharp-Taylor, S., & Fryer, C. S. (2008). Exposure to cigarette advertising and adolescents' intentions to smoke: the moderating role of the developing self-concept. *Journal of Pediatric Psychology, 33*(7), 751–760.

Shaw, J. (1995). Effects of fashion magazines on body dissatisfaction and eating psychopathology in adolescent and adult females. *European Eating Disorders Review, 3*, 15–23.

Sheldon, J. P. (2004). Gender stereotypes in educational software for young children. *Sex Roles, 51*, 433–444.

Shin, N. (2004). Exploring pathways from television viewing to academic achievement in school age children. *The Journal of Genetic Psychology, 165*(4), 367–381.

Shrum, L. J., & Bischak, V. D. (2001). Mainstreaming, resonance and impersonal impact: Testing moderators of the cultivation effect for estimates of crime risk. *Human Communication Research, 27*(2), 187–215.

Signorelli, N. (2001). Television's gender role images and contribution to stereotyping. In D. G. singer & J. L. Singer (Eds.), *Handbook of children and the media* (pp. 341–358). Thousand Oaks, CA: Sage.

Silverman, L. T., & Sprafkin, J. N. (1980). The effects of *Sesame Street*'s prosocial spots on cooperative play between young children. *Journal of Broadcasting, 24*, 135–147.

Silvern, S. B., & Williamson, P. A. (1987). The effects of video game play on young children's aggression, fantasy, and prosocial behavior. *Journal of Applied Developmental Psychology, 8*, 453–462.

Silverstein, B., Perdue, L., Peterson, B., & Kelly, E. (1986). The role of mass media in promoting a thin standard o bodily attractiveness for women. *Sex Roles, 14*, 519–532.

Simon Wiesenthal Center. (2007). *Digital terrorism and hate.* Retrieved March 3, 2008 from http://www.wiesenthal.com/site/apps/s/content.asp?c=fwLYKnN8Lz H&b= 253162&ct=3876867

Singer, D. G., & Singer, J. L. (1990). *The house of make-believe: Children's play and the developing imagination.* Cambridge, MA: Harvard University Press.

Singer, J. L., & Singer, D. G. (1981). *Television, imagination, and aggression: A study of preschoolers.* Hillsdale, NJ: Erlbaum.

Slater, M. D., Henry, K. L., Swaim, R. C., & Anderson, L. L. (2003). Violent media content and aggressiveness in adolescents: A downward spiral model. *Communication Research. 30*(6), 713–736.

Smith, S. L. (2006). Perps, pimps, and provocative clothing: Examining negative content patterns in video games. In P. Vorderer & J. Bryant (Eds.), *Playing video games* (pp. 57–75). Mahwah, NJ: Lawrence Erlbaum.

Smith, S. L., & Wilson, B. J. (2002). Children's comprehension of and fear responses to television news. *Media Psychology, 4*, 1–26.

Smith, S.W., Smith, S. L., Pieper, K. M., Yoo, J. H., Ferris, A. L., Downs, E., et al. (2006). Altruism on American television: Examining the amount of, and context surrounding, acts of helping and sharing. *Journal of Communication, 56*, 707–727.

Smolak, L., & Stein, J. A. (2006). The relationship of drive for muscularity to sociocultural factors, self-esteem, physical attributes gender role, and social comparison in middle school boys. *Body Image, 3*, 121–129.

Sneegas, J. E., & Plank, T. A. (1998). Gender differences in pre-adolescent reactance to age-categorized television advisory labels. *Journal of Broadcasting and Electronic Media, 42*, 423–434.

Snyder, L. B., Milici, F. F., Slater, M., Sun, H., & Strizhakova, Y. (2006). Effects of alcohol advertising exposure on drinking among youth. *Archives of Pediatrics and Adolescent Medicine, 160*, 18–24.

Sobik, L., Hutchison, K., & Craighead, L. (2005). Cue-elicited craving for food: A fresh approach to the study of binge eating. *Appetite, 44*, 253–261.

Somers, C. L., & Surmann, A. T. (2004). Adolescents' preferences for source of sex education. *Child Study Journal, 34*, 47–59.

Somers, C. L., & Surmann, A. T. (2006). Sources and timing of sex education: Relations with American adolescent sexual attitudes and behavior. *Educational Review, 57*, 37–54.

Somers, C. L., & Tynan, J. J. (2006). Consumption of sexual dialogue and content on television and adolescent sexual outcomes: Multiethnic findings. (2006). *Adolescence, 41*, 15–36.

Sparks, G. G. (2001). *Media effects research: A basic overview*. Belmont, CA: Wadsworth.

Spear, L. P. (2000). The adolescent brain and age-related behavioral manifestations. *Neuroscience and Biobehavioral Reviews, 24*, 417–463.

Spoth, R., Greenberg, M., & Turrisi, R. (2008). Preventive interventions addressing underage drinking: State of evidence and steps toward public health impact. *Pediatrics, 121*, S311–S336.

Stacy, A. W., Zogg, J. B., Unger, J. B., & Dent, C. W. (2004). Exposure to televised alcohol ads and subsequent adolescent alcohol use. *American Journal of Health Behavior, 28*(6), 498–509.

Stanford, J. N., & McCabe, M. P. (2005). Sociocultural influences on adolescent boys' body image and body change strategies. *Body Image, 2*, 105–113.

Stankiewicz, J. M., & Rosselli, F. (2008). Women as sex objects and victims in print advertisements. *Sex Roles, 58*, 579–589.

Starker, S. (1989). *Evil influences: Crusades against the mass media*. New Brunswick, NJ: Transaction.

Steinberg, L. (2001). Adolescent development. *Annual Review of Psychology, 52*, 83–110.

Stern, S. R. (2005). Messages from teens on the big screen: Smoking, drinking, and drug use in teen-centered films. *Journal of Health Communication, 10*, 331–346.

Stern, S. R., & Mastro, D. E. (2004). Gender portrayals across the life span: A content analytic look at broadcast commercials. *Mass Communication & Society, 7*, 215–236.

Stevens, T., & Mulsow, M. (2006). There is no meaningful relationship between television exposure and symptoms of attention-deficit/hyperactivity disorder. *Pediatrics, 117*(3), 665–672.

Stobbe, M. (2007). Internet bullying increases for kids. Associated Press. Retrieved November 28, 2007, from http://www.detnews.com

Strahan, E. J., Lafrence, A., Wilson, A. E., Ethier, N., Spencer, S. J., & Zanna, M. P. (2008). Victoria's dirty secret: How sociocultural norms influence adolescent girls and women. *Personality and Social Psychology Bulletin, 34*, 288–301.

Streicher, H. W. (1974). The girls in cartoons. *Journal of Communication, 24*, 125–129.

Substance Abuse and Mental Health Services Administration. (2006). Youth drug use continues downward slide older adult rates of use increase. Retrieved June 6, 2008, from http://www.samhsa.gov/news/newsreleases/060907_nsduh.aspx

Swaim, R. C., Beauvais, F., Chavez, E. L., & Oetting, E. R. (1997). The effect of school dropout rates on estimates of adolescent substance use among three racial/ethnic groups. *Journal of Public Health, 87*, 51–55.

SwansonMeals.com. (2008). *Back in the day...* Retrieved August 1, 2008, from http://www.swansonmeals.com

Tamborini, R., Skalski, P., Lachlan, K., Westerman, D., Davis, J., & Smith, S. L. (2005). The raw nature of professional wrestling: Is the violence a cause for concern? *Journal of Broadcasting & Electronic Media, 49*, 202–220.

Tamburro, R. F., Gordon, P. L., D'Apolito, J. P., & Howard, S. C. (2004). Unsafe and violent behavior in commercials aired during televised major sporting events. *Journal of Pediatrics, 114*(6), 694–698.

Tan, A. S., & Scruggs, K. J. (1980). Does exposure to comic books violence lead to aggression in children? *Journalism Quarterly, 57*, 579–583.

Taveras, E. M., Rifas-Shiman, S. L., Field, A. E., Frazier, A. L., Colditz, G. A., & Gillman, M. W. (2004). The influence of wanting to look like media figures on adolescent physical activity. *Journal of Adolescent Health, 35*, 41–50.

Tepper, C. A., & Cassidy, K. W. (1999). Gender differences in emotional language in children's pictures books. *Sex Roles, 40*, 265–280.

Thomas, M. H., & Drabman, R. S. (1975). Toleration of real life aggression as a function of exposure to televised violence and age of subject. *Merrill-Palmer Quarterly, 21*(3), 227–232.

Thomas, M. H., Horton, R. W., Lippencott, E. C., & Drabman, R. S. (1977). Desensitization to portrayals of real-life aggression as a function of exposure to television violence. *Journal of Personality and Social Psychology, 35*, 450–458.

Thompson, F. T., & Austin, W. P. (2003). Television viewing and academic achievement revisited. *Education, 124*(1), 194–202.

Thompson, K. M., & Haninger, K. (2001). Violence in E-rated video games. *Journal of the American Medical Association, 286*, 591–598.

Thompson, K. M., Tepichin, K., & Haninger, K. (2006). Content and ratings of Mature rated video games. *Archives of Pediatric and Adolescent Medicine, 160*, 402–410.

Thompson, K. M., & Yokota, F. (2004). Violence, sex, and profanity in films: Correlation of movie ratings with content. *General Medicine, 6*(3). Retrieved January 15, 2005, from http://www.medscape.com

Thompson, T. L., & Zerbinos, E. (1995). Gender roles in animated cartoons: Has the picture changed in 20 years, *Sex Roles, 32*, 651–673.

Thomsen, S. R., & Rekve, D. (2006). The relationship between viewing US-produced television programs and intentions to drink alcohol among a group of norwegian adolescents. *Scandinavian Journal of Psychology, 47*(1), 33–41.

Tiggemann, M. (2005). Television and adolescent body image: The role of program content and viewing motivation. *Journal of Social and Clinical Psychology, 24*, 361–381.

Tiggemann, M., & Pickering, A. S. (1996). Role of television in adolescent women's body dissatisfaction and drive for thinness. *International Journal of Eating Disorders, 20*, 199–203.

Titus-Ernstoff, L., Dalton, M. A., Adachi-Mejia, A. M., Longacre, M. R., & Beach, M. L. (2008). Longitudinal study of viewing smoking in movies and initiation of smoking by children. *Pediatrics: Special Issue: Movie Smoking Exposure and Youth Smoking in Germany, 121*(1), 15–21.

Tolman, D. L., Kim, J. L., Schooler, D., & Sorsoli, C. L. (2007). Rethinking the associations between television viewing and adolescent sexuality development: Bringing gender into focus. *Journal of Adolescent Health, 40*, 9–16.

Took, K. J., & Weiss, D. S. (1994). The relationship between heavy metal and rap music and adolescent turmoil: Real or artifact? *Adolescence, 29*, 613–621.

Towbin, M. A., Haddock, S. A., Zimmerman, T. S., Lund, L.K., & Tanner, L. R. (2003). Images of gender, race, age, and sexual orientation in Disney feature-length animated films. *Journal of Feminist Family Therapy, 15*, 19–44.

Tredennick, D. W. (1974). The purpose of this memorandum is to answer the question "What causes smokers to select their first brand of cigarettes?" *Legacy Tobacco Documents Library*. Retrieved May 29, 2009, from http://legacy.library.ucsf.edu/tid/agv29d00

Troseth, G. L., Saylor, M. M., & Archer, A. H. (2006). Young children's use of video as a source of socially relevant information. *Child Development, 77*(3), 786–799.

Trulyhuge.com. (2008). Dr. Size interview. Retrieved April 16, 2008, from http://www.trulyhuge.com/news/tips63a.htm

Tversky, A., & Kahneman, D. (2005). Judgment under uncertainty: Heuristics and biases.

Tynes, B. M. (2007). Role takin gin online "classrooms": What adolescents are learning about race and ethnicity. *Developmental Psychology, 43*, 1312–1320.

UGA.edu. (2008). *Some economic effects of tobacco in Georgia*. Retrieved August 1, 2008, from http://commodities.caes.uga.edu/fieldcrops/Tobacco/econ-effects.htm

Unsworth, G., Devilly, G. J., & Ward, T. (2007). The effect of playing violent video games on adolescents: Should parents be quaking in their boots? *Psychology, Crime & Law, 13*(4), 383–394.

U.S. Census Bureau. (2008). *Population estimates*. Washington, DC: Author.

U.S. Department of Education. (2003). *Computer and Internet use by children and adolescents in 2001* (National Center for Education Statistics, NCES 2004–014). Washington, DC: Author.

U.S. Department of Health and Human Services. (2007). *The surgeon general's call to action to prevent and reduce underage drinking*. Washington, DC: Department of Health and Human Services, Office of the Surgeon General. Retrieved February 12, 2008, from http://www.surgeongeneral.gov and http://www.hhs.gov/od

U.S. Surgeon General's Scientific Advisory Committee on Television and Social Behavior. (1972). *Television and growing up: The impact of televised violence* (DHEW Publication No. HSM 72-9086). Washington, DC: Author.

Valkenburg, P. M. (2004). *Children's responses to the screen: A media psychological approach*. Mahwah, NJ: Lawrence Erlbaum.

Valkenburg, P. M., & Buijzen, M. (2005). Identifying determinants of young children's brand awareness: Television, parents, and peers. *Journal of Applied Developmental Psychology, 26*(4), 456–468.

Valkenburg, P. M., & Cantor, J. (2001). The development of a child into a consumer. *Journal of Applied Developmental Psychology, 22*(1), 61–72.

Valkenburg, P. M. & Peter, J. (2007a). Preadolescents' and adolescents' online communication and their closeness to friends. *Developmental Psychology, 43*(2), 267–277.

Valkenburg, P. M. & Peter, J. (2007b). Online communication and adolescent well-being: Testing the stimulation versus and the displacement hypothesis. *Journal of Computer-Mediated Communication, 12*, 1169–1182.

Valkenburg, P. M., Peter, J., & Schouten, A. P. (2006). Friend networking sites and their relationship to adolescents' well-being and social self-esteem. *CyberPsychology & Behavior, 9*(5), 584–590.

Valkenburg, P. M., Schouten, A. P. & Peter, J. (2005). Adolescents' identity experiments on the internet. *New Media & Society, 7*(3), 383–402.

Valkenburg, P. M. & van der Voort, T. H. A. (1994). Influence of TV on daydreaming and creative imagination: A review of research. *Psychological Bulletin, 116*(2), 316–339.

Valkenburg, P. M., & Vroone, M. (2004). Developmental changes in infants' and toddlers' attention to television entertainment. *Communication Research, 31*(3), 288–311.

van den Berg, P., Neumark-Sztainer, D., Hannan, P. J., & Haines, J. (2007). Is dieting advice from magazines helpful or harmful? Five-year associations with weight-control behaviors and psychological outcomes in adolescents. *Pediatrics, 119*, 30–37.

Van den Bulck, J. (2004). Media use and dreaming: The relationship among television viewing, computer game play, and nightmares or pleasant dreams. *Dreaming, 14*(1), 43–49.

Van den Bulck, J., Beullens, K., & Mulder, J. (2006). Television and music video exposure and adolescent "alcopop" use. *International Journal of Adolescent Medicine and Health, 18*(1), 107–114.

Van Mierlo, J., & Van den Bulck, J. (2004). Benchmarking the cultivation approach to video game effects: A comparison of the correlates of TV viewing and game play. *Journal of Adolescence, 27*, 97–111.

Vandewater, E. A., Lee, S. J. (2006, March). *Measuring children's media use in the digital age: Workshop on media research methods and measures*. Washington, D.C.

Vaughan, K. K., & Fouts, G. T. (2003). Changes in television and magazine exposure and eating disorder symptomatology. *Sex Roles, 49*, 313–320.

Vernadakis, N., Avegerinos, A., Tsitskari, E., & Zachopoulou, E. (2005). The use of computer assisted instruction in preschool education: Making teaching meaningful. *Early Childhood Education Journal, 33*(2), 99–104.

Vidal, M. A., Clemente, M. E., & Espinosa, P. (2003). Types of media violence and degree of acceptance in under-18s. *Aggressive Behavior, 29*, 381–392.

Viemero, V., & Paajanen, S. (1992). The role of fantasies and dreams in the TV viewing-aggression relationship. *Aggressive Behavior, 18*, 109–116.

Vilozni, D., Barak, A., Efrati, O., Augarten, A., Springer, C., Yahav, Y., et al. (2005). The role of computer games in measuring spirometry in healthy and "asthmatic" preschool children. *Chest Journal, 128*(3), 1146–1155.

Vygotsky, L. S. (1978). *Mind and society: The development of higher mental processes.* Cambridge, MA: Harvard University Press.

Wake, M., Hesketh, K., & Waters, E., (2003). Television, computer use and body mass index in Australian primary school children. *Child Health, 39*, 130–134.

Walsh, D., Gentile, D. A., Gieske, J., Walsh, M., & Chasco, E. (2003). Eighth annual mediawise video game report card. *National Institute on Media and the Family.* Retrieved May 7, 2004, from http://www.mediafamily.org

Ward, L. M. (2003). Understanding the role of entertainment media in the sexual socialization of American youth: A review of empirical research. *Developmental Review, 23*, 347–388.

Ward, L. M., & Harrison, K. (2005). The impact of media use on girls' beliefs about gender roles, their bodies, and sexual relationship: A research synthesis. *New Directions in Child and Adolescent Development, 109*, 63–71.

Wellman, R. J., Sugarman, D. B., DiFranza, J. R., & Winickoff, J. P. (2006). The extent to which tobacco marketing and tobacco use in films contribute to children's use of tobacco: A meta-analysis. *Archives of Pediatrics and Adolescent Medicine, 160*, 1285–1296.

Wenglinsky, H. (1998). *Does it compute? The relationship between educational technology and student achievement in mathematics.* Princeton, NJ: Educational Testing Service. Retrieved Novoember 23, 2003, from //ftp.ets.org/pub/res/technolog.pdf.

Wertham, F. (1954). *Seduction of the Innocent.* New York: Holt, Rinehart, & Winston.

Williams, K. R., & Guerra, N. G. (2007). Prevalence and predictors of internet bullying. *Journal of Adolescent Health, 41*(6, Suppl.), S14–S21.

Williams, P. A., Haertel, E. H., Haertel, G. D., & Walberg, H. J. (1982). The impact of leisure-time television on school learning: A research synthesis. *American Educational Research Journal, 19*(1), 19–50.

Williams, T. B. (Ed.). (1986). *The impact of television: A natural experiment in three communities.* New York: Academic Press.

Wills, T. A., Sargent, J. D., Stoolmiller, M., Gibbons, F. X., Worth, K. A., & Dal Cin, S. (2007). Movie exposure to smoking cues and adolescent smoking onset: A test for mediation through peer affiliations. *Health Psychology, 26*, 769–776.

Wilson, B. J., Martins, N., & Marske, A. L. (2005). Children's and parents' fright reactions to kidnapping stories in the news. *Communication Monographs, 72*, 46–70.

Wilson, B. J., Smith, S. L., Potter, J. W., Kunkel, D., Linz, D., Colvin, C. M., et al. (2002). Violence in children's television programming: Assessing the risks. *Journal of Communication, 52*, 5–35.

Wilson, B. J., & Weiss, A. J. (1992). Developmental differences in children's reactions to a toy advertisements linked to a toy-based cartoon. *Journal of Broadcasting and Electronic Media, 36*, 371–394.

Wilson, J., Peebles, R., & Hardy, K. K. (2006). Surfing for thinness: A pilot study of pro-eating disorder web site usage in adolescents with eating disorders. *Pediatrics, 118*, 1635–1643.

Wingood, G. M., DiClemente, R. J., Bernhardt, J. M., Harrington, K., Davies, S. L., Robillard, A., et al. (2003). A prospective study of exposure to rap music videos and African American female adolescents' health. *American Journal of Public Health, 93*, 437–439.

Wingood, G. M., DiClemente, R. J., Harrington, K. F., Davies, S., Hook, E. W., III, & Oh, M. K. (2001). Exposure to X-rated movies and adolescents' sexual and contraceptive-related attitudes and behaviors. *Pediatrics, 107*, 1116–1119.

Witt, S. D. (1996). Traditional or androgynous: An analysis to determine gender role orientation of basal readers. *Child Study Journal, 26*(4), 303–318.

Wolak, J., Mitchell, K., & Finkelhor, D. (2007). Unwanted and wanted exposure to pornography in a national sample of youth Internet users. *Pediatrics, 119*(2), 247–257.

Wood, C., Becker, J., & Thompson, J. K. (1996). Body image dissatisfaction in preadolescent children. *Journal of Applied Developmental Psychology, 17*, 85–100.

Wood, R. T. A., Griffiths, M. D., & Parke, A. (2007). Experiences of time loss among videogame players: An empirical study. *CyberPsychology & Behavior, 10*(1), 38–44.

World Health Organization. (2003). Integrated prevention of non-communicable diseases. (No. EB113/44 Add1): WHO.

WorldHeartFederation.org. (2007). Children, adolescents and obesity. Retrieved May 19, 2008 from http://www.world-heart-federation.org/press/facts-figures/children-adolescents-and-obesity/

Wotring, C. E., & Greenberg, B. S. (1973). Experiments in televised violence and verbal aggression: Two exploratory studies. *Journal of Communication, 23*, 446–460.

Wright, J. C., Huston, A. C., Murphy, K. C., St. Peters, M., Piñon, M., & Scantlin, R., et al. (2001). The relations of early television viewing to school readiness and vocabulary of children from low-income families: The early window project. *Child Development, 72*(5), 1347–1366.

WSBTV.com. (2008). *Georgia law bans retailers from selling "pot candy" to minors.* Retrieved July12, 2008 from http://www.wsbtv.com/news/16186311/detail.html

Yokota, F., & Thompson, K. M. (2000). Violence in G-rated films. *Journal of the American Medical Association, 283*, 2716–2720.

Yurgelun-Todd, D. (1998). Physical changes in adolescent brain may account for turbulent teen years, McLean Hospital study reveals (Press release). Retrieved December 1, 2002, from http://www.mclean.harvard.edu/PublicAffairs/TurbulentTeens.htm

Zhan, M. (2006). Assets, parental expectations and involvement, and children's educational performance. *Children and Youth Services Review, 28*, 961–975.

Zhao, G., & Pechmann, C. (2007). The impact of regulatory focus on adolescents' response to antismoking advertising campaigns. *Journal of Marketing Research, 44*(4), 671–687.

Zielinska, I. E., & Chambers, B. (1995). Using group viewing of television to teach preschool children social skills. *Journal of Educational Television, 21*(2), 85–99.

Zill, N., Davies, E., & Daly, M. (1994). Viewing of *Sesame Street* by preschool children and its relationship to school readiness: Report prepared for the Children's Television Workshop. Rockville, MD. Westat, Inc.

Zillmann, D. (1983). Transfer of excitation in emotional behaviour. In J. T. Cacioppo & R. E. Petty (Eds.), *Social psychophysiology: A sourcebook* (pp. 215–240). New York: Guilford.

Zillmann, D. (1998). The psychology of the appeal of portrayals of violence. In J. Goldstein (Ed.), *Why we watch. The attractions of violent entertainment* (pp. 179–211). New York: Oxford University Press.

Zimmerman, F. J., & Christakis, D. A. (2007). Television and DVD/Videos viewing in children younger than 2 years. *Archives of Pediatrics & Adolescent Medicine, 161*(5), 473–479.

Zukerman, M. M. (1994). *Behavioral expression and biosocial bases of sensation-seeking.* New York: Cambridge University Press.

Zumbrun, J. (2007). *The baby is back on Ferrell's Funnyordie.* Retrieved June 26, 2008, from http://www.washingtonpost.com/wp-dyn/content/article/2007/06/26/AR2007062600530.html

Zurbriggen, E. L., Collins, R. L., Lamb, S., Roberts, T.-A., Tolman, D. L., Ward, L. M., et al. (2007). *Report of the APA task force on the sexualization of girls.* Washington, DC: American Psychological Association. Retrieved May 28, 2009, from http://www.apa.org/pi/wpo/sexualizationrep.pdf

Index